W9-BYB-758

Saints in the
Broken City

Saints in the Broken City

Football, Fandom
and Urban Renewal
in Post-Katrina New Orleans

CASEY SCHREIBER

McFarland & Company, Inc., Publishers
Jefferson, North Carolina

Unless otherwise noted, photographs are by the author.

LIBRARY OF CONGRESS CATALOGUING-IN-PUBLICATION DATA

Names: Schreiber, Casey, author.
Title: Saints in the broken city : football, fandom and urban
    renewal in post-Katrina New Orleans / Casey Schreiber.
Description: Jefferson, North Carolina : McFarland & Company, Inc.,
    Publishers, 2016. | Includes bibliographical references and index.
Identifiers: LCCN 2016037387 | ISBN 9781476662602 (softcover :
    acid free paper) ∞
Subjects: LCSH: New Orleans Saints (Football team) | Football—
    Social aspects—Louisiana—New Orleans. | Hurricane Katrina,
    2005. | Urban renewal—Louisiana—New Orleans. | New
    Orleans (La.)—Social conditions—21st century.
Classification: LCC GV956.N366 S45 2016 | DDC
    796.332/640976335—dc23
LC record available at https://lccn.loc.gov/2016037387

BRITISH LIBRARY CATALOGUING DATA ARE AVAILABLE

ISBN (print) 978-1-4766-6260-2
ISBN (ebook) 978-1-4766-2605-5

Front cover: (top) Exterior of the Mercedes-Benz Superdome, 2013
(iStock); (bottom) interior of the Superdome on opening day of
the Saints championship season, September 13, 2009 (David Reber)

Printed in the United States of America

McFarland & Company, Inc., Publishers
    Box 611, Jefferson, North Carolina 28640
    www.mcfarlandpub.com

To the Who Dat Nation

Table of Contents

Preface

This is a story about the relationship between the Saints football team and the city of New Orleans. From the perspective of fans, we can gain a robust understanding of what professional football means to New Orleans and see how urban residents assign value to their home team. In this analysis, Saints football is not about athleticism, big plays, or the wins and losses associated with sports competition. Rather, this story shows how narratives built around the football team parallel social, cultural and political events as they unfolded throughout the team's tenure in the city.

After Hurricane Katrina devastated New Orleans in 2005, Saints fans used the team to build a narrative of renewal and deliver messages about city recovery. These meaningful local narratives reinforced a connection to the city and created collective identities among diverse urban residents. The "Who Dat Nation" created a sense of fandom that existed outside the confines of the publicly funded stadium on game day as people encountered indicators of Saints fandom through everyday lived experiences. Through shared experiences surrounding Saints football, fans fostered public sociability and meaningful relationships that transcended social differences. In addition, locals embraced the commodification of professional football while also engineering local cultural adaptations to the economic dimensions of sport.

Through the story of the Saints in New Orleans, we can see sport spaces as a combination of symbolism and practice where sporting and urban affiliations are interrelated in complex ways through constructions of identity, culture and commercialism. This work presents spaces of sports fandom as places of empowerment to challenge, renegotiate and rethink difference where sport spaces embody constructions of race,

1

urban place, gender and identity. Spaces of sports fandom can be spaces to negotiate a sense of community identity and foster continuing civil interactions. This provokes discussion about the extent to which sports fan activities influence changes in social interaction across race and gender differences.

The results present new ways of talking about the relationship between professional sports and the city. Research often frames the relationship between sports and city, particularly in North America, in terms of economics as researchers debate the costs and benefits of using public subsidies to build stadiums, retain professional teams, and host mega-events. However, people assign symbolic or intangible values to their home sports teams that cannot be measured through economic frameworks. My research examined the ways in which urban residents created value around a professional sports team that other researchers dismissed as hard to measure. This work started as dissertation research that used the New Orleans Saints as a case study to gain a better understanding of the importance of professional sports to urban residents. The dissertation research incorporated interviews, questionnaires, content analysis and participant observation to provide greater access to the meanings people associate with the experience of being a Saints fan.

Even though I built a dissertation around this topic, my interest in Saints football as a social influencer started before I ever considered entering a doctoral degree program. When Hurricane Katrina struck New Orleans, I was an employee of the Saints football team. It was my first full-time job in professional sports after completing a graduate degree program in sports management. My time as a graduate student was spent under the inspiration of Richard Lapchick. Lapchick is a human rights activist, a pioneer for racial equality, and an internationally recognized expert on sports issues, and is often described as "the racial conscience of sport." He guided me, as he has done for countless others, to view sports as a powerful vehicle to promote positive changes in society with an emphasis on using sports to smash through racial barriers.

In a sense, this book illustrates the culmination of an extended ethnography in which I have played several different roles: a New Orleans resident both before and after Katrina; an employee of the Saints football team; a fan of Saints football; a student of sport in society; a professor of urban studies and public policy; a social scientist; a female fan of NFL football. For me as a New Orleans resident, the events that took place surrounding the Saints football team, the Hurricane Katrina disaster and the subsequent recovery unfolded in real time. My personal memories intermingle with empirical research and I am able to express those perspectives in this book in ways that the constraints of dissertation research did not allow.

I use the Saints football team to present a story about what happened in New Orleans during Hurricane Katrina. I recently realized that many college freshmen do not know what happened in New Orleans during Katrina because in 2005 they were too young to pay attention. I want them to know what happened here and I want readers to know what a sports team can mean to a community.

Beyond the extraordinary circumstances of Katrina, Saints fans continued to build meaningful practices through affiliation with Saints football. The analysis of Saints football fans provides an opportunity to think more critically about the role of sports in city race relations, reconceptualize fandom to include women, and assess how fans respond to the commercialization of football. This is certainly not a typical book about a football team. It is instead part urban history and part social scientific analysis of contemporary issues, using sports as a filter to understand the human condition. Above all, this book tells a story about a battered city and its residents who cover themselves from head to toe in black and gold, the Saints' team colors, and simultaneously offers a new conversation about the relationship between sports and the city.

1

When the Saints Came Marching In

On November 1, 1966, New Orleans' elite gathered in the Pontchartrain Hotel for a press conference announcing that a National Football League franchise had been awarded to the city of New Orleans. The date, All Saints Day, marked the birth of the New Orleans Saints, but the day did not mark the beginning of the relationship between football and the city of New Orleans. One must look back several years earlier to understand how the aspirations of a young professional football league and the actions of city boosters brought the NFL to New Orleans. The thematic elements surrounding New Orleans' efforts to attract an NFL team include politics, race relations, economic development, and city image. These themes reverberate throughout the history of the team's tenure in New Orleans. Beloved sports teams carry a lot of symbolic value. What they symbolize is emblematic of the current events and social structures within which they are located.

A Brief History of the National Football League

Football in America dates back to 1869 when Rutgers University and Princeton University developed a new game based on rugby. By the turn of the 20th century, the game of football was a major attraction for local athletic clubs, particularly in the Pittsburgh area. Former Yale athlete William "Pudge" Heffelfinger received $500 to play in a football game, making him the first person to play professional football.[1] Paying players for their performance marked the beginning of football as a commercialized professional sport, rather than a leisure activity or hobby. Dominant interest in the game shifted from Pittsburgh to Ohio as the new sport seeped into different American cities. Canton, Ohio, remains the site frequently referenced as the birthplace of the NFL, and it houses the Football Hall of Fame. In response to the increased popularity of the game, football organizing bodies struggled to maintain control of a professional league. In 1920 the American Professional Football Association formed to address three problems: dramatically rising player salaries, players jumping from one team to another chasing the highest salary, and teams using college players who were still enrolled in school. Despite the formation of a professional football association led by an appointed president, teams dodged their membership fees and displayed no consistency in the number of games played as each team made its own schedule.[2] As Americans grew fonder of the game, football leaders struggled to maintain organization and operate the sport as a business.

On June 24, 1922, the American Professional Football Association changed its name to the National Football League and fielded 18 teams. Over the next few years the league expanded and contracted, adding teams and then consolidating them to concentrate the best players onto fewer teams. Teams such as the Oorang Indians, Duluth Eskimos, and Akron Pros faded away as teams like the Chicago Bears, New York Giants and Green Bay Packers rose in significance. The league initiated several rule changes to further differentiate the professional style of football from college ball. The NFL formed key practices that define the league today, such as the annual NFL draft of college players and the Pro Bowl.

Fans experienced the sport in new ways in 1939 when the first televised NFL football game aired. Television would forever change professional football. The competition between the Brooklyn Dodgers and Philadelphia Eagles was broadcast to approximately 1,000 television sets in New York.[3] The league saw season-long attendance surpass the one million mark that year. Over the next six years, players departing for service in World War II depleted the rosters of NFL teams and provoked some teams to merge temporarily to sustain league operations. Following the war, the NFL continued to grow and make incremental changes that further shaped the league into a compelling game and thriving business.

1. When the Saints Came Marching In

The year 1950 marked a new era for professional football when the Los Angeles Rams became the first NFL team to have all of its games—both home and away—televised. Other teams followed suit and began to arrange their own deals to put games on television. The growing popularity of both television and football in American culture planted the seed for a bidding war that escalated each year as television networks sought to attract football fans. The first NFL championship game was televised across the nation with the DuMont Network paying $75,000 for the broadcasting rights.[4] In 1955 NBC usurped DuMont as the network for the title game by paying a $100,000 rights fee.

In the early 1960s, professional football leaders pushed for business and political reforms that shaped the modern NFL. Pete Rozelle was elected NFL commissioner and moved the league offices to New York City. Rozelle created a model for professional sports based on the principle that cooperation rather than financial competition would better serve a club's individual interests. Revenue sharing coupled with a national television contract formed the cornerstone of the financial success of the NFL. Rozelle convinced large-market team owners that sharing television revenue would mean financial stability throughout the league and success for everyone rather than disparities between large-market and small-market teams. The previous model relied on each club securing individual television contracts. In 1960 team television deals ranged from $75,000 for the Green Bay Packers to $175,000 for the New York Giants.[5]

U.S. antitrust laws that sought to discourage monopolies and promote free-market competition stood in way of the NFL's growth strategy. In order to establish this profit-sharing idea, which held a potential national TV contract as its key piece, the league would have to bypass antitrust law. A bill legalizing single-network television contracts by professional sports leagues was introduced in Congress. Rozelle "secured the future of the NFL" when his lobbying won congressional approval: the Sports Broadcasting Act of 1961.[6] The NFL became free to implement a revenue-sharing model centered on a single television contract, rather than encouraging local teams to secure individual deals.

In 1962 the NFL entered into a single-network agreement with CBS to telecast all regular season games for $4.65 million annually.[7] Rival network NBC snagged exclusive broadcast rights for the championship game, paying $926,000 for the privilege of televising one game. The bidding war for exclusive rights over NFL broadcasts escalated. Within a five-year time span, the television contract for the NFL ballooned from $615,000 annually to $18.8 million. This growth would not have been possible without the legislative support that legalized the single-network contract. The NFL's power over broadcast media intensified when the legality of the NFL's television blackout within a 75-mile radius of home games was upheld. The blackout rule served to encourage ticket sales within the host city. The league further strengthened its financial and cultural power by forming NFL Films and NFL Properties, the licensing arm of the NFL.

Despite the emergence of the NFL, the American Football League (AFL) still existed as a rival league. Between 1962 and 1965, football players saw a dramatic rise in salaries as the NFL and the AFL competed to obtain the best talent. The war reached a new height in 1966 when the AFL and NFL spent a combined $7 million to sign their draft choices.[8] Caught in a bidding war that would upset the financial balance the NFL desired, the two leagues sought a merger. Under the agreement, the two leagues intended to form an expanded league with 24 teams, to be increased to 26 in 1968 and to 28 by 1970, when the official regular season as one entity would start. All existing franchises would be retained and none would be relocated outside their metropolitan areas.[9] Even though each league kept separate schedules during the transition period through 1969, an annual combined draft and championship game began in 1967.

New Orleans entered the professional football scene at this time. The political clout of Louisiana politicians worked in tandem with the ambitions of the NFL commissioner to both secure the future of the league and to ensure New Orleans would be a part of that action. The AFL-NFL merger required Congress to grant the NFL an antitrust exemption because the merger would otherwise violate antitrust law at the expense of the football players, who would no longer be able to pit the rival leagues against each other in bidding for their salaries.[10] Louisiana politicians Senator Russell Long and House Majority Leader Hale Boggs attached the antitrust exemption to a budget bill and pushed it through Congress on the promise that New Orleans would be awarded the next NFL franchise. Congress passed the bill on October 21, 1966, solidifying the creation of the modern NFL.[11] Eleven days later the NFL announced that New Orleans would be awarded the next NFL franchise.

New Orleans, an NFL City: 1960–2005

New Orleans has always been a remarkable sports city.[12] Culturally and politically, New Orleans established itself as a football town even before the National Football League awarded its 16th franchise to the city in 1966. Louisiana State University and Tulane University were powerhouses in college football. New Orleans hosted the annual Sugar Bowl collegiate championship game every January since its inception in 1934. The Sugar Bowl ranked second only to Mardi Gras in the number of visitors it brought to New Orleans.[13] The Bayou Classic, one of the best-known rivalries in historically-black-college football, has been held in New Orleans annually since 1974. Even high school football dominated local news headlines.

Community leaders wanted to attract professional sports teams and signature national-level competitions to establish New Orleans as a major sports town. This commitment to sports development reflected a trend after World War II, when professional sports leagues spread out of northeastern and midwestern cities and into western and southern areas where population and economic changes increased demand for high-profile entertainment.[14] Post–World War II New Orleans was marked with a declining business district. Political leaders dreamed about strengthening the city through sports-related projects and laid out plans for baseball, football and suburban development. Leaders had every reason to believe that a professional football team would be successful in a football-loving place like New Orleans. To test the city's affinity for professional football, in August 1962 a preseason AFL game was played in City Park stadium. A crowd of 31,000 attended that game and 20,000 people pledged to buy season tickets if a professional football franchise came to New Orleans.[15] Support for professional football gained traction as business and political leaders worked in tandem to shape New Orleans as a premier football destination.

New Orleans was itching for a professional football team during a time of complex segregation-integration issues across the country.

Like most other American social institutions, sports were influenced by a "separate but equal" doctrine manifested from the 1896 *Plessy v. Ferguson* case. Homer Plessy boarded a whites-only railcar at Press and Royal streets in New Orleans to protest state segregation laws that separated black and white spaces on trains and public accommodations. Unfortunately, Plessy lost, and decades of Jim Crow laws ensued in the southern United States. The Supreme Court reversed this decision in 1954, when the *Brown v. Board of Education of Topeka* school segregation case led the Supreme Court to declare that "separate but equal" was inherently unequal. The nation turned its attention towards Louisiana as six-year-old Ruby Bridges, escorted by a phalanx of U.S. marshals, walked through the doors of William Frantz Elementary School in the Upper Ninth Ward neighborhood in New Orleans. She became an icon of desegregation as the first African American child to attend a formerly all-white school in the Deep South. New Orleans thus had been a site for negotiating complex, nationwide racial issues. Sport spaces also served as sites for confronting larger issues of national race relations in the Civil Rights era.

African American athletes participated in football prior to *Brown v. Board of Education of Topeka*, and they served as agents to convince America that integration on the field could lead to integration off the field.[16] Professional football in general was experiencing a period of *reintegration* rather than integration, as blacks and whites had participated in sporting events together prior to the Jim Crow era. Fritz Pollard, the first black head coach in professional football, coached the Akron Pros as early as 1921. Ten years prior to the enactment of a 1956 Louisiana statute banning mixed-race sporting events and mandating segregated audience seating, the Los Angeles Rams ended a twelve-season ban on black players in the NFL by signing Kenny Washington, the first African American to play in the NFL since Joe Lillard and Ray Kemp in 1933.[17] On a national level, the black press considered the reintegration of football one of the top stories of 1946. Some 50 years later, historian Charles K. Ross wrote, "Many black Americans believed that desegregation on the sports field would promote the spirit of equality in other aspects of American life."[18] Across the country, sport spaces served as platforms for negotiating racial changes as America moved through the Civil Rights era of the 1960s.

Despite these changes, southern politicians passed segregationist statutes that further strengthened the Jim Crow customs that seeped into recreational spaces. Louisiana legislators ratified 23 new constitutional amendments, including a 1956 statute forbidding race mixing in social and sporting events. This ban on interracial mixing at Louisiana sporting events reversed national progress that had been made in the decade prior as African Americans began breaking color barriers in professional sports. In comparison to football in the rest of the country, New Orleans' racial progress was significantly lacking.

Racism that played out on the streets of New Orleans threatened New Orleans' image as a tourist destination and premier locale for sporting events. African American football players traveling to New Orleans for an exhibition game experienced a series of incidents of racial discrimination in what was supposed to be a hospitable city. Many of the African American players could not get taxis to pick them up at the airport, they overheard racist remarks from patrons in their hotel lobbies, and jazz clubs on Bourbon Street refused to let them enter.[19]

> Clem Daniels, a standout black player for the Oakland Raiders, stood with some teammates outside the Roosevelt Hotel, waiting for a taxi to the French Quarter. Although six cabs had lined up along University Place, the street that runs in front of the hotel, the drivers all left their cars to avoid serving the black players. After much frustration, Daniels recalled, "Finally we stood in the middle of the street and a cab stopped rather than run us down." Upon reaching the famed Bourbon Street, Daniels and his friends found themselves mocked, insulted, and turned away by bouncers.[20]

Professional football players experienced this type of racism off the field as they traveled with their teammates to competitions in southern cities. The influx of professional football players sparked a racist backlash from Louisianans who believed they represented a potential wave of permanent change rather than being one-time visitors for a sports event.[21] These incidents occurred in New Orleans prior to an All-Star (AFL) football game that had presold over 50,000 tickets. In 1965 black football players from the Buffalo Bills boycotted the AFL All-Star game in New Orleans as a statement against the racist treatment they had received in public accommodations such as taxis and restaurants. This was the first ever boycott of a professional sports game's host city by the players themselves. The game was later moved to Houston.

Not only do national sporting events shine a light onto the host

11

city, they also hold economic significance for cities like New Orleans that rely on a tourism economy. In this instance, racism threatened the economic progress presumed to result from hosting sporting events with national appeal.

The early 1960s was a time when municipal leaders were worried about wounding the city's image with negative publicity surrounding segregation. Accordingly, they focused their efforts on desegregating tourist-oriented facilities.[22] Dave Dixon, who later became known as the father of the Superdome, established the New Orleans Pro Football Club, Inc., and led efforts to attract professional football to New Orleans. He was keenly aware of the role city race relations played in his efforts to secure NFL football for New Orleans.[23] With the increase in both African American athletes and spectators in professional football, New Orleans would have to demonstrate it could accept players, spectators, and media without regard to race.

To test the level of community support for racially integrated sports in New Orleans, a double-header exhibition game featuring the Chicago Bears and the Baltimore Colts was played in an effort to desegregate Tulane University's stadium. Located on private property, the stadium was exempt from racial segregation laws that governed public stadiums. At $8 per ticket, the 1963 exhibition game was the highest-priced football ticket in America for an exhibition game. For the first time in Louisiana history, professional football was played in front of a mixed-race crowd. Seats were sold on a first come, first served basis. The significance of the first come, first served policy was that African Americans could sit anywhere in the stadium. Dixon commented on the importance of this policy:

> I watched this historic ticket-selling drama from six feet away—the first desegregated sports event in the history of the Old South—and our young lady [the ticket seller] handled the situation perfectly. She showed the ticket chart and then stated the words "first come, first served." At that moment our (African-American) visitor asked, "You mean I can sit anywhere I want?" Our young lady answered affirmatively, at which point our "colored" football fan mumbled, "Alleluia."[24]

New Orleans' typically hot, sticky summer weather settled over the 52,000 people in the stadium. During the game, the rain poured, the field flooded, and the game was delayed for two hours while people sought refuge under the stadium. Organizers feared a race riot, but no such thing took place.[25] Dixon had been confident that the people of New Orleans would not have reacted negatively to desegregating football games during this time, and he reported that they ran into very little resistance integrating Tulane's stadium for this event in 1963.[26] The game boasted black attendance of more than 30 percent and was perhaps the most integrated professional football game ever held in the South.[27]

This exhibition game took place to show the NFL that the people of New Orleans were ready to accept professional football against the backdrop of racial progress in America. The social environment seemed ripe for bringing professional football to New Orleans, but racial segregation laws of Louisiana as they existed in the early 1960s remained a barrier to attracting the NFL. According to the Civil Rights Act of 1964, Louisiana's Jim Crow laws were now deemed unconstitutional by federal courts. However, these laws needed to be erased from federal court in New Orleans.

With $6,000 in cash secretly tucked into his pocket, Dave Dixon held a meeting with local black leaders to convince them to assign one of their lawyers to go before the federal bench and represent this cause. After agreeing that a $2,000 fee would help entice this group to take action, Dixon flipped the cash onto the table and the plan was set in motion. Dutch Morial, who would later become mayor of New Orleans, was the young lawyer who represented the matter and got the laws struck down.[28]

Based on the success of the racially integrated exhibition game and changes to local segregation laws, Dixon believed he had convinced the NFL that New Orleans' racial climate was progressive enough to support the increasing national affinity for African American athletic talent.[29] However, a major political hurdle still existed before New Orleans could become the next pro football city. The NFL would have to choose New Orleans over other competing cities to win the next franchise. New Orleans politicians used their legislative muscles to take advantage of the current dilemma facing the commissioner of football—how to legally merge the NFL and the AFL into one league. Louisiana Congressman Hale Boggs and Senator Russell Long pushed the AFL-NFL Antitrust Exemption Bill through Congress on the promise that if they did so, the NFL commissioner would immediately award a franchise to New Orleans.[30] Boggs threatened to vote against the bill until commissioner Rozelle assured him that New Orleans would immediately be granted the next franchise. Praising Boggs's political savvy in this situation, Dave Dixon said, "With that merger, the people of our city made near billionaires out of all NFL owners ... the NFL owes New Orleans, big time."[31]

This type of political conniving that made Louisiana politics infamous resulted in the birth of Saints football in New Orleans. On All Saints Day, November 1, 1966, commissioner Pete Rozelle announced that the NFL's 16th franchise would go to New Orleans. The city paid a $50,000 franchise fee to create the New Orleans Saints. Tulane University pledged to permit a professional team to use its 82,500-seat stadium as an interim facility until one dedicated to Saints football could be built. Within days after the announcement, Dixon lobbied the state to establish a commission empowered to levy a hotel occupancy tax in metropolitan New Orleans and use the proceeds from finance bonds to construct a new stadium.[32] This hotel tax in New Orleans and neighboring Jefferson Parish continues to fund the Louisiana Stadium and Exposition District (LSED). Taxes on tourist commodities such as hotels provided a source of revenue that many different local governments deploy to meet the demands imposed on NFL cities.

Initial excitement for the team could be seen in the line of people queued up to buy Saints season tickets. During the Saints' first season ticket launch on March 8, 1967, they sold 20,000 season tickets on the first day and 33,000 before the first game. September 17, 1967, marked the first Saints kickoff, in front of a sellout crowd of 80,879, against the Los Angeles Rams at Tulane Stadium. Archbishop Philip M. Hannan delivered a prayer that many in attendance may still remember:

> God, we ask your blessing upon all who participate in this event, and all who have supported our Saints. Our heavenly father who has instructed us that the "saints by faith conquered kingdoms ... and overcame lions," grant our Saints an increase of faith and strength so that they will not only overcome the Lions, but also the Bears, the Rams, the Giants, and even those awesome people in Green Bay.
>
> May they continue to tame the Redskins and fetter the Falcons as well as the Eagles. Give to our owners and coaches the continued ability to be as wise as serpents and as simple as doves, so that no good talent will dodge our draft.

Grant to our fans perseverance in their devotion and unlimited lung power,
tempered with a sense of charity to all, including the referees.

May our beloved "Bedlam Bowl" [Tulane Stadium] be a source of good fel-
lowship and may the "Saints Come Marching In" [sic] be a victory march for all,
now and in eternity.[33]

This humorous prayer marked the beginning of New Orleanians creating a distinct fan culture surrounding Saints football.

The Superdome: Icon of a New, New Orleans

Nine years after the NFL announced the Saints had been awarded
to New Orleans, the Louisiana Superdome opened with a dedication
on August 3, 1975, as a 52-acre, 269-thousand-square-foot home to
the New Orleans Saints. Civic leaders involved in the process had been
anxious to design a facility that would outshine the Houston Astrodome.
Like many large-scale urban construction projects, final construction
on the Superdome lagged behind original deadlines for completion and
costs exceeded initial estimates. Construction broke ground for the
Superdome on August 11, 1971. The original plan started as a $35 mil-
lion, 55,000-seat stadium to be built in New Orleans East. It was completed as a 71,000-seat stadium in downtown New Orleans at a cost
of $163 million. The Superdome was supposed to have been ready to
host Super Bowl IX on January 12, 1975. However, it was not ready
until seven months later. Rather than punish New Orleans and move
Super Bowl IX to a different city, the NFL owners committed to New
Orleans, with or without the Superdome. Super Bowl IX, the third
Super Bowl hosted in New Orleans since the championship game was
conceived in 1967, was held in Tulane Stadium that year.

From the beginning, the Superdome emerged as a physical and
symbolic icon of downtown New Orleans' redevelopment, which had
begun in the 1950s. The Superdome was an urban renewal project that
was meant to anchor the downtown corridor, reverse decay and promote New Orleans' image as a major city.[34] Professional sports teams
serve as cultural commodities that politicians and civic boosters sometimes support with generous amounts of public funding in the hopes
of achieving larger urban renewal goals.[35] The Superdome served as a

barrier against blight on the northern end of Poydras Street to encourage investment from there to the Rivergate complex at the southern tip of Poydras by the Mississippi River. Geographer Peirce Lewis wrote, "The Dome would rise twenty-seven stories above the old railroad yards and be altogether the most visible thing in New Orleans—perhaps in the whole South."[36]

On August 9, 1975, the first Saints football game in the Superdome was played against the Houston Oilers in front of a crowd of 72,434. The new stadium was described as the "final piece to [New Orleans'] 'big league' puzzle" and the last jewel in New Orleans' "big league" crown.[37] Observers marveled at the size of the structure, which covered 13 acres and was 27 stories high, and its innovative technology as the world's largest steel constructed room.[38] Historical accounts described the building of the dome as a symbol of the "new, New Orleans."[39] The Superdome stood as a symbol that New Orleans could compete economically with regional metropolitan rivals such as Atlanta and Houston, and was supposed to elevate New Orleans to a status on par with cities like New York and Chicago. The New Orleans *Times-Picayune* listed the building's total economic impact over the first 10 years at $2.6 billion, and noted that "no urban renewal project in the history of the area beneficially impacted the surrounding area more than the mushroom that rose on Poydras Street."[40]

The Saints and the City: Fandom and Funding

Through the years, Saints football developed into its own cultural phenomenon throughout New Orleans. In addition to the normal wins and losses associated with sports, the Saints and the Superdome remained intimately connected to city life. The Superdome was built on the site of a railroad yard and the Girod Street Cemetery. One account of the dome's construction said, "Abandoned for years, [the cemetery's] iron caskets and bones were tossed up by excavation gear in the early 1970s as the crews moved in to build … the Superdome."[41] Unearthed and unidentified skeletons during construction were likely victims of an 1850s yellow fever epidemic and a 1930s cholera outbreak. Urban legends of a cursed Superdome grew, and some speculated that the building was plopped right on top of the burial ground of "voodoo queen" Marie Laveau. Water-cooler talks pinpointed the Saints football team as the main target of a Laveau curse, in which losing streaks were supernaturally linked to the ground upon which the gridiron lies. Voodoo rituals were performed in an attempt to lift the curse from the building and guide the Saints down a winning path. The team continued to lose, and expert practitioners argued that the ritual had been performed wrong as the curse was placed on the field itself, not the building.

In the 1980s, lengthy losing streaks led frustrated fans to don brown paper bags over their heads as a symbol of shame and proclaim their team better deserved the epithet "Aints." In contrast, the "Who Dats" emerged, eager to show support for the Saints. "Who Dat Nation" is the term used to describe a collective identity that encompasses all Saints fans. On game days the Superdome is packed with Who Dats, named for their trademark chant, "Who dat? Who dat? Who dat say dey gonna beat dem Saints?"

In 1984 Saints owner Tom Meachem Jr. announced that the Saints were for sale for a non-negotiable price of $75 million. This value far exceeded the $50,000 franchise fee the city paid to obtain the team in the first place. Nearly 20 years after the inception of the New Orleans Saints, Tom Benson, with Governor Edwin Edwards at his side, announced that Benson had signed a deal to purchase the Saints for $70.2 million. The value of the team increased considerably year after year. In 2014 *Forbes* listed the value of the team at $1.11 billion. This ranking puts New Orleans as number 23 out of 32 teams, whose values vary from $930 million to $3.2 billion.[42]

One of the real stories behind the rising value of NFL teams involves the financial commitments that state and local governments enter into with each team. In the mid–1990s and early 2000s, the Saints organization and the state of Louisiana went through several rounds of negotiating and renegotiating the terms of the contract that kept the Saints playing in the Superdome with New Orleans as their home city. Negotiations were not always amicable, as the government sought to strike a deal that the Saints could live with and the state could afford.

The state of Louisiana and the New Orleans business community remained committed to investing in professional sports in the New

Orleans region. In 1993 a sports bill was passed by lawmakers in Baton Rouge who voted in favor of renovations to the Superdome as well as building a new practice facility for the Saints. The Superdome Commission approved the sale of $14.5 million in bonds to go towards the construction of the Saints' practice facility in Metairie, approximately eight miles from the Superdome in neighboring Jefferson Parish. Within the year, questions arose about whether or not the amount of money generated from a hotel-motel tax directed at supporting professional sports in New Orleans would be enough to finance $80 million in bonds that had been issued to renovate the Superdome, refinance bond debt, and invest in other sports start-up projects.[43] The borrowing and issuing of bonds was a popular mechanism for any municipality financing sport facility construction. The New Orleans region was making a push to increase its status by constructing a new $110 million arena as well as a $20 million minor-league baseball facility. Within this climate, the New Orleans Saints were able to keep tweaking their deal with the state.

In 1994 all parties were seeking a 25-year lease agreement that would keep the Saints in New Orleans through 2018. With Governor Edwin Edwards in the leadership role during this round of negotiations, the state guaranteed it would pay $6 million towards the construction of a new football training facility that the Saints would then be able to use rent-free. The agreement also capped the rent that the Saints would have to pay the Superdome annually at $800,000. At the time, the deal between the Saints and the state was dubbed average for the NFL.[44]

The commitment to using public funds to finance the Saints' progress was not surprising, as the 1990s ushered in a stadium construction boom where nearly half of the professional sports teams in the United States were either playing in a new facility or making plans to build one. Professional sports teams no longer relied solely on private sources of money, such as the team owners themselves, and were increasingly subsidized by state and local governments. The mid–1990s marked a peak in national conversations about professional sports teams relocating to other cities if their home city refused to capitulate to the power of team owners who could use competition between cities to demand subsidies and sweeter deals.[45]

Advocates of stadium building projects justified using public subsidies for sports teams by arguing that facilities and teams provided positive gains to the local economy. Constructing a major sporting facility was said to create new jobs, provide free publicity by turning a city into a popular destination, attract new business, and gain additional tax revenue through lease payments on the building.[46] Much of the academic literature about the relationship between professional sports and the city centers on this economic framework. The conversations focus on the fact that many professional sports teams and facilities, especially in the United States, are heavily subsidized with public dollars despite the overwhelming evidence that shows the economic benefits dip far lower than advertised.[47]

Even though Benson and Edwards inked a deal in 1994 to keep the Saints in New Orleans long-term, doubts about the financial sustainability of keeping professional football in New Orleans resurfaced during the next six years. Benson returned to the negotiating table with two more Louisiana governors as the loyalty between the state, the Saints and the fans of a continuously losing team remained shaky. Saints profits fell as the Saints struggled to sell tickets during a time when the popularity of other NFL teams soared. In 1998 NFL profitability quadrupled with the help of a lucrative television contract. The Saints, however, saw a 40 percent drop in operating income that year.[48] Saints officials complained publicly that their Superdome lease was not competitive with the rapidly rising standards of the NFL and that the lagging ticket sales created financial woes for the team. Fans saw the Saints raise ticket prices year after year while the organization failed to deliver a winning team.

New professional sports threatened to dethrone the Saints as the only professional team in town. The New Orleans Arena opened in 1999 as an incentive to lure professional basketball or hockey to New Orleans. Talk of trying to relocate a National Basketball Association team to New Orleans provoked saber-rattling between New Orleans and San Antonio. While New Orleans threatened to take the San Antonio Spurs NBA team, the mayor of San Antonio threatened to lure the New Orleans Saints to Texas.[49] That same year, the narrative of a losing team record coupled with financial troubles facing both the Saints and the state of Louisiana intensified speculation about whether the Saints would leave New Orleans. In 2000, the Superdome's 25th year, it was described as the most expensive stadium in history in one of the poorest states in the nation.[50] Questions about how to keep an NFL team profitable in a small market like New Orleans reached a head in 2001 as the state of Louisiana, led by Governor Mike Foster, entered into intense negotiations with Saints owner Tom Benson. Benson inked a deal with Governor Foster that resulted in a 10-year lease agreement wherein the state would use public funds to subsidize $186.5 million over the length of the term. This guaranteed the Saints an annual subsidy starting at $12.5 million and escalating to $23.5 million in the final few years of the deal.[51] Like other cities with professional sports teams, New Orleans had to keep up with the growth of the NFL by opening up its public coffers.

Even though Benson and Foster agreed to the broad outlines of a deal that guaranteed revenue payments for the team, the deal did not give the Saints what they really wanted: a new stadium. The Saints organization set their sights on a new stadium as the answer to their financial troubles. Saints executives argued that they could not stay competitive in the NFL without the additional revenue that could be gained from constructing a new venue for football.

A new stadium was the key sticking point throughout the 2001 contract negotiations. The New Orleans business community created the Save Our Saints Advisory Committee to build momentum during this round of fights to keep the Saints in New Orleans. The state argued that the 26-year-old Superdome was still viable. Benson argued that the Superdome was outdated and that a new facility, designed solely as a football stadium, was necessary for the Saints to remain competitive in the NFL. Rather than a generic, domed facility that could be used for multiple types of events and conventions, the Saints envisioned bringing a $450 million retractable-roof football stadium to New Orleans. While an enormous domed facility was an architectural marvel in the 1960s and 1970s, retractable-roof technology was the hottest trend in stadium construction design in the early 2000s. It represented the best of both worlds, where the stadium roof could either be closed during inclement weather or remain open in order to create the atmosphere of an open-air football stadium on fair days.

Negotiations did not go smoothly as the Saints would not give up their request for a new stadium. State officials offered counterproposals centering on renovations to the Superdome, added deadlines into the contract for when they would provide more concrete decisions on the stadium issue, and created a task force to study the feasibility of a new stadium. At this point in the relationship, the state sunk $75 million into stadium renovations to make the Superdome more profitable for the Saints. The Saints were receiving millions in taxpayer subsidies every year, but the stadium issue had not exactly been resolved. In addition, the 2001 deal signed by Benson and Foster did not silence the threat of team relocation, as there were escape provisions in the contract that would have allowed the Saints to move if they were not satisfied with their financial prospects or with stadium accommodations.

The Saints organization compiled a development team of architectural, real estate and consulting firms and busied itself in creating a vision for a new stadium. An architectural firm worked on stadium design, favorable economic impact reports were commissioned, and several locations were identified and analyzed as potential sites for the new stadium. The Saints had spent years crafting their own plan for sports-led urban redevelopment without much cooperative input from Mayor Marc Morial and other government officials. One of their favored sites in 2001 was the Iberville public housing complex, which they proposed to demolish in order to build a 40-acre sports complex off of Canal and Rampart streets that would represent a $1 billion revitalization of the Tremé neighborhood.[52] This particular plan never gained traction, as political and community backlash coupled with stalled financial negotiations strained the Saints' relationship with New Orleans in the few years prior to Hurricane Katrina. The Saints organization took actions, such as the identification of potential new stadium building sites, with a conviction that they were going to get what they wanted or else move their city's beloved team elsewhere.

When New Orleans politicians aided the NFL in 1966 in winning congressional approval to operate outside of antitrust laws, these actions sealed the role of the government as "a powerful enabling, but non-profit-sharing, partner" to the NFL.[53] The uneven power structure embodied in that legislation continued to guide the relationship between local governments and professional sports teams. The intention of the NFL had always been to maximize profit for a small number of member teams. Improving economic conditions for host cities was not the core mission of the NFL, despite the willingness of taxpayers and local governments to fund teams with public subsidies based on the hope that professional sports would economically benefit home cities. Scholars overwhelmingly concluded that the economic impact for home cities does not outweigh the public subsidy costs of acquiring and retaining professional sports teams and stadiums.[54] NFL teams were continuously promoted as being a public good that benefits the city as a whole, despite the reality that NFL franchises are privately owned businesses.

A problematic relationship developed between local governments and NFL owners. Cities paid the tab while team owners generated personal wealth. The threat of team relocation coupled with the monopoly status of the NFL left cities little choice but to invest public funds into stadium building to retain sports teams and attract national events. The alternative would be to risk losing the beloved home team to another city with a better financial offer.[55] The city of New Orleans had already lost the New Orleans Jazz basketball team to Utah in 1979. State and city governments impose local sales taxes, borrow and issue bonds, and dedicate millions of dollars in annual payments to keep their home sports teams.

This burden weighed heavily on Louisiana when Governor Kathleen Blanco took office in January 2004. Within months of taking the helm, Blanco fired out pleas to Tom Benson to renegotiate the Saints' lease agreement, insisting that the state simply did not have enough money to pay the Saints. Saints officials stood firm in their insistence that a contract is a contract and expected the state to live up to its agreement to pay the annual fee to the team, which would soon balloon to $23.5 million. The Saints were viewed as being totally unreasonable with the demands they had made during Governor Murphy J. Foster Jr.'s tenure, and the organization was equally uncompromising in their dealings with Blanco, even walking away from negotiations and calling off talks. Repeated attempts through the 2004 football season to have a rational discussion about the sustainability of using large public subsidies to fund Saints football produced no results. Tom Benson held the upper hand in negotiations and broke off all talks with Blanco in April 2005.

1. When the Saints Came Marching In

By 2005 the growth of the NFL into a cultural and financial powerhouse left Louisiana struggling with its role as the "enabling, yet non-profit-benefiting" partner of the NFL. Despite the growing success of the NFL and the steep price Louisiana was paying to retain a team, by 2005 the team had never sold out the Superdome on a season ticket basis. Fans' love for the Saints was constantly challenged as the Saints played for 21 years before celebrating their first winning season and 35 years before winning their first playoff game.[56]

In 2004 and 2005 the Saints organization had a very poor relationship with the New Orleans public. The local papers documented sour relationships between the Saints owner and state officials, as the public subsidy deal became more of a burden to fund. Years of losing seasons coupled with poor internal team management disheartened Saints fans, and one result was dwindling ticket sales to home games. Impending local television blackouts of games plagued the 2004 season due to minimum attendance requirements at individual games. Despite the lagging ticket sales, NFL marketing reports often ranked Saints fans among the most loyal in professional sports. This honor was due to their rate of attendance at games when stacked up against number of losses throughout the teams' history. Saints fans credited themselves as being a people who can persevere. The team lost almost every season, but the fans kept coming back every season. They had faith that the team could be better next season. On August 17, 2005, the New Orleans *Times-Picayune* reported that Benson was ready to resume talks with Governor Blanco to try to resolve the stalemate.

The Saints rolled out a new advertising campaign at the start of every season. In 2005 the theme was "You Gotta Have Faith." A television commercial showcased vintage Saints bumper stickers and a series of slogans used throughout team history. It celebrated the loyalty of Saints fans in New Orleans throughout the team's 39-year history and ended with a shot of a bumper sticker that displayed the word FAITH. It was with this hope and faith that the Saints entered into the 2005 season. Friday night, August 26, 2005, was the last game the Saints would play in the Louisiana Superdome before Hurricane Katrina changed everything.

2

Hurricane Katrina and the Shelter of Last Resort

On Friday evening, August 26, 2005, the New Orleans Saints played a preseason game in the Superdome against the Baltimore Ravens. At the time, I was an employee of the New Orleans Saints. I bounced from one suite to another in my role as a corporate sponsorship manager and visited with clients on behalf of my employer. I paused briefly to notice that the televisions in the suites were broadcasting some type of weather report. The Saints lost that night, 21–6. The next day, city residents were fully occupied in decisions about whether or not to evacuate from Hurricane Katrina.

Hurricanes and other severe summer storm activity plague the entire Gulf Coast region every year, particularly during the Atlantic hurricane season, which lasts from June 1 through November 30. New Orleans' position along the Gulf of Mexico leaves the city lying in the pathway of as many as ten named storms every year. The history of New Orleans as a target for hurricanes worked against citizens as Katrina approached. Many had grown complacent about the constant hit and miss threats of summer storms. The expense and time it took to evacuate every time a storm entered the Gulf was considered an annoying burden, rather than a life-saving measure, particularly when the storm changed course and residents who struggled through traffic abruptly turned around to get back to normal responsibilities. This was the case in 2004 with Hurricane Ivan. Traffic congestion spanned 50 miles, causing a 12-hour delay.[1] Ivan, just one year prior, prompted many to scrutinize whether or not they wanted to go through that again as Katrina churned in the Gulf.

Looming storms were seen not necessarily as threats but rather

24

as a way of life. Lifelong New Orleans residents felt that since they had survived hurricanes before, they had no reason to believe they could not ride out the storm again. Homeowners and business owners wanted to stay so they would be able to repair any damage from winds or waters right away. The compulsion to protect private property was strong. The decision whether or not to evacuate was not an easy decision for New Orleanians and one that was not made without consulting family, employers or other social connectors such as church leaders. The saying "If one of us doesn't go, none of us go" is an accurate descriptor of how families in New Orleans felt about hurricane evacuations.

As Hurricane Katrina traveled through the warm waters of the Gulf of Mexico, it grew massively, reaching Category 5 status as it swirled closer and closer to New Orleans. Complacency faded as people began to realize that this might not be just another storm. During a press conference, the mayor advised citizens, "We're facing the storm most of us have feared."[2] Many people packed up their belongings and fled the city. Many others did not.

On Saturday, August 27, the New Orleans Saints football players and coaches evacuated to California, arriving early for their next pre-season game. Many of the lower-wage workers of the Saints organization, like the ticket sales staff, stayed in New Orleans. They were not invited to evacuate with the players, coaches and scouts and were called and told by upper management to be prepared to return to work selling game tickets on Monday morning. One young man who worked for the team told me he was not going to evacuate because he couldn't afford to do anything that might cause him to lose his job. A young woman who worked in ticket sales planned to go to her office in the Superdome to ride out the storm if it got bad. During previous storms it was not uncommon for a few Saints employees to stay in their offices in the Superdome instead of their apartments to ride out a storm.

I had driven all night with friends, arriving at a motel in Houston around 10:00 on Sunday morning. We waited in the motel parking lot for several hours before being allowed into our room. The area was thick with other evacuees from New Orleans. I had listened to the radio all night while driving in the car. Sometime around 3:00 a.m. we were able to pick up a radio station signal. I remember hearing the words "definitely a Category 5, definitely aimed right at New Orleans." That was when my little group of friends started making phone calls. I called and interrupted "hurricane parties" among friends who had planned to stay in New Orleans to ride out the storm. Hurricane parties included copious amount of alcohol along with the usual supplies of canned goods and flashlights needed to prepare for a storm. Anyone who went to bed on Saturday night thinking the storm would not be so bad woke up Sunday morning and heard a very different story as soon as they turned on their TV or radio.

At 9:30 a.m. on Sunday, August 28, New Orleans mayor Ray Nagin ordered the first-ever mandatory evacuation of the city of New Orleans. New Orleans had already implemented the contraflow plan for those who had voluntarily evacuated prior to Sunday. The contraflow plan turned all lanes of interstate traffic into one-way routes out of town. The states of Louisiana and Mississippi worked cooperatively in contraflow, in order to utilize shared interstate systems to evacuate as many as 1.2 million people from the greater New Orleans area.[3] The U.S. evacuation model focused on the individual automobile as the method of escaping hazards. This reliance on car ownership automatically would leave many citizens behind when an evacuation order was issued. In New Orleans, many residents did not own cars. Prior to Katrina's landfall, as many as 127,000 people did not have access to cars when the mandatory evacuation was announced.

Not everyone had the resources necessary to evacuate ahead of the storm. Consider the different types of people who compose an urban population for whom evacuating would be difficult or impossible: homeless; victims of domestic violence hiding from an abuser in a women's shelter; someone needing frequent medication or regular dialysis treatments; hospital patients; tourists staying in hotels after the airport discontinues operations; someone without enough money to fill the car with a tank of gas; someone who refuses to leave her home because no shelter or hotel will let her bring her pets. Those without means have few choices and must either stay at home or seek out government-designated shelters. The Superdome, a venue built for football, became New Orleans' government-designated shelter.

The Shelter of Last Resort

Nagin announced the Superdome would open as the refuge of last resort. Nowhere else in the city would be capable of sustaining winds higher than a Category 3 hurricane level. Officially, the Superdome would open to take people with special needs. The *Times-Picayune* reported the following message: "Nagin said the city would open the Superdome as a shelter of last resort for evacuees with special needs. He advised anyone planning to stay there to bring their own food, drinks and other comforts such as folding chairs, as if planning to go camping." The reality did not resemble camping in any way.

For me, this scene played on a tiny television in a motel room in Houston, Texas. I watched on the television as people queued up, waiting to get into the dome. The news reports calmly advised people to bring enough supplies to last for a few days. Some people shuffled towards the Superdome with a few bags of supplies. Many of the arms I saw carried nothing. The images on the TV showed throngs of people with no belongings at all, let alone a few days' worth of supplies. And then I watched as the rain started pouring down on them, soaking people as they waited outside in a lengthy line trying to get into the shelter. I discovered later that it was intense security screenings that were taking so long in getting the people into the dome and out of the weather. Crowds formed before dawn on that Sunday. The last person did not make it into the building until around 10:30 p.m. A reporter described the scene:

> Clad in T-shirts, shorts and flip-flops, the evacuees wound their way to the front lobby, where they were submitted to a thorough security search. Soldiers probed every cooler, plastic bag, backpack and suitcase that entered the building. They asked the able-bodied people to clasp their hands behind their heads and patted them down. They searched cuffs, hems and seams and then waved metal-detecting wands to scan for weapons, drugs and alcohol.[4]

This was not the first time the Superdome was used as shelter from a storm. Hurricane George in 1998, Hurricane Ivan in 2004 and Hurricane Dennis in 2005 all prompted opening the Superdome to city residents seeking shelter from an approaching storm. About 14,000 people sought shelter from Hurricane George in 1998. Due to a city-wide curfew imposed by then mayor Marc Morial, residents complained the Superdome felt like a prison rather than a refuge from the storm.[5]

The previous experiences in using the dome as a shelter were mostly uneventful, with news reports citing such minor crimes as theft of furniture and property damage committed by people staying in the Superdome. During Katrina, although the security searches were thorough, little else was organized to care for the tens of thousands of people seeking shelter. The city was ill prepared to manage the Superdome as a shelter. Supplies such as food and toilets were much lower than what had been requested by Superdome management. The necessary support personnel were not in place in advance of the storm. Federal Emergency Management Agency (FEMA) medical disaster teams, for example, were not scheduled to arrive for several days.

The mood across the city was ominous. On the news Governor Kathleen Blanco donned a serious facial expression and asked residents who chose to stay to write their Social Security number on their arm in permanent marker. She implied this would make it easier for emergency personnel to identify dead bodies. Those planning to weather the storm at home were reminded to include an axe as a necessary supply. The axes were for chopping a hole through the attic to escape onto the roof should flood waters rise to that height. Families had conversations about who could and could not swim, in case circumstances came to their very worst. People accepted that the storm was coming. Hurricane Katrina made landfall at 6:30 a.m. on August 29, 2005.

The wind and water assaulted the city. Power went out, while emergency generators did what they could. Plumbing failed and toilets overflowed, filling the Superdome with an overpowering foul stench. Those in the Superdome had no way to bathe, brush their teeth, change their clothes or even relieve themselves decently. They were provided with some military-issue MREs (meals ready to eat) but not provided with information.[6] At 6:00 a.m. on Monday, August 30, the roof panels of the dome started tearing away. Katrina left gaping holes in the roof of the Superdome, soaking the inside of the building with rain, condensation, and doubt about the strength of the building to protect those inside.

Evacuees inside the dome were not allowed to leave. Five hundred National Guard soldiers sent to contain the situation held them inside.

By Monday thousands more people entered the dome, trying to escape the destruction outside. Estimates put the number of people who sought shelter in the Superdome from 24,000 up to as many as 41,000. In the confusion and chaos of the storm, it was difficult to gather an accurate count.

At first, city residents breathed a sigh of relief because the city had avoided a direct hit as the eye of the storm made landfall a little east of the city. But the temporary relief turned to terror when the levees broke. People left behind in the city suspected that the water was coming in over the levees, rather than from hurricane rains. The city relied on a system of levees and floodwalls for protection against the water surrounding it. Geographically, New Orleans resembles a bowl flanked by water with the Mississippi River on one end and Lake Pontchartrain on the other. This leaves the city susceptible to flooding. Water that enters the bowl does not flow out on its own and disappear. Excess water has to be pumped out. To address this issue, 22 drainage pumping stations in New Orleans ran 24 hours a day, 7 days a week.[7] Some amount of street flooding is common in New Orleans even during afternoon showers as the pumps work to mitigate the overflow.

Water was rising so rapidly in the city it could not have been from storm rains alone. People reported hearing a "boom" and thinking that it was an explosion. In the Lower Ninth Ward neighborhood, it is possible the boom was the sound of a barge hitting the concrete floodwall and crashing through the levee, providing a massive gateway for waters to devastate the neighborhood. Some residents believed they had heard dynamite exploding and thought it was done intentionally to flood the predominantly black neighborhood. On the face of it, this may sound like an irrational conclusion, but New Orleans has mechanisms in place to divert floodwater from one area by directing it to another. New Orleans leaders had a history of intentionally dynamiting levees downriver from the city during the 1927 and 1965 floods,[8] which resulted in flooding predominantly black neighborhoods in order to preserve the city's business core. Although nothing like this happened in 2005, the residents' suspicions served to reinforce not only the lack of information about what was really happening in the city but also the vast distrust city residents had toward their government.

On Tuesday, even though the storm winds and rain had passed, water continued to rise due to levee breaches. Rising water threatened to kill the back-up emergency generator supplying the Superdome. Standing water prevented supply trucks from entering the area and essentially turned the Superdome into an island. Cell phones began to fail. Not just in the Superdome, but any phone number with a 504 area code had trouble completing calls or getting a signal. Breakdowns in communication had a terrifying effect. For those inside the Superdome, it meant they did not know what was happening outside. Some reports came sporadically over the radio. Eventually, enough information was gathered to know that people were trapped in attics trying to escape the rising floodwaters, and calling for help. Not knowing what was happening to neighborhoods, to homes, to friends and family who had decided not to leave, was terrifying. Not knowing when they would be allowed to leave the Superdome was troubling, and the people became frantic.

Mayor Nagin visited with Superdome management and informed them that levees had been breached throughout the city, water was pouring in and they would have to be prepared for everyone to stay in the Superdome for several more days. I spoke with one member of SMG, the Superdome management group, several months after Katrina. We were both sitting in the Saints' makeshift office in the Alamodome in San Antonio, Texas, getting ready for the Saints to play one of their "home" games of the season. As an operations employee at the Superdome, he had stayed in the Superdome when Katrina hit. He told me about something he called the 14-point list. He said they had given Mayor Nagin a list of 14 things they would need in order to sustain people in the Superdome in Katrina's aftermath. The list contained items such as diapers and portable showers and toilets. He referred to it infamously as the 14-point list because, he recalled, they never received a single item.

He shared with me that the staff had been evacuated from the Superdome prior to the organized evacuations of the masses of people huddled inside. The New Orleans Police Department and National Guard decided to pull out of the building and evacuate SMG and Centerplate (the Superdome's food service operation) staff and their families. Their small group was marched to a helicopter by National Guard soldiers with guns lowered, pointed towards the crowd of people as the soldiers backed up to the helicopter. I was told several months after Katrina that one woman I used to work with during Saints games, one of Centerplate's top executives, had left New Orleans and would never return again. She had been too traumatized by her experiences inside the Superdome during its time as the shelter of last resort.

As Hurricane Katrina's winds pummeled New Orleans and the levee breaches flooded the city, the Superdome became known as the "shelter of last resort," as documented by thousands of media accounts. It was first uttered as a matter-of-fact statement from the lips of the mayor and within days morphed into an emotionally charged term with a variety of intense connotations.

Local news stories published the week Katrina made landfall revealed different metaphors used to describe the Superdome during this building's time as a negative icon for New Orleans. On August 29, 2005, the *Times-Picayune* referred to the dome as "ground zero," marking the Superdome as the epicenter of the Hurricane Katrina disaster. Descriptions of the situation in the Superdome started out somewhat mildly, as the local media only hinted at the inadequacy of conditions inside. The *Times-Picayune* reported, "The Dome was set up as a divided safe haven, with one side of the facility for the disabled and medically ill, where food and water and emergency personnel were plentiful. For the masses of residents, however, there was the other side, where all that was provided was a concrete stadium built for athletes and spectators."[9]

Words and phrases used to describe the Superdome included: "a sprawling building meant more for touchdowns than emergencies"; "safe haven"; "makeshift shelter"; "a place to ride out the storm"; "tightly guarded by young men and women in army fatigues"; and "last resort."[10] As the days clicked by, the language used to describe the conditions in the Superdome became more intense. According to reports, "More than 25,000 refugees were housed in the sweltering Superdome, saying that the Dome was filthy and smelled bad."[11] Later that same day, Louisiana's "most famous roof began to fail" as Hurricane Katrina left the "CBD landmark in tatters" and the Superdome's "iconic curved roof" was stripped away.[12] No longer describing the scene as a safe haven or shelter, the media began describing this place as an intolerable refuge. According to news reports, "The Superdome resembled a scene from

31

the Apocalypse ... a hellish environment of short tempers, unbearable heat and the overwhelming stench of human waste."[13]

Part of the tragedy of Hurricane Katrina is that much information about the damage that could be caused by a massive hurricane and subsequent levee failures was known ahead of time. The Louisiana State University Hurricane Public Research Center conducted a fictitious "Hurricane Pam" simulation the year before Hurricane Katrina struck that predicted with scientific certainty much of what would come to pass. President George W. Bush and FEMA officials have been criticized for having these reports in advance of Katrina and ignoring the warnings. When Hurricane Katrina did make landfall, it was not a direct hit on the city of New Orleans. It touched down east of the city. Even though Katrina was a Category 5 storm, reports say that Katrina had weakened to a Category 3 or even Category 1 when it hit certain areas. This adds evidence to the argument that the levees failed due to flawed engineering or poor maintenance rather than being slammed by an Category 5 natural disaster. People felt that they had been lied to about the level of protection that the levees offered the city. In the minds of many New Orleanians, the Army Corps of Engineers became villains in the story of the human-made tragedy of the levee failures. The disaster was compounded by failures at all levels of government in response to Katrina as well as the subsequent policies that served to slow the wheels of recovery. Even more astounding was the indifference shown towards a predominantly black urban population. Citizens were trapped inside the Superdome for five days before relief efforts were organized enough to begin to evacuate them. The Superdome became emblematic of the failed government response.

During these days, images in the media showed New Orleans as a place of destruction and terror. New Orleans during Katrina was defined by visuals of levee breaches, flooded streets, devastated houses, and residents being rescued from rooftops as helicopter crews lowered baskets to carry them away. Racial disparities in New Orleans came to the forefront as the country watched New Orleanians trapped inside and around a building that had been meant for football. A single image of the people in the Superdome made one reality very clear—the majority of people left stranded in New Orleans during Katrina were African American. One person who experienced Katrina from inside the dome said, "You could count the white people in the rest of the Superdome on one hand. I say 99 percent black and poor. I know everybody else feels like we weren't in a major city in America, our country."[14] The scenes of New Orleans residents suffering near the Superdome, the Convention Center and along Interstate 10 kicked off a national discussion about race. Those who were left behind in New Orleans were disproportionately African American, poor or elderly. The indifference shown toward New Orleans was equated to indifference toward black Americans.

During a live televised Concert for Hurricane Relief, rapper Kanye West went off script and told viewers that "President Bush doesn't care about black people." West is known for his outrageous comments, but in this instance, for those who could not shake the images of a predominantly black city forsaken by their own government, his words felt right. Lingering issues of structural racism in America came to the forefront in an unlikely place—a venue that was meant for football. New Orleans had used racially integrated football games as proof in 1965 that New Orleans could be a city of racial progress. Forty years later, the scene inside the Superdome during Katrina proved the opposite. A thin veil lifted to expose to the rest of the world harsh realities of what it meant to be black and poor in 21st-century America.[15]

Rumors about what was taking place in the Superdome were rampant. News reports of armed gangs roaming the halls of the stadium, murders and rape led people to picture a city shrouded in darkness and chaos. Those in charge, such as the mayor and police chief, did little to dispel the rumors and perpetuated some of the worst of them to national media outlets. New Orleans residents still marvel at the vast differences between what the media reported in the days after Katrina and their actual experiences. The media criminalized New Orleanians, particularly if they were black, as disaster management policies sought to reinforce prison-like conditions within government-sanctioned shelters and turn evacuation measures into a military operation rather than a relief effort.

Limited oral histories exist documenting what the experience was like for those in and around the Superdome in the days following Katrina. These accounts suggested that the lived experiences were different than any tidbits news reporters provided to the rest of the world to consume. The people sheltering inside the Superdome told of a grueling and terrifying experience. They were confined, surrounded by a sickening stench and suffocating heat with little food and water for several days. Those inside described the Superdome as a prison, with the people inside being held at gunpoint, rather than a shelter from the storm. One man whose testimony was included in an oral history of Katrina said, "We thought we was going to a shelter, but it was more of a prison."[16] Another man wrote, "What began as a place of rescue had turned into Alcatraz Prison. We could not leave. We could not escape the horrific odor of human waste that spread throughout the building."[17] People described the extensive search of their belongings upon entering the Superdome as one way of illustrating the prison-like management of the shelter: "As we were waiting in the incredibly slow line, some of us were amazed that here we were going into a homeless shelter and they were thoroughly searching us as if we were criminals."[18] Some say that Louisiana suffers from a "culture of incarceration." Unfortunately, this culture extended into disaster management policies.[19]

A common theme that ran through each account of being in the Superdome involved people fearing for their lives, believing they would be murdered at the hands of the military personnel occupying the dome. One man said, "I believe with all my heart the military was going to kill us."[20] The militarization of disaster response continued to criminalize New Orleanians. "People were forced out by gunpoint. People think that the rescue mission was not a military mission, but this was a military operation. People with guns telling you what to do, when to do it, where to stand, what not to do. Everywhere."[21]

As evacuees faced these external forces, their internal stories and experiences reflected a sense of community and family support. One overwhelming similarity between different accounts of being in the Superdome focused on people relying on each other, helping each other out, and sticking together. "Everybody was trying to hold each other up. If it wasn't for just everybody trying to pull together and save each other, then a lot more of us would have died. We all we had."[22] The idea of creating tiny support communities was evident in another firsthand account of someone stranded in New Orleans after Katrina who said, "When individuals has to fight to find food or water, it meant looking out for yourself. But when these basic needs were met, people began to look out for each other, working together and constructing a community."[23] Constructing a sense of community was important for New Orleanians in this dark and desperate situation. Some people in the Superdome turned to spiritual singing and clapping and walked the concourses singing "This Little Light of Mine."

People were left in the hellish conditions of the Superdome for four days before evacuations began. When it was time to evacuate the Superdome, there was confusion about the process. Pictures showed barricades constructed like three-sided cages full of people waiting to board buses. They were arranged into a line. Some reports say they were separating men into one line and women into another. There used to be a bridge between the Superdome and the New Orleans Center building next door. Known as the "Bud Bridge" during Saints games, it hosted live music on a stage and provided a space for tailgating fun. During Katrina, that space crowded with people thinking that was the way to the buses that would take them out of their miserable environment. People crowded to the bridge, packing themselves into line, desperate to get on a bus. People spent as long as two nights on that bridge waiting for evacuation in sweltering summer heat.

When the buses finally came, the city and the dome were emptied. In an almost matter-of-fact tone, one newspaper reported that "by early evening the Superdome was expected to be empty."[24] People were ushered onto buses without knowing their destination and were essentially cast out of the city on a one-way ticket. As the last of the residents drifted away from New Orleans, no one had any guarantees about when they would return or how they could rebuild their home. The tattered Superdome remained soaking in the center of a wrecked and water-logged city.

The San Antonio Saints

Within days after the storm hit, the Saints football and business management team moved operations to San Antonio, Texas. Within a week all personnel who chose to remain employed with the team, including myself, gathered in San Antonio to piece together an NFL season. All players, coaches and staff members lived in hotels, paid for

35

by the team for the first couple of weeks, before finding their own living quarters throughout the greater San Antonio area.

Eleven days after Katrina made landfall, all Saints employees—from ticket sellers to legal counsel—who had congregated in San Antonio in a timely fashion were invited to travel on the team's private plane to Charlotte, North Carolina, for the Saints' regularly scheduled football game against the Carolina Panthers. Including women staff members, such as myself, on this trip was a rare exception to Benson's long-standing rule that women were not allowed on the Saints' airplane. Private buses greeted the airplane in Charlotte, where a police escort guided the Saints to a hotel. As the team buses rolled up to the hotel, people stood behind ropes leading up to the hotel entrance. These people were fans of the Saints. They had gathered to get a glimpse of the football players as they walked from the bus into the hotel lobby. One man in the crowd cried out, "Deuce, Deuce! I lost everything. I don't have anything left but I have you." Deuce McAllister was a star player for the Saints. In that moment, a connection to his favorite player and to the Saints was what the man reached out for to feel connected to home.

The next morning, before the football game, several members of the Saints staff visited a shelter in Charlotte that had taken in hundreds of New Orleans residents. Donning shirts bearing the Saints logo, they shared teary-eyed exchanges with displaced residents as each recounted how their homes were all gone. Several employees from Outback Steakhouse set up at the shelter to serve lunch to everyone housed there. Sunday church services were held in a tent erected outdoors. On that particular Sunday afternoon, more than 600 shelters across the country were set up with televisions to enable evacuees to watch the Saints game.

On Sunday afternoon, September 11, 2005, the Saints embarked on their first regular season game since Hurricane Katrina struck the Gulf Coast. The Saints played against the Carolina Panthers at Bank of America stadium in Charlotte, North Carolina, in front of a crowd of 72,920. As the Saints players ran onto the field, the fans from the opposing team greeted them with heartfelt cheers and standing applause rather than boos. Homemade cardboard signs offered love and support for the Saints and the people of New Orleans. This touching gesture was very different from the typical "my team will destroy your team" propaganda that normally litters the stands at NFL games. Mardi Gras beads that were sold on the concourses during the game raised money for hurricane relief efforts. The players went through the motions of a regular NFL competition, but knew they were playing to uplift the spirits of a city that had just been destroyed. John Carney kicked a 47-yard field goal with three seconds left in the game to bring the Saints and the devastated Gulf South an emotional victory. The final score was New Orleans 23, Carolina 20. The winning moment was captured on the cover of *Sports Illustrated*, which sported a photo of Saints kicker John Carney in a victorious embrace with quarterback Aaron Brooks. Saints owner Tom Benson had an oversized version of the photo printed for each member of the Saints staff to keep as a memento of the game.

On Monday night, September 19, 2005, the Saints prepared for a game against the New York Giants. With a destroyed Superdome festering back home, the game that had originally been scheduled for New Orleans was moved to Giants Stadium in New York in front of a crowd of 68,031. Even though the Saints were in New York, the NFL counted this as a "home" game for the Saints. The event became part of the NFL Hurricane Relief Weekend to generate donations for Hurricane Katrina victims. A telethon featuring more than thirty NFL players raised $5 million for the Bush-Clinton Katrina Fund.[25] During a nationally televised message, football players from a variety of NFL teams wore black t-shirts emblazoned with the Saints black-and-gold fleur-de-lis logo that bore the words "Be a Saint." It was a rare and touching occasion to see players who would normally be rivals wearing an opposing team's logo in order to show support for the city and residents of New Orleans. This is just one example of an outpouring of support that sports organizations showed towards victims of Hurricane Katrina.

The sports world showed yet more support for the people of New Orleans. "Coaches Caring across America" was created to help rebuild the Gulf Coast by working with Habitat for Humanity. The Southeastern Conference (SEC) and its twelve collegiate member institutions donated $1 million to various Hurricane Katrina relief efforts. The National Basketball Association donated $2 million to relief efforts while the National Hockey League and Major League Baseball each donated at least $1 million to the Red Cross.[26] Philanthropic giving from all sources, not just sports, that poured into Katrina relief efforts totaled $6.5 billion. This was more than double the amount of charitable donations collected for either the 2004 South Asian tsunami or 9/11.[27] People involved in sport continue to support efforts to rebuild New Orleans through service projects. NBA Cares offers opportunities for basketball players, family and alumni to work on service projects in conjunction with hosting NBA All-Star Games. In addition, the Hope for Stanley Alliance brings college students and participants in the sports industry to New Orleans for service projects to assist in recovery efforts. Since 2006 Hope for Stanley has worked on 122 houses and provided 800 volunteers. No other organization outside of Louisiana has worked there more often.[28]

After the first couple of games on the road, for the remainder of the 2005 NFL season, the Saints operated out of San Antonio rather than New Orleans. The Saints executive offices and practice center, a state-owned facility in Metairie, Louisiana, escaped the storm undamaged but were taken over by FEMA as a base of operations for disaster response.

Many feared that the Saints would make San Antonio their permanent home. During this time, New Orleans' other professional sports team, the Hornets NBA basketball team, took up residence in Oklahoma City. People began to wonder whether the "city that care forgot" (as New Orleans is sometimes called) would become the "city that sports forgot" with both professional teams operating in other cities. Experts at Tulane University anticipated that there would be no way for New Orleans' economy to recover enough after the storm to support professional sports, let alone two professional sports teams. By professional sports standards that rely on the size of television markets, New Orleans had been a small market in the hierarchy of cities even before the storm. Rumors had circulated before Katrina that the state of Louisiana could not afford to keep up with public subsidy payments necessary to secure the Saints' future in New Orleans.

Deciding where to play Saints games that had originally been planned for the Superdome in 2005 was a contentious decision. The San Antonio business community had welcomed Saints owner Tom Benson with open arms and open wallets. He had business interests in San Antonio and a positive reputation there. From a logistical and financial standpoint, it made sense to him to play all "home" games in San Antonio. Saints president Arnie Fielkow persuaded Benson to stage some of the games in Baton Rouge because he felt that it would be important psychologically for the people of New Orleans to have the Saints play as close to their city as possible. People needed to know the Saints had not abandoned them. Fielkow understood the emotional connection between New Orleans residents and the Saints. As a result, the Saints scheduled three "home" games in the Alamodome in San Antonio, Texas, and four "home" games in Tiger Stadium at the Louisiana State University campus in Baton Rouge.

The Saints' business operations, temporary offices and weight training facilities were housed in the lower levels of the Alamodome in San Antonio until they had to vacate the building to make way for amateur athletics events that had already been scheduled to occupy the building prior to the Saints' unexpected arrival. The Saints personnel shifted offices to an abandoned sewer and water building on the edge of downtown San Antonio. The Saints players practiced wherever they could find space, including the football fields of local high schools. One afternoon, the players ran drills in an abandoned parking lot outside the old city water building. They continued to try to play the game of professional football, not knowing when or if they would return to New Orleans. Many members of the Saints organization thought the team was never going back to New Orleans.

When the Saints players had time off from their practice schedule, many of them visited shelters full of Katrina evacuees in San Antonio. Saints community outreach programs were fully operational throughout their host city. San Antonio residents showed an outpouring of positive support for the team. The ticket sales phone lines rang faster than sales staff could answer, a marked difference from the previous NFL season when the Saints ticket office had struggled to sell tickets to games in New Orleans. Local San Antonio businesses eagerly bought sponsorship packages and suites for the games that would be played in the Alamodome. The San Antonio Chamber of Commerce encouraged local businesses to support the Saints by purchasing suites, club tickets and sponsorships. These efforts were intended to demonstrate to the NFL that San Antonio was a city worthy of having its own NFL franchise. This positive relationship between the Saints organization and the city of San Antonio strengthened rumors circulating among Saints fans that Benson intended to relocate the team to San Antonio permanently. San Antonio was one of many cities that had always lingered in the background during contract negotiations between the Saints and the state of Louisiana as a possible relocation site if the state could not meet Benson's demands. After Katrina, fans saw more than a rumor of the threat of team relocation. They saw their beloved home team living and playing football in San Antonio. The San Antonio business community was doing everything possible to prove that they were a city that could financially support professional football in the manner that Tom Benson wanted.

On Sunday, October 2, the Saints played the first of three scheduled "home" games at the Alamodome. The crowd numbered 58,688 and included some fans who traded in their Superdome season tickets for tickets to the game in San Antonio. Some fans were mistakenly let through the entrance gates with their season tickets printed before Katrina for the game in New Orleans. Others who came to watch the game were San Antonio residents who hungrily bought up tickets to watch NFL football in their hometown. New Orleans won the game that day, 19 to 7, against the Buffalo Bills. To commemorate this event and victory, Tom Benson ordered replica game balls to distribute to his staff members, each personalized with their name. The second game in the Alamodome took place during week six of the NFL season on Sunday, October 16, 2005. Attendance was 65,562 as the Saints lost to the Atlanta Falcons by three points.

New Orleanians were desperate to see the Saints return to Louisiana. On Sunday, October 30, 2005, the Saints played their first game in Louisiana since Hurricane Katrina. Baton Rouge swelled with Katrina evacuees, given its proximity to New Orleans. The competition against the Miami Dolphins took place in front of a 61,643-person crowd at Tiger Stadium in Baton Rouge. This stadium is normally home to the Louisiana State University football team. The game was also a welcome home for Miami coach Nick Saban, who had coached the Louisiana State football team for the previous five seasons. In many ways, the game served as a type of bizarre homecoming for regional sports fans. The Saints lost 21 to 6 that day, and Saints fans lost a little more faith in their team.

2. Hurricane Katrina and the Shelter of Last Resort

The second game at Tiger Stadium in Baton Rouge had a much more sparse crowd than previous games as the Saints' losing streak continued when they fell to the Chicago Bears 20 to 17. Game day attendance peaked at 32,637, which is extremely low for an NFL game. Low attendance could have been a reflection of the growing turmoil both within the Saints organization and between New Orleans Saints fans and their beloved team. Editorial writers pleaded for the Saints to return to their home city. Fans were enraged at the possibility that the Saints could relocate permanently to San Antonio. But Tom Benson was comfortable in San Antonio. Rumors intensified that the Saints would abandon New Orleans and make San Antonio their new home. These rumors produced an extremely negative backlash from the fans against Benson.

Residents of New Orleans were suffering from the emotional trauma brought on by Hurricane Katrina, the levee failures, being displaced from their homes, and watching their city seem to perish. Some of this anger was directed at Benson as people worried that he would choose not to bring their football team back to New Orleans. The intensity of negative feelings between the New Orleans community and Tom Benson could be seen in the debris that lined city sidewalks. Following Katrina, everyone in New Orleans had to dispose of household refrigerators, which had sat abandoned for weeks or longer in the smoldering heat of the Louisiana summer. A funky stench clouded the outdoor air in New Orleans for months after the storm. The smell was attributed partly to the vast number of refrigerators sitting on the curbs. More than one of these refrigerators, left abandoned on the side of the road awaiting trash pickup or debris removal, had been spray painted with the message "Tom Benson inside." The vitriol was such that Benson and his family shielded themselves from the angry fans in Baton Rouge with additional hired security.

The financial operating losses for the Saints organization were significant for the games played in Baton Rouge. In retaliation Benson fired top Saints executive Arnie Fielkow, blaming Fielkow for persuading him to play home games in Baton Rouge. Fielkow became a type of martyr to Saints fans, having lost his high-level executive job with the Saints organization because of his outspoken and publicized efforts to keep the team near New Orleans. New Orleans voters elected Fielkow to president of the New Orleans city council the following year—despite it being his first time running for any political office and despite the fact that he is a Chicagoan, not originally from New Orleans.

Attendance at Saints home games in Baton Rouge did not pick up through the 2005 season. The Saints lost 10 to 3 against the Tampa Bay Buccaneers on December 4, 2005, in front of a crowd of 34,411. The Saints lost their fourth and final Baton Rouge game on Sunday, December 18, 2005, against the Carolina Panthers. Attendance at this game was the worst yet, at 32,551. (In comparison, the average attendance at 2005 NFL regular-season games was 66,455.)

The Saints played their final game in the Alamodome in San Antonio on December 24, 2005. They lost by one point to the Detroit Lions in front of a crowd of 63,747. At the end of the 2005 season New Orleans had logged only three wins and thirteen losses during the regular season. In the week between Christmas and New Year's Day, instead of celebrating a routine holiday season, those in tune with the Who Dat Nation teetered on the edge of their seats, waiting for an official announcement about whether the Saints were going to stay in San Antonio or return to New Orleans.

Benson seemed to prefer San Antonio and intended to sit down with the San Antonio mayor to talk about long-term prospects. The San Antonio business community and media outlets confirmed that they wanted to be the Saints' permanent home, not just a temporary host city. On the other hand, Louisiana officials declared that FEMA personnel were ready to vacate the Saints practice facility in Metairie, and said it was ready for the Saints return to Louisiana. NFL commissioner Paul Tagliabue insisted that going back to New Orleans was just the right thing to do. Tagliabue also persuaded Benson by agreeing to heal some of the Saints' financial woes using mechanisms such as league cost-sharing, emergency funds, or insurance. A subsequent commitment to repair the Superdome sealed the deal. Governor Blanco fast-tracked funding for Superdome renovations while Superdome management committed to a construction schedule intended to put the Saints back in the dome for the 2006 season. In January 2006 the Saints organization packed their bags, waved goodbye to San Antonio and headed back to New Orleans. While in San Antonio, the Saints struggled through many roadblocks that resulted in a losing football season. And at that time, New Orleans residents were encountering many obstacles in their fight to rebuild home.

Scope of the Katrina Disaster

Katrina and the breached levees flooded 80 percent of the city, with some areas under more than 20 feet of water. The water remained in the city, painting a scummy line across everything it touched. The waterline did not mark the highest point of flooding, but rather indicated where the storm sludge settled, lingered and stewed with debris until the broken levees were dammed and pumps could push out the water. One of the most compelling sights that burned into my memory during my first trip back to New Orleans in October after the storm was the waterline that stretched on for miles and miles. It was as if someone had taken a picture and drawn a singular line across everything. Houses, fences, cars, telephone poles, trees, anything on a typical urban street was covered by the exact same line. Inside homes, mold crept up the walls. The waterline streaked the city and remained as a symbol of how bad the flooding had been.

The estimated storm damage tallied between $135 billion and $200 billion.[29] In many ways, Katrina was the worst storm the United States ever faced. At least 986 Louisiana residents died during Katrina, with over 1,500 deaths as the most commonly quoted figure. It is difficult to pinpoint the exact number of Katrina-related deaths. Many feel that suicides due to post-traumatic stress disorder or medical conditions that worsened from storm-related stress are indirectly the result of Katrina. Nevertheless, they are not included in official counts.

The extent of physical damage varied from neighborhood to neighborhood, with some areas receiving one foot of flooding while others were submerged in over 15 feet of water. Vast expanses of many New Orleans neighborhoods were inundated, making Katrina the largest residential disaster in U.S. history.[30] The urban landscape, particularly in hard-hit neighborhoods like the Lower Ninth Ward, Desire and New Orleans East, were covered in empty concrete slabs that had once been homes. I pointed out countless "steps to nowhere" to volunteers who came to New Orleans in the months following Katrina—the homesites where the only thing left standing was the front staircase because the force of the floodwaters washed away the house. Katrina damaged more than one million homes in the Gulf Coast region. About half of these damaged units were located in Louisiana, with New Orleans alone experiencing damage to 134,000 housing units.[31] This number represents 70 percent of all occupied housing units in the city. In other words, 70 percent of New Orleanians did not have anywhere to live.

In addition to flooded homes, city infrastructure and transportation suffered massive losses. Several dozen segments of the Interstate 10 bridge had fallen into Lake Pontchartrain. Louis Armstrong International Airport, which sees 10 million travelers per year, was closed for more than two weeks. New Orleans hotels suffered major damage. Perhaps due to its position adjacent to the Superdome, images of the Hyatt Regency hotel, with windows blown out, was a popular picture used to convey the scope of disaster. The Audubon Zoo, which rests on some of the highest ground in the city, escaped mostly unharmed, but the Audubon Aquarium suffered massive losses. The facility's emergency generators failed and the aquarium lost nearly all of its 10,000 fish, which could not get enough oxygen and cooked in the rising water temperatures. City Park, which has served as a prominent recreation facility for generations of New Orleanians, was swallowed up underneath eight feet of water representing $43 million in damages.[32] Water sat in the park for three weeks and destroyed 2,000 trees, including the famous collection of live oaks.

Charity Hospital closed its doors. Schools were almost nonexistent. A month after the storm, only eight out of 126 Orleans Parish school buildings were deemed usable.[33] In neighboring St. Bernard Parish, all 15 schools were under water and suffered major damages. In Plaquemines Parish, six out of nine schools were completely flooded. In addition to the physical damage to the school system, thousands of teachers were displaced and teachers were expected to find employment in other cities.

These are only some examples that outline the scope of Katrina's damage. They serve to show that all components that comprise a city—housing, transportation, recreation, medical facilities, school systems, and government services—needed to be rebuilt. Trying to wrap your head around the magnitude of rebuilding was dizzying. It required more than the fortitude of an individual family willing to gut out their flooded, moldy house and refresh the roof, siding, interior walls and plethora of household items that had been infused with lifelong memories. Questions lingered about who would come back to New Orleans.

Doubt as to whether the Saints would return to New Orleans paralleled doubts about who would or could return to New Orleans after Katrina. More than one million people throughout the Gulf Coast region fled Katrina. At their peak, hurricane evacuee shelters housed 273,000 people. In September 2005 nearly 100,000 evacuees were housed in barracks-style shelters across 26 states.[34] One month after the storm, up to 600,000 households were still displaced.[35] It was speculated that as many as 300,000 of them could end up permanently displaced. Cities that had welcomed and aided displaced residents immediately after the storm grew weary of the burden of extended hospitality and turned against New Orleanians. Many residents who evacuated from the Superdome had been taken to yet another massive sports stadium, the Astrodome in Houston, Texas. As the months clicked on and New Orleanians were still not able to return home, Houston news media blamed crime on New Orleans "refugees." Calling displaced residents of the Gulf Coast "refugees" further worked to diminish their status as citizens of the United States and strengthened feelings that the people of New Orleans had been forsaken by their own government. The phrase "right to return" materialized as citizens of New Orleans were hammered with messages that questioned whether New Orleans or certain parts of New Orleans should be rebuilt at all.

The scene inside the Superdome during Katrina was one that brought poverty, racism and failed government response to the forefront. The outrage towards these injustices faded too quickly as a commitment to rectify these wrongs disappeared. In the immediate aftermath of Katrina, national news media pumped story after story across America about the plight of New Orleans. Across the country, as people far removed from the storm tired of hearing stories from New Orleans, the term "Katrina fatigue" was coined. Katrina fatigue sent a message that people outside of New Orleans either no longer cared or refused to accept the breadth of social injustices linked to disaster response and recovery. As the rest of the country gave way to

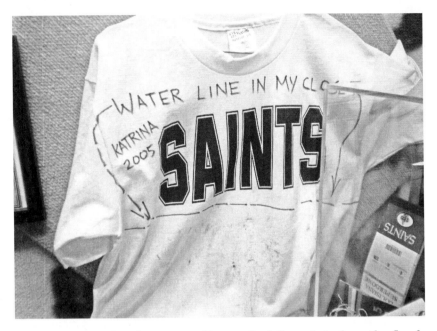

After Hurricane Katrina, a waterline marked the point where the flood-waters settled. This T-shirt illustrates both the impact of the waterline and the extent to which New Orleanians combined Saints football with Katrina narratives. Image taken at the Katrina museum inside the Super-dome in 2009.

"Katrina fatigue," New Orleanians wrestled with a very slow recovery process where Katrina was not just a disaster, but rather a wound aching to be healed.

Symbolism of the Superdome

The Superdome stood as an emblem of all that went wrong. The mighty Superdome, "the popular symbol that had communicated pride in the city's progress, now became a symbol of civic failure," one historian wrote.[36] The Superdome as a space of meaning and memory delivered messages about the city of New Orleans, but, despite its status as a massive architectural and city icon, these were not positive city images.[37] After Katrina, New Orleans needed a positive symbol of recovery to rally around. The need to transform the Superdome from the shelter of last resort during Hurricane Katrina into a symbol of hope for the recovery was strong.

Football offered a platform for changing the narrative where stories of winning replaced stories of failure and people could talk about something that united them across races instead of divided them. One did not have to be present in the Superdome in the days surrounding Katrina to mourn the condition of the city and feel sympathy for the heartbreak of fellow humans. A tremendous sadness blanketed the city after Katrina, and the citizens of New Orleans were looking for something, anything, to feel positive about. They found a common rallying point when the Saints returned to play football in the Superdome in 2006. No commitment to eliminate racism and structural disparities gained the same momentum as rallying around Saints football.

The city of New Orleans made a conscious effort to invest in rebuilding the Superdome and bring the Saints back to New Orleans. The decision to repair the Superdome came while schools, hospitals and homes still sat in disrepair. Even though the decision to repair a sports facility came more swiftly than a commitment to repair other basic civic services, the seeming frivolity of celebrations provided some relief during a time when despair was the enemy. Ignoring criticism from the rest of the nation, New Orleans staged Mardi Gras in 2006 despite the displacement of many residents, heavily damaged infrastructure and questions regarding the capacity of the police force to monitor normal parade routes. New Orleanians needed Mardi Gras to express their post–Katrina emotions and regain a cultural definer of the city. Mardi Gras 2006 was unique in the volume of parade themes, floats and spectator costumes that expressed a myriad of issues connected with post–Katrina recovery. Mardi Gras 2006 was not a frivolous waste of resources, but rather a celebration that helped heal the psyche of New Orleanians. When the NFL announced the Saints would return to New Orleans, the city prepared for another important celebration.

NFL commissioner Paul Tagliabue visited the Saints' makeshift facilities in San Antonio in January 2006 and informed Saints employees the team would be returning to play in New Orleans for the 2006 season. The commitment to renovate the Superdome was a massive

Steps to nowhere marked the New Orleans landscape after Katrina. This image was taken in the Lower Ninth Ward neighborhood in October 2007 (photograph courtesy Jennifer Beaver).

undertaking. In February 2006, 27 Louisiana business leaders joined together to support the Saints' return to New Orleans and started the Saints Business Council. The council was an effort to rally civic leaders and support the Saints in the sales of tickets, suites and sponsorships. In turn, the NFL promised to promote the city of New Orleans through nationally televised games. The Saints Business Council signaled a commitment from business and city promotional leaders to support the return of professional sports to New Orleans.

The psychological hold the Superdome, as the shelter of last resort, held over the city needed to be changed into something that offered hope instead of symbolizing despair. For the Saints organization and for the Superdome, out of disaster came opportunity. According to Paul Tagliabue, this was a chance to make the dome better. This rhetoric about coming back better and stronger paralleled sentiments linked to the larger recovery of New Orleans that said New Orleans should not only be rebuilt, but also made better than it was before the storm. The Superdome and the Saints were the perfect vehicles for crafting positive narratives of renewal.

The physical presence of the Superdome in downtown New Orleans had been significant since its initial construction. Especially in post–Katrina New Orleans, physical spaces took on an important meaning within the narrative of renewal. Every restaurant reopening or neighbor's porch light turning on was a small victory. The magnitude of the Superdome both physically and symbolically gave it a citywide significance: if one bar reopening was a sign that one block could recover, then something as big as the Superdome reopening was a sign that the whole city could recover.

The Superdome restoration project was unprecedented in American stadium history. A Katrina exhibit in the Superdome showcased large posters whose captions offered statistics about the scope of repairs the Superdome required. Water from the storm invaded the 2 million square feet of interior space, causing damage to ceilings, walls, floors, electrical equipment and scoreboards. The Superdome management group had nine months to complete $187 million in renovations. The project included replacing 800,000 square feet of ceiling tile, 700,000 square feet of drywall, and 1.6 million square feet of flooring. Crews hauled away 4,000 tons of debris and pumped 3.8 million gallons of water out of the stadium garages. Suites, concession areas, and club lounges were all gutted and completely rebuilt. Repairing the Superdome's iconic roof cost $32 million and involved replacing 440,000 square feet of metal decking atop a 270-foot roof with a severe slope. It took 144 days and has been described as the world's largest reroofing job.

The newly repaired Superdome with its gleaming white roof contrasted with the majority of its surroundings, as the rest of the city did not enjoy the same swift recovery. Although this contradiction existed, it did not undermine the psychological and emotional importance that New Orleanians attached to the Saints' return to New Orleans. In a speech delivered to students at the University of New Orleans, Doug Thornton, the executive director of SMG, the management company that operates the Superdome, said he knew if they failed to get the dome ready and failed to have the Saints game on September 25, 2006, it would have changed the city's history. Thornton offered the following insight:

> I think we all knew that not rebuilding the Dome would be a huge psychological blow to the city. It would have taken a while to tear it down, so it would have sat

right there in downtown New Orleans, abandoned and in ruins. You can see the Superdome from almost every direction when you come into the city. What do you think it would have done to the heart of the people if it had just sat there rotting? And then, if it did come down, what would be here? For a long time there'd be nothing: just a big, gaping hole in the middle of the city.[38]

The narrative of renewal surrounding Saints football was rooted in real emotions and experiences of New Orleans fans that reflected a local football culture which was present in New Orleans before the dome reopened.

As the city reconstructed its storm-damaged infrastructure, the Saints organization reconstructed their talent on the field. Excitement grew among Saints fans leading up to the start of the 2006 season as the Saints welcomed a new coaching staff and promising players. In January the Saints named new head coach Sean Payton as the 14th head coach in club history. In March the Saints signed former San Diego Charger Drew Brees as the new quarterback. During the NFL draft, the Saints picked Heisman Trophy winner Reggie Bush in the second round, setting off excitement throughout the Who Dat Nation. Not only were the Saints coming back, it looked like they were coming back as something different, something better than the losing team they had been before.

That Monday Night Game

On Monday night, September 25, 2006, the Saints returned to play in the Superdome for the first time since Hurricane Katrina. The New Orleans *Times-Picayune* communicated the anticipation leading up to the game and captured the significance of this moment for the city's recovery: "For the past year, life has been defined by what has been lost. Tonight in the Superdome, life will be defined by something regained."[39]

For the first time in franchise history, the Superdome was sold out for the entire season and official attendance counts reached 70,003. One fan described her decision to buy season tickets as a way of showing she was "coming back to New Orleans with a vengeance" after Hurricane Katrina exiled her to Baton Rouge for six months.[40] People bought season tickets not just to see the games but also to show a commitment to New Orleans. The press box was so full of credentialed media that a space for overflow media members was set up in the arena next door. The night was anticipated to be a seminal moment in the recovery of the city and in the history of the Superdome. The *Times-Picayune* said:

> The Saints return to their home field to play a nationally televised football game that has come to embody the rebirth of one of America's most beloved cities. And while many parts of New Orleans and the surrounding area still bear the deep scars of the horrific damage inflicted more than a year ago by Hurricane Katrina, tonight's party against the Atlanta Falcons provides a welcome respite from the often depressing grind of everyday life for those who call this area home.[41]

One man who became a Saints fan when he moved to New Orleans in 2006 said he thought having the Saints in New Orleans lifted morale and made people happier. He explained that the morale boost may have kept people here who otherwise might have left or not come back to New Orleans. He said of post–Katrina New Orleans in 2006, "It kind of sucks here but I'm happier now so I'm going to stay. And seeing people happier might attract other people."[42] Another fan said, "The steam, the momentum of coming back and rebuilding had kind of worn off and people were realizing how tough it was going to be. And right then, the Saints returning to New Orleans was something that made everyone feel better."[43] The local paper talked about Saints games in post–Katrina New Orleans, saying, "Just milling around, soaking it in, being a part of it because there was better than being home, because home might be a trailer, a gutted house or a slab."[44]

Thousands of fans, even those without tickets, swarmed to the festivities taking place around the Superdome. Free concerts and the "NFL Experience," which includes inflatable games for young people to play, attracted crowds to the areas outside the Superdome. More so than the staged festivities, people felt the need to reclaim the spaces around the Superdome as a site of communal joy rather than communal despair. Individual tickets sold on the streets for prices inflated beyond $1,000 for a single ticket. For those who could not enter the Superdome, many fans gathered in public spaces throughout the city to watch the game with other New Orleanians. One local bar named Lucy's pro-

jected the game onto the wall of a nearby building as people poured
out of the overcrowded bar onto the streets.

Overshadowing the concerts and football festivities was the idea
of coming home to something positive in a time when much of New
Orleans' focus had been about all the things that had been lost—homes,
loved ones, neighborhoods. This event was a way to connect displaced
people with their home. One man who talked about the importance of
that game shared the following experiences:

> I don't believe that the Saints saved the world and saved New Orleans after Kat-
> rina but that first game back did mean something to me. I was sitting in Tupelo,
> Mississippi, wondering if I was ever going to come back to New Orleans for
> real. I mean it was serious consideration for all of us. When I did get back to the
> house, I was living with my roommate and my mom was staying with us because
> her house was wiped out and I just remember seeing on TV that they had
> signed Drew Brees. So they hadn't drafted Reggie Bush yet but they had signed
> Drew Brees and the reason we got season tickets was for that game. I haven't
> missed a Saints game since then.[45]

U2 and Green Day, the star musical talent performing during the
game, moved Saints fans to an emotional mix of passion, sadness, and
hope with a medley of the punk song "The Saints Are Coming" and
the classic folk song "House of the Rising Sun." Goose bumps covered
the skin of those listening when the first line of the latter was changed
to "There is a house in New Orleans they call the Superdome." Tears
streamed down cheeks upon hearing the words, "I cried to my daddy
on the telephone how long now until the clouds unroll and you come
home." By the time the drumbeats hastened and the guitars amplified
to belt out the refrain "The Saints are coming, the Saints are coming,"
fans shook in a frenzied excitement and emotional catharsis. For
months afterwards, I would hear that song pop up on cell phones of
New Orleanians who had downloaded it for their ring tone.

People who talked about that Monday night game have trouble
finding words to describe what they were feeling. One interviewee said,
"It was like a huge deal. I think I might have cried for it. I can't even
tell you why I have so much emotion about it. There's just a lot of emotion that's involved with it that's uncontrollable and there's some weird
place that I can't even tell you where it's from."[46]

The intensity, joy, and magnitude of the Saints being back in New
Orleans were real for the people in the city. People who recalled their

experiences at Saints games talked about how the first game back in the Superdome meant more to them and was more important to the people of New Orleans than when the Saints went on to win the Super Bowl a few years later. One man said, "I went and it was the coolest sporting event I've ever been to in my life. I didn't go to the Super Bowl but even if I had gone to the Super Bowl—and I refer to the Saints Super Bowl as *the* Super Bowl—so even if I had gone to that, you still will never match that same feeling because it wasn't just a football game."[47] That feeling grew more pronounced after Katrina, according to several fans.[48] One fan said, "Being around here in 2006 I think was kind of something special."

The Saints beat the Atlanta Falcons 23 to 3 that night. The Saints defense registered five sacks throughout the game. During the game Steve Gleason blocked a punt by Atlanta's Michael Koenen only one minute and thirty seconds into the game. Saints player Curtis Deloatch recovered the blocked punt in the end zone for a touchdown. This blocked punt and subsequent touchdown set the tone for the on-field performance that would follow.

Steve Gleason's blocked punt is a game highlight that every Saints fan remembers when recalling the importance of that Monday night game. Several years later the Saints erected a monument on the grounds of the Superdome that paid tribute to Steve Gleason's blocked punt and memorialized that moment of collective joy. The blocked punt symbolizes a collective joy, a collective victory rather than the collective misery of Katrina.

With that explosive football game, the Saints solidified themselves as a symbol of renewal. Dave Dixon wrote, "It would be an extraordinary moment full of symbols: New Orleans rising from the dead, in prime time on your TV set, at the very spot in the days following Katrina where a nation had watched horrible scenes of a city swimming, of its people begging for help."[49] Such headlines as "They're Home. There's Hope," were frequently seen. One publication called the Superdome "the prettiest vision in a city so desperately in need of beauty."[50] While giving a lecture to students in a sport management class at Tulane University, elected official Arnie Fielkow said, "The first Saints game back in the Superdome truly served as a catalyst that sparked the rebuilding of New Orleans." That game was a mega-event that served as a vehicle for delivering messages about the recovery of New Orleans.

One fan explained how the Saints were important to New Orleans because they gave people a renewed faith in the city, especially post–Katrina. "After Katrina, the Saints gave me hope that we as a city could scrape, scratch and claw our way to the top. Attending the first home game back in the dome showed that as a city we are a family first and everything else comes second."[51] Another person explained, "They are our Saints. When nobody thought we could make it past Katrina, we did. Nobody ever gave them credit as a football team and they earned it."[52] One person said, "There was a lot of judgment here then. I remember people talking in the news about the Saints playing a game. And everyone was like, 'Why are the Saints playing? The city's been devastated, what are they thinking?' You know, but really people needed something to normalize their lives a little bit. And something positive to join in with one another."[53]

Katrina was not simply a disaster but more like a wound aching to be healed. Every success surrounding the Saints dabbed a little bit of ointment on that wound to help people feel better. The Superdome experienced rebuilding and recovery at a rapid pace, which was in direct contrast to the neighborhoods surrounding it and the citizens struggling to rebuild their lives years after the storm. Narratives of renewal can be contradictory as they can obscure, in this case, the uneven city redevelopment after Katrina, even as they offer hope and healing to the community.

3

Saints Win the Super Bowl

The Saints' 2006 season was one of the most spectacular in the 40-year history of the team. They finished out their 2006 post–Katrina "Domecoming" season with a heartbreaking playoff loss to the Chicago Bears. That NFC Championship game was the only hurdle between the Saints and the 2007 Super Bowl. Fans were desperate to make that season a true Cinderella story to complete the narrative of how the Saints came back to New Orleans post–Katrina and won it all for the city, but it was not to be. Instead, the game served as a reminder to New Orleanians that they were all alone, struggling to rebuild a great city in a country that did not understand them. The Saints fans who traveled to Soldier Field in Chicago for that playoff game were greeted with heckling from Bears fans that evoked images of Katrina in their battle cries against the Saints. Some taunting from fans of the opposing team is expected at sporting events, but using Katrina-related words and signs crossed the line for New Orleanians. The most infamous sign held by a Chicago Bears fan read "BEARS FINISHING WHAT KATRINA STARTED." New Orleanians were still displaced and scattered throughout the country, but the national broadcast of the game put Katrina-themed game signs on display for all to see. Another sign said "CATEGORY FIVE DEFENSE" and Saints fans who were at the game reported threats, taunting and even snowballs hurled in their direction.[1] The Katrina-related "jokes" in this context felt colder than the snowy weather pummeling the playing field that day.

The Road to Recovery

Despite the Saints' attempt to leave losing seasons behind them and reinvent themselves as a new and better team, they could not quite shake their past. This narrative parallels the city of New Orleans, whose future relied upon confronting realities of the past. The political, geographic and social history of New Orleans shaped an uneven recovery from Hurricane Katrina. Layer upon layer of challenges presented themselves as residents looked to rebuild and recover after the storm.

New Orleans has often been written about as a racially exceptional city composed of French, Spanish, African and Native American cultures. In addition, there were Creoles, a mixed-race ethnic identifier that is problematic to define. The outward projection of New Orleans as a place of exquisite food, jazz, and racial exceptionalism prevails where celebrations are ingrained in local culture and serve as a way of life. This dominant narrative wraps New Orleanians up into one festive package. If we peel back the layers of the dominant narrative that blankets the city, we can see contradictions that lie underneath.

Images of poor and predominantly black people huddled in the Superdome during the storm alerted the nation that Katrina had disproportionately affected poor, black neighborhoods. Post-disaster reports that more precisely measure damage done to New Orleans neighborhoods further show that the storm's impact was disproportionately borne by the region's African American community, by people who rented rather than owned homes, and by the poor and unemployed.[2]

The port of New Orleans used to be the main economic driver of the region. In New Orleans oil and gas, shipping, and tourism were the leading industries. Tourism generated billions of dollars annually for the Louisiana economy, and the state relies on New Orleans to drive those numbers. Ironically, tourism accounts for the lowest average wage of all New Orleans economic sectors. Relying on a tourism industry that pays minimal wages provided little economic opportunity for city residents. Poverty rates in New Orleans are high.

Geographically, New Orleans sits in a bowl, surrounded by water and built on soil that is essentially the consistency of gelatin. Its location on the Mississippi River made New Orleans attractive for transportation and commerce, but also left it prone to flooding. The physical geography came face to face with New Orleans' historic social landscape, where social inequalities presented themselves spatially in the city. Historical segregation patterns shaped the urban landscape where many whites occupied areas of the city in higher elevations and left predominantly poor and black neighborhoods in low-lying areas. These predominantly African American and poor neighborhoods were more vulnerable to flooding than their geographically superior counterparts.

The condition of post–World War II American cities lead to increased residential segregation. The federal government subsidized highway construction and suburban home ownership, which contributed to white flight and disinvestment in the urban core. As businesses and wealthier residents fled the city, those left in inner cities were mostly black, faced high concentrations of poverty, and suffered from dwindling resources to maintain or improve infrastructure and civic services. Even though New Orleans is touted as a racially exceptional city of multiculturalism, the city was no exception to this pattern of American urban residential segregation. What did emerge in New Orleans were strong family networks rooted in particular neighborhoods. Neighborhood identity is strong in New Orleans. To live in Gentilly, Lakeview, Uptown or the Lower Ninth Ward means something not only in terms of race, income or other demographics, but also in terms of identity and family. People wanted to return home to their own neighborhoods. However, not everyone in New Orleans had the same opportunities in New Orleans' post–Katrina rebuilding plans. Policy choices affecting who could return, to which neighborhoods, and with what forms of assistance, would shape the future of the city.

The phrase "right to return" materialized as New Orleanians had to prove they had a right to come back home. Certain government leaders perpetuated the idea that New Orleanians deserved what they got during the storm and fueled ideas that not everyone in the city should be able to return. Former state representative Richard Baker of Baton Rouge said, "We finally cleaned up public housing in New Orleans. We couldn't do it, but God did."[3] This statement solidified a sentiment that many low-income residents feared: that those in power would do what they could to prevent them from coming home.

New Orleans never did reopen its major public housing complexes. In December 2007 the New Orleans city council voted to demolish the shuttered public housing complexes, known as the Big Four. The council meeting was contentious, with many residents and protestors locked outside the council chambers while police armed with pepper spray erected barricades and contained the situation through their freedom to arrest protestors for disturbing the peace. Affordable housing became a serious concern for those looking to return to New Orleans as the rents skyrocketed.

Obstacles continued to mount for people trying to repair their houses. The Road Home Program, set up to assist residents in receiving government funds to repair their houses, was a bureaucratic disaster. The Road Home Program assessed the money paid out based on the home's pre–Katrina value, not what it would actually cost to rebuild a house. When Road Home checks finally did make it to those who needed them, they were often not adequate to rebuild houses. Funds were automatically taken out to pay down mortgage balances rather than fix the damaged house. Fraudulent contractors ran off with home-owners' checks, never making the repairs. Insurance companies sent in assessors who brashly informed people that their homeowner's insurance did not cover damage due to flooding. I stood in one man's living room, looking up at his ceiling fan whose blades curved and hung down like branches of weeping willow because they had been warped by floodwaters. His insurance assessor said they would only cover damage that occurred above the water line.

Faced with these layers of complex challenges in city rebuilding, New Orleanians gravitated towards the elements of the city that they loved. They needed something to feel good about. In 2009 the Saints gave the city something to celebrate.

We Are the Champions

In 2009 the Saints enjoyed their most successful season in franchise history. They rose to a record-breaking 13 game winning season, went to the playoffs for the first time since 2006 and won Super Bowl XLIV. A unique level of excitement grew throughout the city. This time period demonstrated an extreme case of Saints fans, nicknamed "Who Dats," spreading into what seemed like a citywide phenomenon.

As the Saints crept towards a 13 and 0 season record, the excitement surrounding football could be seen in every corner of the city. With each win on the road, throngs of fans lined up along Airline Highway to welcome the winning team back from another victory. With each win in the Superdome, fans screamed a little louder, cheered a little harder, and filled their closets with more and more black and gold clothes. Even when it was not game day, Saints symbols covered the city.

A small church sign read, "JESUS IS UNDEFEATED AND SO ARE HIS SAINTS." Saints-themed songs were heard on local radio as the winning season inspired various musicians to create a new slew of Saints songs. It seemed as if fans tuning in to local radio stations heard a new "Who Dat" song every week. A song called "Halftime" by the Ying Yang Twins became an anthem for the Saints in 2009. The song played in the Super-dome every time the Saints scored a touchdown. "Halftime" became a favorite song for Saints fans and could be heard throughout New Orleans. One local Walgreens store played the song on a continuous loop. A woman standing in line at the Walgreens said she never got tired of hearing that song.

On any Sunday morning in 2009 while the Saints played, every cashier in Rouses supermarket donned a Saints jersey instead of a uniform shirt. While pushing a shopping cart through the grocery aisle, instead of hearing the usual music that fades into the background or daily specials broadcast over the speaker system, shoppers heard score updates about the Saints games. Many businesses instituted "black and gold Fridays," allowing employees to wear Saints-themed black and gold clothing to work instead of standard business attire. New Orleanians covered themselves, their homes and their cars in Saints merchandise. One person even put a Saints jersey on a fan being buried in her coffin.[4]

Instead of an ordinary recess at a local elementary school, the students and faculty raised a Saints flag in the schoolyard and second-lined their way to the playground.[5] The second line is a New Orleans parading tradition and cultural expression. The main line or "first line" of the celebration includes a brass band and official members of the parading club. The "second line" includes everyone who follows the main line, dancing and celebrating. They are often depicted waving white handkerchiefs in the air. Rooted in New Orleans' traditional African American social aid and pleasure clubs, second lines are deployed in various formal and impromptu celebratory displays. To celebrate and second-line for the Saints became a common practice.

A devastated house sits among overgrown lots in the Lower Ninth Ward neighborhood in October 2007. The Superdome experienced rebuilding and recovery at a rapid pace after Katrina, in direct contrast to the neighborhoods surrounding it and the citizens still struggling to rebuild their lives years after the storm (photograph courtesy Jennifer Beaver).

Local news writers published an abundance of Saints-related stories that appeared on the front page, in the living section and the money section of the local newspaper, not to mention the actual sports pages. Articles about topics such as the dire condition of health care in Louisiana were squeezed to the margins to make way for a front-page feature on how to scream and cheer louder and longer in the Superdome. Saints fans scrambled to buy copies of the *Times-Picayune* newspaper when they published a "Super Saints" edition.

Rather than focusing on each Saints win as just a big football game, the people of New Orleans felt an indistinct joy—some called it magic and talked about how there was a feeling in the air and something positive in the atmosphere. The citywide explosion of positive emotions was evident as New Orleanians spent weeks reveling in the Saints' victories, with the Super Bowl itself being only one of many days of celebrations. A two-week period of celebrations surrounding the Saints' first Super Bowl appearance included the NFC Championship game in the Superdome, Saints players riding in a Mardi Gras–style parade, a New Orleans–style jazz funeral, and one quirky event where men paraded through the streets wearing dresses. These events coincided with annual Mardi Gras celebrations. One interviewee said, "That's something I will never forget, that feeling of those two weeks. Since Katrina and all that. You know? It's weird; it really did have a good effect on us and especially in '06. That made a big difference in people's morale. Oh my God did it."[6]

As New Orleans residents talked about the Saints' winning season, they chose this football team to represent them and to deliver messages about their hopes and dreams for their community. The ubiquitous media coverage of big NFL events did not create this hype but rather was a reflection of a collective feeling experienced by the New Orleans community.

During the week of January 24, 2010, Superdome employees painted the NFC Championship logo onto the field for the first time in team history in anticipation of the Saints–Vikings matchup. The Saints had never been to the Super Bowl and had never before participated in an NFC Championship game with home field advantage. Some fans felt that this game would be the most exciting sporting event in New Orleans history. The Saints wanted to win the game to stake their claim as the best team in the NFC. But the storyline surrounding the game was that the team was playing for something more. They were playing for a fan base that had been faced with disappointments throughout team history when the Saints logged several losing seasons. The *Times-Picayune* wrote, "They'll be playing for the 10-year-old boy who wears a Reggie Bush jersey in sandlot games at Harrell Playground. They'll be playing for the Black-and-Gold-crazed teacher at Trist Middle School in St. Bernard. They'll be playing for the senior citizen who just completed rebuilding her house in the 9th Ward that Hurricane Katrina pummeled."[7] The Saints' victories gave New Orleanians something to celebrate together and stood in stark contrast to the communal misery of Hurricane Katrina.

It is difficult for Saints fans to find words to describe their feelings about the NFC Championship game played in New Orleans at the Superdome. The *Times-Picayune* asked fans to submit playoff pep talks for publication. One fan wrote:

Katrina could not stop us; we fought to come home. Corruption could not stop us; we fought to expose it. Dallas did not really stop us; we fought back valiantly. Any other team that comes to the Dome will see a city and a team that refuses to be defined by others. The naysayers may have forgotten who we are, because they did not know us to begin with. We will define who we are. We are New Orleans. When others count us out, we Finish Strong.[8]

On the evening of January 24, 2010, the only thing standing between the Saints and the Super Bowl was seasoned quarterback Brett Favre and his Minnesota Vikings. The game was plagued with fumbles and interceptions, a tug-of-war between the two teams with the score remaining close. Tension built as the game went into overtime. Saints fans held their breath as Saints kicker Garret Hartley sent the football towards the goalpost. The ball passed through the uprights, and with that 40-yard field goal in overtime the Saints were on their way to the Super Bowl. The Superdome reverberated with overjoyed Saints fans. The euphoria spilled out onto the streets as fans rushed out to hug, high-five, and bask in the positive mood shared by anyone they encountered.

The morning after the Saints won the NFC Championship game, some homeowners awoke to discover their daily paper stolen from the front lawn. A 75-cent copy of the paper sold on eBay for over $10. Demand for the paper was so strong that the newspaper produced two additional printings.[9]

New Orleans prepared for the Super Bowl in unique ways. One event that highlighted the citywide celebrations of the Saints was the Buddy D Dress Run. On January 31, 2010, thousands of men (and women) donned dresses and paraded through the streets of downtown New Orleans. This spectacle took place because beloved local sportscaster Buddy Dilberto, more commonly referred to as Buddy D, vowed he would walk through the streets of the French Quarter wearing a dress if the Saints ever made it to the Super Bowl. Although Buddy D had died in 2005, thousands of New Orleanians gathered as either dress-wearing participants or spectators to honor Buddy D's promise and celebrate the Saints' first Super Bowl appearance. Quirky parades that call for community participation are a common sight in New Orleans. From costumed pub crawls to more reverent second-line parades, these participatory jaunts through neighborhood streets are ingrained in New Orleans culture. However, the large number of people who showed up to stand on the sidewalks and watch something as seemingly frivolous as the Buddy D Dress Run was astounding.

All types of people turned out for this event—white men with graying hair and beards, women shouting the Who Dat chant, two tiny children in pink coats waving Saints flags, a Latino man wobbling in high heel shoes, a dog wearing a tutu. A black man with a spiky hairstyle sat in a wheelchair with a Saints blanket draped around his shoulders. Men, women, young, old, black, white, Latino, Asian, disabled, and able-bodied—all crowded together in a sea of black and gold. Who Dat chants proliferated, as well as improptu versions of "When the Saints Go Marching In." People danced, cheered, snapped pictures, waved black-and-gold flags, sipped beers or cocktails, and twirled gorgeous black-and-gold parasols dripping with feather boas.

Amid this euphoria, while walking down the street in a gold sequined dress and long blond wig, one man rhetorically asked, "Who wants to move from New Orleans now?" Doubts about whether to return to New Orleans post–Katrina, whether or not to stay and face the mammoth task of rebuilding, or whether to move somewhere easier were questions that residents had spent the past few years asking themselves. For this wig-wearing man to comically address the issue in the midst of the parade underscores the reality that the emotions New Orleanians felt during these celebrations were intertwined with their ideas about what it takes to feel recovered. A local editorial writer covering the parade explained the concept in another way: "I realized what an utter triumph this parade represented—not only for the Saints but for our city itself. After almost five years of struggle to break Hurricane Katrina's psychological chokehold, New Orleans is finally getting back to abnormal."[10]

The city spent the next week preparing for Super Bowl day. Mardi Gras parades changed their regular schedules in order to avoid conflict with game time. An Orleans Parish Civil District Court judge ordered a trial delay in light of the Saints' trip to the Super Bowl. Ochsner Hospital distributed infant clothing printed with the words "Where Saints fans are born" to any babies born there during the weekend the Saints played in the Super Bowl.[11]

When Super Bowl day finally arrived, formal or informal Super Bowl parties proliferated. Press releases flying out of the Super Bowl offices in Miami named Miami, the host city of Super Bowl XLIV, the best place to watch the game. New Orleanians disagreed. The New Orleans newspaper anticipated that even though the game was being played in Miami, the real party would take place in New Orleans. Saints fans agreed it would be a special night in the city. Much to the disappointment of many residents, mass screenings for the game in New Orleans—such as in the Superdome or even small local movie theaters—would not be possible as the NFL said that would violate copyright laws. After Saints fans packed the local Prytania Theater in Uptown New Orleans to watch the NFC Championship game, the theater owner received "cease and desist" letters from the NFL.[12] Venues and planned gatherings all around New Orleans, from hotels to clubs to large block parties, weighed whether or not to let the NFL stance on mass viewings deter their Super Bowl party plans. Nevertheless, plenty of local places—from daiquiri shops to boutique hotels to Bourbon street bars—offered gathering spots for Saints fans to watch the game together. People wanted to watch Saints football surrounded by fellow New Orleanians.

Intermingled with the more routine weekly worship services, parishioners attending Sunday morning church that day whispered prayers for their football team. The final Mardi Gras parade of the day, whose start time had been moved up hours earlier than normal to accommodate the Super Bowl, finished rolling in the early afternoon. In different corners of New Orleans, people put on their game day outfits, which might consist of anything from an officially licensed Saints jersey to a homemade black-and-gold costume. One woman I saw wore a shimmery black-and-gold leotard complete with tassels. A tiny sequined top hat perched on her head. This ensemble resembled a trapeze performer's costume more than a typical football fan's outfit.

I met some friends at a bar on Magazine Street before proceeding to a Super Bowl party at someone's house in the Irish Channel neighborhood. The bartender applied sparkly gold makeup to her eyelids and then offered the small pot of gold dust to the other women sitting at the bar in case they wanted to increase their visible team spirit. The bartender said she was relieved we were there. She was afraid no one was going to come into the bar because they would all choose to stay home around their own TV or a more intimate Super Bowl party. All

A Saints-themed storm trooper carries the flag of the Who Dat Nation during a Mardi Gras parade in New Orleans in 2010. Symbols of Saints football fandom were woven into the fabric of the city.

over town people huddled around television sets as the Saints embarked on their first ever Super Bowl journey.

People watched the game from bars or living rooms, clapping, cheering, holding their breath, and praying. The party I attended had separate rooms for different types of Saints fans. One TV was reserved for those who were dead serious about watching every action in the game and did not want to be disturbed by large crowds talking about anything other than football. The other room held a big-screen TV and the atmosphere was more relaxed, for people who wanted to do a little socializing while watching the Super Bowl. A kitchen full of food separated the two rooms. Two men decided they were going to do a tequila shot every time the Saints scored. One woman passed around a prayer candle similar to the ones found in local voodoo shops that might display a picture of a Catholic saint. Instead, a picture of Drew Brees was scrolled around the glass tube. This woman made everyone touch the candle for good luck before setting it on the coffee table. Saints fans expressed their fandom in different ways, but everyone came together to root for the Saints.

As soon as the game clock ran down to zero, and people were certain the Saints had just won the Super Bowl, people burst away from the televisions and out into the streets. Cheers erupted all over town as people made their way through the streets, migrating towards the French Quarter. It seemed as if everyone ran out into the streets to share their joy and excitement:

> It had to be shared. It was almost as if it didn't happen unless you saw other people's reactions to it. It had to be proven that it happened. We had to go interact with other people to make sure it happened. Yeah. I don't know that we ran out into the street. I think we kind of levitated out to the street. I don't know that I could have *not* gone out into the street after both those things [NFC Championship win and Super Bowl win]. It's inexplicable.[13]

The local paper described the atmosphere in New Orleans that night as the "Who Dat celebration of a lifetime" and quoted a fan as saying, "We figured if we are going to do it right, we are not going to sit in front of a TV with six people. We had to be on Bourbon Street."[14] People danced on top of cars that were stuck in traffic headed downtown. Pedestrians walked down the streets and high-fived people hanging out of car windows. I watched one man clamber onto every porch along a single block and kiss every woman who was standing in her doorway. His friend shouted, "You can't just go around kissing everyone's mama!" But he could kiss and hug and rejoice with strangers because the normal rules of social propriety had been effectively suspended for the celebration.

People proudly reminisce that there was no violence in the city during the night the Saints won the Super Bowl. One woman explained, "You're on Bourbon Street and you're being pushed and shoved and there's so many people trying to move through and not a single fight. Not a single harsh word. Everybody was loving each other. It was more amazing than anything I have ever seen. This city and the Saints—I can't, I mean—I'm speechless most of the time because it is just so amazing to me."[15]

Crowds of people standing outside bars were so massive that they all but blocked the streets to vehicle traffic. One police car rolled up to an overflowing corner bar and turned on his lights as a warning. In contrast, another police car drove by the same bar, waving a Saints T-shirt out of his trooper window and honking. One woman recalled the scene:

> Oh my God. It was incredible. The energy that night. It was madness. It was like a ghost town because everybody was glued to some kind of TV. But then as soon as everyone knew we won it was like mad spillage out into the streets. People were crazy. Grown men were crying. I remember that the most. Men who were strangers to each other were embracing each other and hugging like crazy people.[16]

One Saints fan explained why she ran out into the street after the game: "Because I couldn't contain myself and neither could the bar. There was not enough room in the bar to contain me and my excitement. I wanted to high-five everybody that I possibly could. It's that transfer of energy thing. I had it. Everybody else had it."[17] Another woman described her experiences and feelings on Super Bowl day by saying, "We watched it in the warehouse district at a friend's condo and then we walked into the [French] Quarter and I have never seen—I mean it was bigger than Mardi Gras down there, but it was locals—and it was the most amazing thing I have ever seen."[18] She said, "It was truly, truly the city of love. I mean there was so much happiness and so much joy and it was the truest moment of New Orleans ever coming together."[19]

The communal euphoria continued beyond Super Bowl night. New Orleans welcomed their championship football players home from the Super Bowl in Miami with a special parade. A Mardi Gras–style parade carried the Saints players and staff members through downtown New Orleans. Locals nicknamed the 2010 Mardi Gras season "Lombardi Gras" (after the Vince Lombardi Trophy, the official name of the Super Bowl trophy) as the Super Bowl celebrations combined with Mardi Gras festivities. The multitude of people making their way into New Orleans prompted a local reporter to say, "Tuesday's Saints parade triggered a Hurricane evacuation in reverse," as the streets stood bumper-to-bumper with cars making their way into the city.[20] This comment exemplifies how New Orleans directly contrasted the joy surrounding Saints events with the sorrow from Hurricane Katrina. Another reporter said, "Folks, we're experiencing a period of non-stop category five euphoria."[21]

In the hours before the Super Saints Parade, from the top of Interstate 10 looking towards Uptown, I saw droves of people walking towards downtown to secure a parade-watching spot. Along the parade route, streets, sidewalks and the wrought iron balconies above overflowed with people. The balconies, dripping in traditional purple, green and gold Mardi Gras decorations, also displayed large black-and-gold Saints flags. The Super Saints parade resembled a Mardi Gras parade with *more*: more people condensed into a small area, more flashing camera lights from the crowd, and more excitement. People were giddy with the hope of catching beads or a plush football from Saints quarterback Drew Brees. A DJ set up near the parade belted out a play on words, "Welcome to Drew Orleans, LaBreesiana," as Brees approached on top of a float carrying several members of the Saints offensive line.

In addition to this parade, New Orleanians had their own ways of celebrating the Saints success that were derived from local cultural practices. Saints fans staged a funeral for the "Aints." The Aints tradition started in the 1980s when losing seasons caused embarrassed Saints fans to cover their heads with brown paper bags and nickname their losing team the Aints. For the second-line funeral, fans carried a fake black-and-gold coffin with the words *Aints No More* scrawled across the sides. They hoisted the coffin onto their shoulders and carried it through the streets, symbolizing the burial of the team's losing history. This second line of Who Dats featured jazz musicians and fans wearing homemade shirts and toting brown paper "Aints" bags to lay to rest. A horse-drawn hearse completed the procession to bury the brown paper relics. As fans paraded through Tremé into neighboring Faubourg Marigny, this second line provided another moment to reflect upon what the Saints meant to New Orleans. As one woman explained, "It is beyond words how this city has come together in the last couple of weeks—more so than, I don't know, even after Katrina."[22]

The Saints winning Super Bowl XLIV solidified a narrative of renewal around the team that began with their 2006 return to New Orleans post–Katrina. The months of excitement surrounding the Saints' winning season in 2009 offered positive experiences that brought New Orleanians together. At this time, the euphoria worked to heal the community, give people a positive shared experience and build a collective identity. Throughout this time people paused to reflect on life in New Orleans after Hurricane Katrina and how Saints football played a role in recovery.

Believe, Believe, Believe: The Role of Saints Football in New Orleans' Recovery

In 2006 Spike Lee directed a documentary about Hurricane Katrina's devastation of New Orleans titled *When the Levees Broke: A Requiem in Four Acts*. Lee also directed a follow-up documentary about New Orleans' recovery in 2010 titled *If God Is Willing and da Creek Don't Rise*. The opening scene featured local actress Phyllis Montana LeBlanc reciting a passionate monologue while wearing a white Saints jersey emblazoned with the number 88. The first several minutes of the documentary showed scenes of Saints fans from the Super Bowl in Miami as the song lyrics "Black and Gold to the Super Bowl" kept cadence in the background. Various notables appeared in the film expressing optimistic observations, among them Saints player Deuce McAllister, former secretary of state Condoleezza Rice, and the Archbishop of New Orleans, Gregory Aymond, who talked about the Who Dat spirit and New Orleanians being a people of perseverance.[23]

Jumping to a shot of crowds partying in the French Quarter, Lee's documentary captured someone saying, "This city needs this more than anything. It's a rebirth." Another person in the crowd commented, "When you're down it's good to have something to rally around."[24]

These scenes from the documentary reflected themes about the role of Saints football in New Orleans' recovery. Fleshing out the dif-

Inside the Balcony Bar in New Orleans, Saints fan Holly Mahony pauses while the bartender applies glittery gold eye shadow to her lids prior to Super Bowl XLIV. City residents shared communal enthusiasm for Saints football in many ways.

ferent ways in which New Orleanians interpreted the role of Saints football in the recovery of New Orleans requires building upon a collection of messages from various sources. On one hand, the tourism industry disseminated images to a national audience in order to promote the idea that New Orleans was recovered enough to be a vibrant place for tourists. On the other hand, New Orleanians created messages for other New Orleanians about the city's recovery. These fostered a narrative of renewal rooted in real emotions and experiences. From fans to football players, coaches to television anchors, newspaper articles to documentaries—any number of information outlets linked the Saints to New Orleans' recovery and built upon one another to instill a narrative of renewal through Saints football.

The Saints became instrumental in the story of New Orleans' recovery because they are intimately connected to the city and represent New Orleans. This connection to place lies at the heart of why people talked about sports teams and events as meaning more to them than just a game. Illustrating this idea, one woman said, "They are so much more than a football team. They are part of the city, and they give hope and joy to lift up the fans."[25] Another New Orleanian describing Saints football said, "It's less about the actual game and more about the indomitable spirit of the city behind the team."[26] The *Times-Picayune* reported, "The rest of the NFL is playing football. The Saints are waging some kind of crusade. They're playing not just for themselves, but for a city, region, and fan base desperate for spiritual renewal."[27]

As the Saints became a championship team, the narrative of the Saints as a symbol of spiritual renewal for the post–Katrina city was delivered to national audiences. Standing in the Superdome after the NFC Championship game in 2010, Saints coach Sean Payton delivered a speech, saying, "This stadium used to have holes and it used to be wet. It's not wet anymore. This is for the city of New Orleans."[28] This narrative reached the top ranks of American leadership when the winning Super Bowl team visited the White House where President Obama told the Saints, "This team took the hopes and dreams of a shattered city and placed them squarely on its shoulders."[29] The team presented Obama with a Saints jersey that had the number 44 stitched on the back. Obama is the 44th President of the United States and the Saints had just won the 44th Super Bowl.

Both the marketed city images and the messages that New Orleanians fostered amongst themselves contributed to creating the narrative of renewal. Saints players were able to tap into the essence of New Orleanians' inward messages and deliver something more than a packaged, marketed image during their Super Bowl interviews. This underscored the prevalence and importance of how these narratives helped heal the community in numerous ways. In this case, the Saints players themselves served as messengers for explaining to the national media how their team meant something for Saints fans and the recovery of New Orleans.

NFL press conferences held during Super Bowl XLIV captured messages from Saints players. The NFL media center operates in the city hosting the Super Bowl every year and involves a flurry of information sharing and provides a hub for disseminating press releases. During Super Bowl press conferences, players are usually asked questions related to the football game itself. In addition to talking about the details of football, Saints players interviewed by the media in Miami prior to Super Bowl XLIV talked about the idea of the Saints playing for the people of New Orleans. The media asked questions about the city, the team, and Katrina. In addition, Saints players talked about the importance of playing this game for a people who had been through so much turmoil, even when they were not asked directly about Hurricane Katrina.

When talking about his teammates feeling pride in New Orleans, center Jonathan Goodwin said, "It's a special place, and the fans are like no other. All the time they're telling us we inspire them, and they inspire us. It's definitely a great bond between the city and the team."[30] Goodwin was asked if coming to New Orleans post–Katrina was a concern:

> Definitely after the storm coming down there, me and my wife had some concerns. But coach Payton and Loomis and those guys did a good job of telling us that the city would come back, and we could be a part of helping the city come back. That was something that really interested me. I believed in the city of New Orleans. Fortunately the city is fighting back and improving each and every year.[31]

This player latched on to the idea of the team being able to help the city come back. His comments reinforced the city-team connection and reinforced the narrative that this connection can be used to help the city recover. This narrative was so strong that cornerback Tracy Porter mentioned Hurricane Katrina when asked by the media prior to Super Bowl XLIV on how special it feels as an NFL player to be at the Super Bowl. Porter could have talked about how being at the Super Bowl was a personal honor or important for his career as a professional player. Instead, his thoughts turned to the people of New Orleans and how they have endured since Hurricane Katrina:

> It is definitely very special to be here. The turmoil with Hurricane Katrina along with the struggles the Saints have had since they have been in existence and not ever making it to the Super Bowl…. It is a feat all in its own, but nothing will be more special than to win the trophy and bring it back home.[32]

These players acknowledged the symbolic meaning of the game and recognized that New Orleanians had feelings of post–Katrina recovery linked to the Saints' participation in the Super Bowl. Saints safety Darren Sharper shared his thoughts on the connection between Saints football and New Orleans:

> I don't think that can be stated enough. The fact of what we have done for the city, the community, New Orleans and the whole state of Louisiana and even going beyond that with the Saints fans, people who have been displaced out of New Orleans and have not had a chance to come back. This season has meant a lot for all of them. It's meant a lot for us to be able to touch their lives and bring a little bit of happiness to them. Besides the fact of what they went through with Hurricane Katrina, but beyond that and before that, what they've gone through with this organization and struggles that they've had. Us playing for the community can never be understated.[33]

Sharper touched upon the idea that Saints football helped displaced people connect with home. He mentioned that the team's success touched the lives of people who had not been able to return. This need to feel connected to New Orleans was particularly strong during this point in Saints and New Orleans history because of the fact that Katrina had displaced so many people. In American culture, football serves as a particularly effective way for people to feel connected to home. Sports fandom offers a way for people in the United States to rekindle lost local identities.[34] The need to rekindle a connection with New Orleans was particularly strong after the Katrina disaster. Prior to the storm, city residents were forcibly and physically removed from New Orleans. There existed a great need to be reconnected with New Orleans. Saints football served as a platform for creating this feeling of connectedness to the city.

During a Super Bowl XLIV press conference, quarterback Drew Brees talked about this Super Bowl's impact on New Orleans, considering the effects of Hurricane Katrina:

> It is important for not only the people in New Orleans, but I think the people around the country because you do understand how much it means to that community and what they've been through. Our success as a team over the last four years, but especially this year, has been tremendous just in regards to giving so many of the members of that community hope and lifting their spirits. There is still a lot of work to be done there in regards to the rebuilding and the recovery post–Katrina. There are still a lot of people in some pretty dire straits. For us to be able to have the success we're having, it just does so much for that community as far as bringing everyone together. There's a bond that we have with our fans—between our organization and our fans—that's truly special. This has been, obviously, a storybook season for all of us—a 13–0 start and a lot of firsts. It was our first time to host an NFC Championship game and the first Super Bowl appear-

ance in the 42-year history of the organization, so we have a lot to play for. We don't look at it as extra pressure. We look at it as a sense of responsibility, and we really gain strength from our fans from the "Who Dat?" nation and from the people of New Orleans, just knowing that their spirit is with us.[35]

In a way, it was important for outsiders to understand something about New Orleans and what the people of the city had been through. The part of America that showed "Katrina fatigue" or suggested New Orleans should not be rebuilt, or accused citizens of being refugees and thugs, did not understand New Orleans. People who had not seen what it was like right after Katrina or realize how hard it was to try and rebuild did not understand the perseverance, strength and faith that propelled the people to continue in the face of adversity. Residents wanted their sports team to deliver messages about their identity.

This coffin was the centerpiece of a mock funeral procession staged by Saints fans. The second-line celebration was held in 2010 to bury the "Aints" after the Saints won Super Bowl XLIV. The Aints were born in the 1980s when several losing seasons provoked discouraged Saints fans to don paper bags over their heads in shame. The coffin is shown here at the Saints Hall of Fame museum in the Superdome.

In his speech Brees recognized the importance of the Saints in giving the community hope and uplifting their spirits as a factor in New Orleans' recovery. One man interviewed in the paper explained this phenomenon by saying, "Throughout the buildup of the Super Bowl, people kept saying 'believe, believe, believe.' This is what keeps people rebuilding their houses; the belief that the city will come back. The Saints are a symbol of this."[36] One man talked about how having the Saints back and winning gave him the momentum to start gutting his Katrina-soaked house:

> Like I said, my old house is just twenty feet from the trailer. I had so much adrenaline built up after the first game that I had to do something, so I went in the house and started hauling stuff out. We had been waiting for weeks for the guys to come get this stuff out so we could get some work done, to start rebuilding in there. Well, I guess thanks to the Saints I at least got the trash out of my house.[37]

Defensive tackle Sedrick Ellis answered a question about the team providing hope for the New Orleans area after the hurricane:

> It's really great to be in that atmosphere with those people who have gone through so much with the storms and the things that hit down there, and still have the gumption and the pride to live the way they do every day is amazing. I'm definitely proud to be a part of that and it really means a lot.[38]

Ellis's comments reflect messages that New Orleanians wanted delivered through their football team. The Saints' success allowed New Orleanians a chance to tell the world that they are people who can persevere, who are resourceful and can rebuild. New Orleanians did not just want their city's name in the national media. They wanted the Saints and the NFL to deliver messages that said something substantive about the character of New Orleans. One Saints fan put it this way:

> I think a lot of people misunderstand New Orleans and by coming to New Orleans for the NFL, if for no other reason they're coming for the NFL, and that's a way to get them here and to maybe understand what our city is about because there is still all this Katrina backlash five years later, almost six, and it's pretty hurtful to me as a citizen and born and raised here person. Yeah. There's a lot of ignorance about our city and if by having an NFL team, which most of the rest of the world can understand. They can relate to sporting affiliations and by coming to New Orleans, our quirky city as fabulous as it is, people will finally get it. If it takes sports to get it, to get us, to come here, so be it.[39]

Reporters asked head coach Sean Payton about the city of New Orleans and the team rebuilding together:

> The relationship with the fans I think is unique. There is a city that really has been very close to this team through a lot of hard times. After Katrina, when the Saints were able to get back and play in the Super Dome, certainly there was some symbolism that evening. I think playing good football and giving them something to be proud of is important. With as visible as many of our players are in the community, and many of them are just because of the logistics of where they live, I think all of those things make it positive and make it pretty special.[40]

Coach Payton saying it is important for the community to have something to be proud of is a reflection of how New Orleans needed a narrative of success, pride, and winning to replace a narrative of losing and failure. Television producers inserted footage of flood-ravaged streets into national telecasts of Saints football games. The images of disaster were juxtaposed against images of sports victory. There was a conscious effort to rebuild and rebrand the Superdome after Katrina and use that symbolic space to project winning narratives. But there were also messages connected with winning in the Superdome that New Orleanians could use for themselves to escalate civic pride and to use as bragging rights. This was important as a marketed message aimed at tourists. It was also important for residents who had been hurt when they were told in the days after Katrina that their home, their city wasn't worth rebuilding.

When the Saints won the Super Bowl, New Orleanians were able to boast that not only could they recover from Hurricane Katrina, they could also rise to the top. One news article describing the mass celebrations around New Orleans for the Super Bowl said, "More than four years after Hurricane Katrina wrecked this city, severely damaged the Dome and left unprecedented damages, some questioned if New Orleans would ever recover, let alone party like this."[41]

For many New Orleanians, their enduring struggle was not the storm itself but rather the roadblocks faced in a rebuilding process that stretched on for years. Immediately following this disaster, some outside observers opined that New Orleans should not be rebuilt. So, not only were people rebuilding their homes and businesses, they were also struggling to prove that the city was worth trying to salvage. One woman explained how important she thought the Saints were for showing the world that New Orleans is a vibrant community:

It has really, I think, brought the city together. It's brought a sense of hope for us as well as I think the rest of the country when they saw we won the Super Bowl or that we had our sporting teams come back. That's what gets a lot of people from other parts of the country and other parts of the world to come in and see that New Orleans is viable. But for us it means more to me, more to us, than just a sporting event. It means the people are seeing New Orleans as a fabulous place to be. And that we're back and we're not under water.[42]

The people of New Orleans clung to their football team as something that they had regained for themselves and for the city. Rumors about the Saints permanently moving to San Antonio following Katrina intensified the feeling that the football team was something else almost lost in the storm. The feeling that the Saints belong to the people of New Orleans strengthened the association between the team and the city.

New Orleanians acted possessive towards their football team and expressed a feeling of ownership over it. A sign that hung in the New Orleans airport exemplified this possessiveness. This sign depicted a large Saints football helmet. Below the black-and-gold football helmet were the bold words "OUR SAINTS," the word *our* being capitalized and underlined as if to prove a point to the throngs of visitors arriving at New Orleans airport. One fan said the Saints are important to New Orleans because "the particular history of the team's losses and wins has endeared them to New Orleanians. They're ours, so we love them no matter what."[43] The Saints represented what was happening in the city where rooting for the Saints became a way to root for the city itself.

As people expressed what Saints football means to them, the narrative of renewal continuously resurfaced, contrasting the euphoria of Saints victories with the devastation from Hurricane Katrina. People connected with their football home team as a way to connect with their city. Residents continued to talk about Hurricane Katrina as they talked about what it means to be a Saints fan and why the Saints are important for New Orleans. The messages delivered about New Orleans recovery through Saints football represented not only individual fans' emotions but also a collective of New Orleans people.

A piece of artwork adorned the brick wall of the Corner Bar in New Orleans' French Quarter. Instead of a standard canvas, the artist used a wooden door—presumably from a New Orleans home—as the medium for his brushstrokes. The word KATRINA scrolls along the bottom of the door in shades of watery blue. The word SAINTS arches across the top of the door in black and gold. Below the black-and-gold words WORLD CHAMPS, a replica of a New Orleans historical building marker is covered with what some locals refer to as the "Katrina cross" or "Katrina tattoo." Following Hurricane Katrina, a ubiquitous symbol spread across the city as every house in New Orleans bore spray paint in the shape of an X indicating the house had been inspected by a search and rescue group. The artist used orange spray paint in his interpretation of the Katrina cross on this piece of artwork. Along the left side of this door, a rendition of the Lombardi Trophy—the official name of the Super Bowl trophy—rests on top of a pile of crawfish. Mirroring this, along the right side of the door is an image of the green New Orleans streetcar that runs along St. Charles Avenue. This one colorful piece of artwork captured visually the extent to which New Orleanians intertwine Hurricane Katrina and the Saints into a narrative of renewal.

As this painting suggests, in the years following Katrina, the Saints became an integral part of New Orleanians' consciousness. Talk of Hurricane Katrina infiltrated New Orleanians' stories about Saints football. In 2005 the Superdome became the worldwide symbol of the Hurricane Katrina disaster. When the Saints returned to the Superdome in 2006, this symbolism transformed into one of hope. As the Saints played that Monday night game in the Superdome, it became a powerful symbol that what was broken could be repaired—a symbol not just of football and the dome but of the renewal of New Orleans. This rebirth was not only attributed to the physical repair of the Superdome but rather one of the spiritual renewal of the people of the city. This narrative began prior to but intensified during the Saints' Super Bowl–winning season.

Messages about New Orleans' recovery showed how a sense of community or collective identity with the Saints is strong and contributed to a narrative of renewal that united New Orleanians around rebuilding the city after Katrina. The NFL and media outlets latched on to the Cinderella story of the Saints, where winning the Super Bowl concluded their narrative arc as "a Katrina story with a happy ending."[44] However, the storyline of the Saints in New Orleans extends both before and after Hurricane Katrina, and the Saints' Super Bowl win did not mark the end of recovery for New Orleanians. Rather, it opened the door to understanding how New Orleanians continue to build collective experiences around Saints football. It opened the door for the emergence of the Who Dat Nation.

4

We Are the Who Dat Nation

What is a Who Dat? The simple answer is that Who Dats are Saints fans. They were nicknamed from a chant heard at football games in New Orleans that goes, "Who dat? Who dat? Who dat say dey gonna beat dem Saints?" Rather than remaining reserved for hardcore fans, the catchphrase spread across New Orleans as countless people turned their attention towards a winning Saints team in 2010. The 2009–2010 NFL season marked a time when New Orleans people needed to feel connected to their city and to other city residents. Saints fans developed a type of community referred to as "Who Dat Nation." Constructing the Who Dat Nation was a way Saints fans built a special connection to the city. Even though the events of winning the Super Bowl five years after Hurricane Katrina devastated New Orleans marks an extraordinary time in both city and football history, the continuing ability to use Saints football as a way to connect with other people remains important beyond the exceptional framework of post–Katrina recovery.

Participating in activities associated with the Who Dat Nation united diverse urban residents under a collective identity that represented the city of New Orleans. In her analysis of social-spatial relations in the public realm, Lyn Lofland said, "There is no question but that the connections that humans forge between themselves and places are somehow coupled to the connections they forge between themselves and other humans in those places."[1] The human–place connections forged through the practices of people who gathered together to engage with Saints football exemplify this sentiment. The Who Dat Nation offered both an identity about being New Orleanians and a way to engage with other urban residents through Saints football-related activities and emblems.

4. We Are the Who Dat Nation

The Who Dat Nation developed as a symbolic or imagined community that fostered ideas about community cohesion and helped people feel connected to place and to each other. In addition, the Who Dat Nation involved social interactions. The collective experience of watching Saints football carved out spaces for interacting with socially diverse people in a positive way. Both the idea of the Who Dat Nation and the interactions feed off of each other and strengthen one another. This is reinforced on game day and also outside of game day in the more routine aspects of daily life. Fan practices extend beyond game day, beyond sports stadiums, and beyond team attachment. Behaviors that were fostered through game day rituals became woven into everyday lived experiences.

New Orleanians used association with Saints football to interact and build relationships in an urban environment characterized by segregated social patterning. The collective experience of watching Saints football carved out spaces for interacting with socially diverse people in a civil and positive way. Fan practices created a space of positive interaction and mutual understanding to which everyone had access through fandom. Sociologist Elijah Anderson created the term 'cosmopolitan canopies' to describe city places where people are able to interact cooperatively and gain an appreciation of others' differences.[2] While giving a lecture at Tulane University, Anderson repeatedly called the cosmopolitan canopy "an island of civility in a sea of segregation." Civil spaces formed around Saints football fostered the type of cooperation and understanding that Anderson described as being important for civic engagement.

The Who Dat Nation developed in a way that contained both symbolic relevance and practices of engagement. Anyone had access through fan practices. Sport spaces are fluid where the Who Dat Nation was a space to speak about relevant concerns. Racial narratives became a part of the recovery narrative as people recognized the ability of Saints football to provide shared experiences that united diverse urban residents regardless of race. The desire to see racial unity in New Orleans was a significant issue in this time period. Sport spaces offered a platform to negotiate racial unity through face-to-face interactions. The following descriptions of how Saints fans experienced game day demonstrate how the spaces of sports fandom manifested among those who gathered to watch football in New Orleans.

81

The Game Day Experience

When I stepped on my front porch to retrieve the Sunday paper, the neighbor a couple of houses down stood outside attaching two Saints flags to his car windows. On this particular Saints game day, as the bus rolled up to the stop where I regularly catch a ride downtown, the words GO SAINTS scrolled across the lighted marquee on the front of the bus rather than the words ELYSIAN FIELDS and the number 55 that normally flashed in lights to indicate the route for this bus. As the doors opened I noticed the bus driver wore a Saints jersey over his transportation uniform.

Tailgating spaces during Saints home games tended to be centralized within a handful of city blocks near the Superdome. Parking lots often provided the settings for tailgate parties. Parking in the Superdome garages was reserved, purchased like a season ticket, for $20 per spot per game. The parking lots closest to the Superdome filled up early with cars or were kept clear of all cars to accommodate private parties. This scarcity of space to actually park a car meant that people did a lot of walking on game day from further out in the city to get near the Superdome. People left from their houses, from a far out parking spot, from a bus or streetcar stop, from a hotel, or from a bar and all walked in droves towards the Superdome. The journey through city streets towards the Superdome before Saints games provided a setting that was alive with sights, sounds and smells all brewing in anticipation for the football game.

The city blocks surrounding the Superdome transformed on game day into a large party. Police officers poised at each intersection, waving batons to coordinate the flow of cars with the waves of pedestrians walking across the city sidewalks. Stretching out from the Superdome for several blocks the city felt like an outdoor party. Music from large, personal speaker systems covered every area. The soundscape created from outdoor speakers along with smells emanating from barbeque cookers seemed to unify an outdoor space that spanned several city blocks. It looked like a series of private parties taking place in a public space. Some of these spaces were tightly secured and regulated while many resembled more informal gatherings of friends in parking lots and sidewalks. Tailgate parties surrounding the Superdome looked like little bubbles of private spaces. Hovered under tents, around cars or near personal RVs, all these groups of fans were unified in purpose. They all celebrated the Saints game. They were unified under a canopy of noise, aroma, and the sight of black-and-gold jerseys and costumes.

Groups of people gathered around their parked cars in lots that provide just enough room to carve out spaces to set up tents, grills, chairs, and drink coolers. Mostly, the scene involved people standing around with their friends. People mingled for hours, listening to music, drinking and eating, dancing, or chatting with friends. Talk of football, Saints trivia, reflecting on past games, or discussing how much each player is liked or hated gave people who don't know each other something to talk about. At one of these parties a man confided in me that talking about football gave him something to say to the "high powered lawyers" around him—a group of people whose high incomes and political influence were so far removed from his own that he couldn't imagine what else they would have in common.

Amongst these stationary parties, people walked in constant streams along the sidewalk and streets for hours leading up to kickoff. Two women weaved in and out of the groups of people offering pralines for sale. Two men walked up and down the streets, through parking lot areas selling black-and-gold T-shirts. A few open-air buses circled the city blocks, blaring music and providing the passengers a mobile party experience. Heads turned as loud music blared from these mobile parties. People clad in Saints jerseys danced and dangled out of the moving bus. The walk to the Superdome surrounded me with hoards of people all moving in the direction of the impending football game. I glanced in the windows of a Subway sandwich shop in a building across the street from the Superdome. Almost everyone in there was wearing a Saints jersey, except for one man asleep at a table. He was homeless and found an opportune time to take a quick nap indoors as the streams of Saints fans rendered him mostly invisible.

A row of RVs, positioned for pre-game festivities near the dome, lined an entire edge of parking lot along Loyola Street. One group looked like they were going to camp out in that parking lot through the entire game. An elaborate set up with a tent, grill, tables, and chairs all provided enough entertainment to sustain the group throughout the duration of the game. The words *Happy Birthday* decorated a paper sign stuck onto the side of the RV. Several people sat in a circle of chairs under a pop up tent as if re-creating their living room on the searing asphalt. Another RV housed a smoker grill big enough to serve a modest sized restaurant. Several tents and tables set up to serve food. Although the city layout of New Orleans did not provide the same expanses of grassy fields that other stadiums boast for tailgating festivities, people found these small niches to conduct traditional tailgate parties.

Champions Square served as the official, controlled and commercialized pre-game party space. Champions Square, the newly developed party area outside of the Superdome, entertained fans on their way into the game. This space also attracted Saints fans that wanted to join festivities near the Superdome but did not have a ticket to the game. A one-block stretch of LaSalle Street had been permanently closed to vehicle traffic to accommodate Champions Square. 30-foot high photos of sports heroes were on display including Drew Brees, Michael Jordan, and Muhammad Ali. Hoisted high in the air above the music stage, the Saintsations cheerleaders danced in scaffolding boxes surrounding the several story high projector screens. They resembled cage dancers in an exotic night show. A grand staircase led up to the gate C Superdome entrance. People without tickets were welcome to sit on the steps and watch the game as it projected on an enormous viewing screen.

During the pre-game festivities local musicians like Rockin' Doopsie performed on stage. Saintsations cheerleaders walked around selling their calendars. Saints fans posed for pictures with other Saints fans that wore elaborate costumes. There was a large crowd at Champions Square but you could move through it freely. One Seahawks fan at Champions Square caused a little bit of a crowd to gather around him as he performed crazy dance moves that were acrobatic in nature. Sponsored by Verizon, the space contained food vendor booths, carnival-like cotton candy stands, drink stands, and NFL apparel sales. Portable potties lined the sidewalk and the entire area was monitored by Superdome security.

When the Saints played at home in the Superdome, 73,000 spectators wedged themselves into stadium seats to watch the game. The stadium seats were so close to each other that when everyone packed into their assigned seats there was no way to avoiding touching the people that sit on either side of you. When everyone stood to cheer, I was forced to take a step back, leaning against the folding stadium seat as the back of my knees press against it. The two men on either side of me were so close, their shoulders almost touched each other, leaving no room for all three of us to fit side by side. The seats and hallways in the dome were always crowded to the point of restricting movement.

Despite these intrusions into personal space, Saints ticket holders enjoyed the atmosphere in the Superdome. They wore costumes, cheered for their team, taunted fans of the opposing team, drank beer, high-fived each other, and—only in New Orleans—they stand up and get crunk. "Stand up and get crunk" are the repetitious lyrics in the song *Halftime* by the Ying Yang Twins. The Saints players adopted this song as an unofficial team anthem in 2009. Since then, Who Dats have been seen dancing, wiggling, throwing their arms in the air and swaying their hips and rocking their shoulders back and forth whenever this song belts over the Superdome loud speakers. Whenever the Saints scored a touchdown, fans jumped to their feet when they heard the first few beats of this song as their cue to celebrate. Seeing tens of thousands of fans reacting to this song in unison can be comical. Saints fans that I talked to said they never tire of it. It played on the radio, popped up at dance clubs, and echoed through the streets during tailgate parties.

The night before one Saints game, I warned a few out-of-town guests that when in the Superdome they would be expected to "get crunk," meaning they would need to stand up from their stadium seats and dance with other Saints fans when the words "Stand Up and Get Crunk" played over the loudspeakers. They informed me after the game that they enjoyed watching a woman sitting in their section displaying her personal "get crunk" dance. She gladly shared her dance moves with them after each celebratory football moment to include them into the Who Dat Nation. Interactions between strangers are common in these sport spaces.

In the moments leading up to the first kickoff, music blared and a voice boomed over the loudspeakers announcing Saints star players. The team ran out of an inflatable tunnel set up in the end zone and skipped through a line of cheerleaders waving shimmering gold pom-

poms. Small blasts of white-hot fireworks shot up from the field as Saints fans stood, clapped, cheered and whistled. During the pre-game and halftime shows, entertainment and sponsorship elements replaced the players on the field, giving fans a constant stream of sensory stimulation. During the first game of the 2010 season, Saints owner Tom Benson, members of his family and the Saintsations cheerleaders rode into the stadium on a parade float bearing a giant replica of the Lombardi trophy. Tom Benson held in his hand the prize for winning the Super Bowl—the real Lombardi trophy.

Prior to kickoff, the Saints team captain raised a fist in the air as a signal for all 73,000 fans in the Superdome to simultaneously engage in three rounds of chanting "Who dat? Who dat? Who dat say dey gonna beat dem Saints?" One visitor to New Orleans heard all the fans chanting "Who dat?" in unison after the coin toss. When she asked what was happening, I explained that it was a new tradition Drew Brees had started by calling for a press conference and asking Saints fans to chant "Who dat?" three times when he raised and lowered his arm as a cue before opening kickoff. She admired the display of solidarity and wished her home basketball team had a similar gesture to unify and excite fans.

A certain amount of cooperation was necessary among those sitting together in the Superdome. Anytime someone needed to exit their stadium seat to use the restroom or get snacks, it required the entire row of people to stand while the passing person shimmied across the slender aisle. Every time my seat flopped down it grazed the leg of the person seated next to me. People returned to their seats carrying newly purchased beers or nachos at the cost of $8.50 each. One man mentioned to me that he does not think anyone can go to a game in the Superdome without spending about $100 on food, drink or souvenirs. This conveyed the idea that even if you have already paid for the game ticket, the act of going to the game itself can still be expensive. Some people admittedly snuck flasks of alcohol into the Superdome. Two women showed me how they tucked makeshift flasks into their bras, nestled into areas of the body where the security guards will not touch them during the mandatory search conducted before entering the stadium.

A snapshot of section 630 in the Superdome showed a cross-section of Saints fans with diverse characteristics. As I sat in my seat, to my right sat a large African American man who appeared to be in his thirties. Next to him sat a trio of white men of various ages. To my left was a young white couple. In the row behind me, I could hear a group of eight to ten speaking Spanish during the game. Three middle-aged white men sat in front of me. One of these men always wore the same camouflage-patterned LSU cap with a fishing hook speared into its brim. One man who sat off to my left often brought his tiny blond, blue-haired son to the game and parked the boy on his lap. One small, frail woman with puffy white hair sat next to a woman in a wheelchair in the front row of section 630, where some of the few ADA-compliant seats in the Superdome were located. Amidst these regulars, some seats contained new people at each game. During one game a whole row of African American Atlanta fans sat in front of me. Seven out of this group of nine were women.

As all these fans navigated the halls of the Superdome, walking through the crowds of people reminded me of a documentary of penguins huddled together for warmth against the icy environment. People packed shoulder to shoulder, butt to belly, trying to move forward without being stepped on. I was impressed with the way one elderly woman navigated the crowd. With her wrinkled face, gray hair, and bright yellow T-shirt that said something about "roadkill," she didn't appear to have any problems in the overcrowded concourse.

The ride back home after the game provided a time to reflect on the less frenzied aspects of city life on Saints game day. In contrast to the "Saintsmania" that existed in and around the Superdome during the pregame festivities, there was something so ordinary about riding the bus home from the game. At the bus stop, my husband and I stuck out as anomalies in our Saints jerseys. A tourist from Europe stopped and asked which bus would take her to the French Quarter. As we waited for the bus, a woman on her phone cursed loudly at the person on the other end of the call, saying she wanted her stuff back. People got on and off the bus in work uniforms—a polo shirt bearing a grocery store logo, a white cook's uniform. The fact that it was Saints game day did not take everyone away from his or her daily routine of taking the bus to and from work. The bus was as quiet as the streets around the Superdome were loud. Within the confines of the bus, it almost seemed like any other day in the city—although, as I looked out the bus window, I saw a sprinkling of stores throughout the French Quarter displaying black-and-gold apparel on the sidewalks and in their store entrances. As I arrived home and took a few minutes to sit on my front porch, I could hear the neighbors across the street talking about Saints football.

Many people choose to watch Saints games at local bars. The Rendezvous bar, for example, held so many patrons that maneuvering across the floor required a polite shuffle so as not to knock into anyone. The Saints preseason game was to kick off in about 45 minutes. The lone billiards table that consumed a majority of the floor space in this small bar, usually a hub of activity on any other night, had been covered with a crude wooden plank so people could set down their drinks or lean on the surface without ruining the green felt. A small, fat plastic baby doll painted shimmering gold perched on a pub table in front of a man with sandy-colored hair and freckles, a loyal Rendezvous bar regular. This doll somewhat resembled an oversized king cake baby. (A king cake baby is a small plastic doll no bigger than a quarter that is hidden inside a king cake, a popular and traditional Mardi Gras treat.) When I asked about the gold baby, the man matter-of-factly replied, "It's the touchdown baby." It was hoisted into the air and rubbed by those near it in the bar in celebration of Saints touchdowns throughout the game. This gold baby was one Saints fan's good luck charm. Other items passed around groups of Saints fans ritualistically to bring the team good luck have included a glowing pillar candle bearing quarterback Drew Brees' image and a homemade voodoo doll fashioned to resemble a member of the opposing team.

As I looked around the room, I saw few people wearing officially licensed Saints jerseys, but many people wore Saints T-shirts purchased from local New Orleans shops. These shirts provided less expensive wardrobe options for Saints fans with displays of black-and-gold fleurs-de-lis, favorite players' uniform numbers, or slogans like KREWE DU DREW (for quarterback Drew Brees) or SHOCK IT TO ME (for tight end Jeremy Shockey). A wide varity of people could be seen wearing identical Saints shirts. A small, dark-skinned man in skinny jeans sporting a mohawk hairstyle with piercings in his ears and nose wore the same Saints T-shirt as a young, polished white girl who looked like a university student.

Fans gather in Champions Square prior to a Saints game in New Orleans in 2010. Three fans wear "We Dat" bags over their heads to acknowledge the past fan behavior of the Aints and reinvent the tradition as something that celebrates wins rather than condemns losses.

Some people trickled out onto the sidewalk and scattered themselves along Magazine Street to continue chatting, drinking, and socializing while the Saints were in motion. The Balcony Bar down the street from the Rendezvous was less crowded. Even though the game had started, one could still find an empty chair. After the Saints scored a touchdown, one stranger talked to me because he found it amusing that we had both been cheering for a football player named Beaver. Touchdowns, scores, or other good plays provoked strangers to interact. Clapping, cheering, high-fiving, or booing a referee all happened simultaneously among game watchers throughout the course of the night. These game moments gave people a cue that it was socially acceptable to interact with the people around them, especially if they also wore black-and-gold Saints clothes.

Wearing the team colors indicated cohesiveness among an otherwise diverse group of people. Whether jerseys, T-shirts or costumes, everyone, even the people working at the bar, wore Saints gear. One young woman working behind the bar at a local haunt called Handsome Willy's wore a gaudy black-and-gold sequined dress more fit for a beauty pageant than slinging beer. Several T-shirts paid tribute to the Saints with wording such as "Breesus is my homeboy," "Bree Peat" and "WWBD? What Would Breesus Do?" One woman wore a black shirt that read "Qui Ça?" in gold letters, translating "Who Dat?" into French. Everywhere I looked, I saw a variety of outfits, all in black and gold. A trio of men in elaborate costumes posed for pictures. One was the Gris Gris man, a fan whose consistent wearing of an elaborate costume to the Superdome earned him a place in the 2010 Super Saints fan calendar. His friend was dressed like coach Sean Payton and mimicked him perfectly with a whistle hanging around his neck, a clipboard tucked under his arm, a logo visor resting across his forehead and a Motorola headset covering his ears.

At a neighborhood bar called Finn McCool's one man with a scraggly graying beard sat quietly at the bar, sipping one Bud Light after another and craning his neck to watch every Saints play. He wrapped his own insulated drink holder around each beer bottle. Bringing your own drink holder to a bar or festival is not an uncommon practice in New Orleans, a city where open containers of alcohol in public places are allowed. He stood out from the rest of the bar crowd in the sense that he seemed to be one of the only people there by himself, rather than with a small gathering of friends. In a full bar he was completely surrounded by other people and surrounded by their conversations. However, he seemed mostly content to watch the game rather than talk to anyone around him. About two feet away from this lone creature, three or four women occupied neighboring barstools. They watched the game but they talked to each other too, leaning in close, putting their lips right next to the other's ear so their words would not be lost in the noise from multiple television sets. It was impressive that anyone could converse in such a roar of constant sound. Periodically, a woman with a high-pitched, throaty voice led the multitudes of people in the Who Dat chant.

Saints fans flocked to Handsome Willy's prior to Saints home games. It was the kind of bar where people stopped by on their way to the Superdome to have a drink, get a burger, and do some pregame celebrating. Handsome Willy's was nestled downtown near the Super-dome and medical district. Housed in a small red brick building, it stood almost isolated amid the industrial grayish-white medical build-ings. Its close neighbors included a cemetery, the remnants of a public housing project, and a small pizza place. In contrast to the vacant build-ings and barren streets shadowed by Interstate 10, Handsome Willy's was alive with people, colors, and a general fun atmosphere. Secured behind a wooden fence, an open-air patio hid from the vast blacktop parking lot surrounding it. Picnic tables, shade umbrellas, and an out-door bar and grill station welcomed Saints fans. A paper sign advertised breakfast burritos for $3. Bartenders served up plenty of beer and a specialty drink called Handsome Juice.

Many people do not leave their homes to experience a Saints game. Instead of trekking to the Superdome or to a sports bar, some experi-ence public spaces of sociability near their homes. For example, a couple of people on Franklin Avenue were setting up a tent and TV outside of their house to watch the game. A truck parked in the neutral ground as a way of delineating an otherwise empty plot as a party space. (The neutral ground is the grassy strip of land in the middle of a wide street that most American cities call the median.) An abandoned school with boarded-up windows loomed across the street. The marquee on the decrepit pink building read AUG 2005 ENROLLMENT, an eerie reminder that no children have been able to return to that school since Hurricane Katrina. This was a poorer, slower-to-recover area of town. The tent was set up on the sidewalk, as though it were a block party. These more intimate gatherings occurred in different pockets of town on game day, but it was not unusual to see small social activities taking place on the neutral grounds of this neighborhood even when the Saints weren't playing. Sometimes a handful of men played horseshoes. Other times a group sat outside in metal folding chairs, just visiting with each other. Setting up a tent and TV in this same neighborhood space to watch the Saints game served as an extension of their urban lifestyle, far removed from the luxury suites or elite club seats in the Superdome. These bubbles of sociability in different parts of town contributed to a citywide sense of unity on game day.

Game day inside the Superdome.

Beyond Game Day: Collective Identity and Everyday Practice

These observations could be applied to any Saints game day experience when fans gathered together inside the Superdome, at local bars or on city streets. People reacting simultaneously to game plays, high-fiving, chanting "Who Dat," dancing to the "Get Crunk" song, or wearing black-and-gold Saints outfits were all indicators of football fans acting as a collective. Regardless of the places where people watched games and whom they watched with, their celebrations all displayed similar characteristics. The football crowd seemed to accept certain tacit rules of behavior, especially inside the Superdome where people were required to be so physically close to one another. Chants and songs may hold different meanings for each person, but they have become an integral part of constructing place-related collective identities.[3]

These collective representations displayed cohesiveness in an otherwise multifarious crowd. People with different demographic or socio-economic characteristics carried out all these physical displays of similarity—wearing team colors, chanting songs, and communal fan behaviors. The Saints fans I observed included men, women, African Americans, Latinos, children, elderly, gay, straight, or disabled. Although this list is not exhaustive, these different types of people were united under the common interest of rooting for the Saints. These findings were consistent with collective-identity literature that portrayed sports as having the power to unite people across social barriers and build place-related common identities.[4]

The concept of the Who Dat Nation did more for the New Orleans community than simply creating the appearance of similarity during Saints games. The collective acts contributed to the creation of a Who Dat identity that transcended football games, was on display throughout New Orleans daily life and fostered an imagined community among

More than 73,000 people crowd into the Superdome on a Saints game day. New Orleanians foster collective identity through wearing team colors or chanting and dancing in unison.

New Orleans residents from diverse circumstances. The imagined community of the Who Dat Nation was both an idea and practice where the concepts of a collective and the opportunity for interaction strengthened one another. Collective identity and imagined community are powerful concepts.[5] The Who Dat Nation developed as an imagined community where New Orleanians fostered person-to-person and person-to-place connections. Behaviors such as shouting "Who dat?" that were fostered through game day rituals became woven into everyday practices. They became influenced by and reflective of a broader New Orleans culture.

Interviewees attributed the emergence of a Who Dat language as concrete evidence of how the Saints provided diverse urban residents with a common point of understanding and communication. The words "Who Dat" infiltrated city culture, rather than just Saints culture, and became part of the local lexicon. One interviewee said you can walk down the street and shout out "Who dat?" and a stranger will answer back. One fan explained that "Who Dat" replaced hello and even replaced "Throw me something, mister!" during Mardi Gras parades in the time period when Super Bowl mania swept the city. In October 2010 the *Times-Picayune* published a Who Dat Dictionary as a humorous guide to the new language. The dictionary both poked fun at the proliferation of the Who Dat phrase and spoke to the phrase's significance in local culture: "Rare, universal joy over the Saints' newfound success has created a new common language and solidified a shared identity."[6]

The powerful circumstances surrounding the Saints' first Super Bowl spread this Who Dat language onto a citywide level and developed it as a lingering part of local culture. It was a language born as a football chant but reflective of New Orleans cultural traits, emphasizing that New Orleanians have a certain way of speaking or certain local phrases that would not be found in other communities. In proper English, the chant "Who dat say dey gonna beat dem Saints?" could be read as "Who are they who believe that they might beat those Saints?" The very language of the Who Dat chant was reflective of New Orleans culture.

The more mundane ways that Saints symbols were woven into daily life reinforced the idea of the Who Dat Nation as a collective identity rooted in symbolism and practice. New Orleanians reaffirmed collective action through the everyday experience of seeing Saints emblems around town or hearing the Who Dat chant. The songs associated with Saints wins could be heard all over town, from dance clubs to popular radio stations. Instead of listing drink specials, chalkboards outside bars bore Saints-themed phrases such as "Who Dat, Repeat Dat." Driving by a local daiquiri shop, I saw the marquee advertising a Sunday Who Dat special. A few weeks later their marquee read "Now Hiring Who Dats." As I sat in the waiting room of my dentist's office, a man and a boy walked past, both wearing Saints T-shirts and caps. As I walked my dogs around the neighborhood, we crossed paths with a man walking a large pit bull. The pit bull was wearing a gold Saints jersey. Colorful murals covered dingy concrete walls in various city locations. A mural on Orleans Avenue bore a black-and-gold fleur-de-lis, the words "Home of the N.O. Saints," and was still streaked with Katrina's distinct waterline.

During a New Orleans neighborhood festival called Gentilly Fest, an entire family encircled a long banquet table on the grassy field near a stage. This family listened to the musicians on the stage rather than huddling around a TV to watch the Saints game. However, they all wore white Saints jerseys. They looked unified in their jerseys like Saints football was something the family celebrated communally—even though watching the actual game was not their priority that day.

When sports fans discussed why they like watching professional football, most of them mentioned athleticism, competition and strategy of the game. When asked about Saints football, people described community. They said the Saints meant something more than football. They talked about using the Saints to feel connected to the city of New Orleans.

Fandom as a Gateway to Build Relationships

The social interactions that occurred through the rituals of watching football built relationships that transcended the game. Shouting "Who dat?," wearing black and gold and dancing to "Stand Up and Get Crunk" were not only indicators of collective action but also became tools that people used to interact with others. Football watchers built different types of relationships through the game day experience. Three different types of relationships found in the football crowd included family, friend groups, and strangers. Movement between the three relationship levels was fluid. People could move between these levels throughout the course of a game or season. Strangers could be welcomed into semiprivate tailgate-party areas. Strangers who sat near each other in the Superdome or frequented a neighborhood bar could become friends. Groups of friends formed symbolic families or communities. Newcomers who had moved to the city post–Katrina could use Saints football to connect with other city dwellers. We called them "New Dats."

Although having Saints football in New Orleans provided a way for urban residents to share a brief moment of Who Dat happiness with complete strangers, many people placed importance on the less fleeting relationships they built with the people they watched games with. For some this meant the family you were born into and for others this meant a "family" that you built with other Saints fans who happened to sit near you during a game.

Fans emphasized the importance of using football to enhance family ties. Saints games were family events. One could easily find small children perched on a grownup's lap in the Superdome. One Saints fan discussed his determination to continue the family tradition of sharing his season tickets with his own children because he knew how special the memories could be. Another person quoted in a news article explained how growing up, Saints games meant four or five hours out of every week that he knew he would be with his dad.[7] In November 2010 the *Times-Picayune* featured an article on kid Saints fans and described the Saints experience as being a family event "where football is one of the few things that pulls us together each week" as a family.[8] One fan who mentioned the things he enjoyed most about watching football simply stated, "It brings family together." Another described the importance of sharing Saints games with his children, saying, "Our fans love seeing their section 'neighbors' in the Superdome," and felt his kids should be a part of that.[9] One fan stated that the thing she enjoys most about watching professional football is "the three- to four-hour family I acquire during that afternoon."[10] In various ways, urban residents were forming collective, familial bonds through Saints football games.

Saints games became a time to build friendships. One woman who I talked to had season tickets with her very best friends and—as a matter of ritual—she must sit in between them. It was easy to spot friend groups at neighborhood bars when people gathered to watch Saints games. They sat in close proximity to each other and mostly socialized with the friends seated at their table or in a cluster of barstools. Tailgate parties around the Superdome felt like semiprivate events taking place in public spaces. However, as people shared football spaces the opportunity arose to foster new friendships. One Saints fan said during an interview, "I bought my tickets in 2006 for the reopening of the Dome; I just picked two random seats together in the very upper terrace. I was sitting next to a very charming young couple and we quickly became friends and our whole section had such a dynamic that we all became very close friends and started gathering together in bars and at people's home for the away games."[11]

Socializing with other people who like the same team was an important reason why fans enjoyed watching football. A news article published in January 2011 highlighted the numerous celebrations that took place during the games: "Saints fans form football families when they watch big games at their neighborhood bars," and "Who Dats are looking for gathering places outside their homes to share in the black and gold bonding and communal hell raising that are standard at every Saints watch party."[12]

One interviewee shared a story that highlighted the importance that people placed on the relationships that they built through Saints football. She was part of a group that named themselves "The Missing 1200." This name referred to 1,200 Saints season ticket holders whose seats were removed to make room for interior Superdome renovations that increased the number of luxury suites and relocated the press box. When they eliminated her seating section, she compared it to the demolition of a neighborhood:

> A lot of us were new ticketholders starting in 2006 for the rebirth of the Saints, the rebirth of the city, all of that, and we came together and we became our own little community within the community so that's one of the things you have in the Dome. You have neighborhoods up in the Dome. You have groups of people who may just sit there with whoever they came to the game with and then you have lifelong friendships that are forged and yeah, I mean you basically demolished our neighborhood. I mean really you just said if we can, we'll put you here

but if we can't then you just can move to another city and never come back to this city. We were all pretty upset about it.[13]

The language this woman used compared her Superdome seating section to a city neighborhood, exemplifying the extent to which New Orleanians drew parallels between Saints fan practices and the city at large within a post-disaster recovery context. Her words reflect a spirit of New Orleanians taking the initiative to rebuild community, where social relationships are a valuable part of what defines community.

In addition to the family and friend group relationships that people built, the Who Dat Nation generated sociability among strangers. Social scientists emphasize behaviors among strangers as a key component to understanding cities and city life.[14] People move through cities obeying a tacit social code that requires them to ignore or even fear strangers. It takes something slightly out of the ordinary to encourage strangers to interact with one another. Some are described as "open persons" who because of certain characteristics are seen as more available for an encounter than others.[15] Wearing a Saints jersey made someone an open person. Someone who recently moved to New Orleans and had never before given the Saints much thought, told me that he got "Who Datted" for the first time. He had received a Saints jersey as a gift and he wore it to the grocery store. He said a man in the parking lot said "Who dat?" to him and offered up a fist bump. The man then proceeded to talk about details of the Saints game that had been played earlier that day. My friend confessed to me that he was relieved he had watched the game that day, otherwise he would not have had a clue what the man in the parking lot was talking about.

Triangulation, a term used by sociologist William H. Whyte, is defined as a process by which some external stimulus provides a linkage between people and prompts strangers to talk to each other as though they were not strangers.[16] Displaying Saints-related symbols prompted strangers to talk to each other and share something positive in common. The simple act of wearing a Saints jersey to complete daily chores like going to the grocery store opened up strangers to talking to one another. People could identify with strangers within different city places even outside of the fan spaces formed on game day. Almost every activity that Saints fans engaged in generated sociability. Even people who watched games alone at home might talk about game plays with neighbors or coworkers. People left their homes wearing Saints gear, decorated their porches with Saints flags, or bought a Saints-decorated cupcake from the local bakery.

One challenge facing contemporary cities is a disconnect between diverse residents. Lofland said, "A crucial dynamic of the public realm emerges from the fact that not only do many of its inhabitants not 'know' one another in the biographical sense, they often do not 'know' one another in the cultural sense. The public realm is populated not only by persons who have not met but often, as well, by persons who do not share 'symbolic worlds.'"[17] The Who Dat Nation created a "symbolic world" for people in New Orleans that allowed strangers to interact and begin to know one another regardless of their neighborhood affiliation or other social identifiers. The act of wearing a Saints jersey, for example, gave two strangers a sense of connection. A sports jersey delivered information about the person wearing it. Two strangers wearing sports jerseys who met on a city sidewalk could assume information about each other. They could make conclusions about what geographical location a person is tied to, that the person shares a common interest in the sport, and that the person shares a fan culture or shares similar narratives.

In different ways, Saints fans built relationships during a football game and during interactions that took place throughout normal routines of daily life. In addition to placing value on Saints football as a way to build different types of familial and friendly relationships, New Orleanians talked about the value of building community cohesion across New Orleans' racial divides.

Breaking Through Racial Barriers

Saints fans articulated the need for community cohesion. When interviewees and survey respondents were asked to talk about the ways in which they thought the Saints are important for New Orleans, many of the answers involved the concept of uniting people. This indicated recognition of the historic political, geographic and racial barriers that existed among the diverse urban population that comprises New Orleans. The formation of the Who Dat Nation was important for New

Orleans because it built community cohesion across historically segregated social patterning. The presence of Saints football in New Orleans prompted exceptions to the ingrained social boundaries in myriad ways.

Saints fans saw value in using football to bring the community together in a positive way. Their words conveyed this message. For example, when asked in what ways the Saints are important for New Orleans, one fan responded, "It brings the community together and bonds us." Another used the words "motivation, inspiration, and community involvement" to describe why she thinks the Saints are important. To further reinforce the idea that people felt the Saints promoted positive feelings for New Orleans collectively, one fan simply stated that "just bringing everyone together" was important and that "it helps the people to feel good about something New Orleans." Another fan said the Saints were "a common theme that everyone from the city can rally around regardless of background." The Saints "bring everyone together" and were "a common rallying point for the city."[18]

The celebrations taking place after the Saints won the Super Bowl highlighted a particularly dramatic example of New Orleanians feeling community cohesion in connection with their football team. One fan described this feeling:

> I think it's something that was a true victory for the city of New Orleans. We've been waiting so long for it and we weren't the last NFL team to ever win a Super Bowl. There are still some out there that never have [won a Super Bowl], but it's the one thing that no matter what your race, creed, or color, ... what we all in this city wanted more than anything else ... was a Super Bowl win and so you couldn't have anybody that could say anything negative. It was a purely positive thing for every member of society in the city of New Orleans.[19]

As another enthusiastic Saints fan explained, "The Saints are what ties every New Orleanian together—near or far. People can have different favorite local restaurants or bands or places to watch parades, but *everybody* loves the Saints. It gives us something to collectively root for, celebrate, and commiserate about."[20] This fan suggested that having the Saints in New Orleans united people in a way that is unique to sports teams, rather than other celebratory or social events such as parades or dining out at restaurants. One fan said the Saints were important for New Orleans because "civic and cultural pride is most easily manifested in a sports team to root for." This fan described sports as a cultural phenomenon that had mass appeal regardless of different individual tastes.[21]

Even people who were not lifelong or die-hard fans insisted that the Saints were important in bringing the New Orleans community together. One fan admitted, "I am new to New Orleans but I think that the team really brings the city together. It provides the community with a team to cheer for and helps them be closer." Another explained, "I wasn't really a sports fan before I fell for the Saints. But that team has been a sort of great equalizer for New Orleans—the one thing that everybody can love." Another person said, "It's a way to connect that seems to be a little more universal than a lot of other things. Take any kind of weirdo freak nerd who's not even into sports, never played in their life and boom, all of a sudden you start talking about the Saints and they're into it. It's crazy that way. Sense of pride I guess, sense of belonging. It's because people need something to hold onto that brings people together."[22]

This sign posted outside a grocery store in the Gentilly neighborhood of New Orleans demonstrates how informal Saints-related symbols spread throughout the city. People encountered Saints football fandom through the course of their daily activities even when it was not Saints game day in the Superdome.

While these fans focused on the mass appeal of a sports team, others addressed fandom's ability to unite a community across social divides based on socioeconomic status. The participants in this study made it clear that they believed the Saints bring people together regardless of social divides. One person said, "The Saints provide a central point on which just about everyone in the city can get behind regardless of ethnicity, social background, income levels or anything else."

Race repeatedly emerged as the particular social divide across which the Saints could help people unite. For example, one fan said the Saints "help hold people together; race isn't an issue between fans." The local paper picked up on the possibility that the Saints could bridge some kind of gap in city race relations and said, "A new dialogue has emerged in New Orleans race relations. The Saints' first Super Bowl berth could prove to be emblematic of a turning point in the infinitely more tortured story of race in the Crescent City."[23] The article went on to describe "the concept of the Who Dat Nation, a post–Katrina phenomenon that has tied together Orleanians, suburbanites and displaced former residents of all ethnicities, ages and socioeconomic classes based on their love of the Saints."[24] In this case, not only were people demonstrating a collective identity, they also believed that this collective engagement could make a difference.

One person explained the phenomenon and said, "I feel like anything that is going to bring people together and transcends any kind of lines is a good thing. And for some reason sports, and specifically Saints football is like that here. It doesn't matter; people are fanatical about that thing. And they will see past *anything* if you are a Saints fan and they are a Saints fan." The newspaper echoed the sentiment, saying, "The Saints are good for everybody. This blurs all the lines—racial, income, social status, everything."[25]

Sociological research and mass media narratives commonly use sports as a microcosm of society to better understand or even influence race relations. Sports can be an extremely powerful catalyst for promoting positive changes in society and smashing through racial barriers.[26] Influential football player and coach Bill Curry describes a phenomenon that occurs between members of a football team who are working towards common goals that he calls "The Miracle of the Huddle."[27] The miracle of the huddle occurs when players of all races, nationalities, religions, and backgrounds transcend their differences and come together to accomplish a goal as a team. The way that Saints fans talked about football, especially in referencing the Super Bowl–winning year, certainly sounded like the New Orleans community had experienced the miracle of the huddle. Rather than being strictly a phenomenon for athletes, Saints fans insist these powerful unifying forces are possible among fans of an NFL team in a contemporary American city. One man who experienced the "Aints" funeral that took place to honor the Saints' Super Bowl win described the event by saying, "It done a whole lot for the city because it made the city fall in love. It doesn't matter what color you is. Everybody is embracing each other, hugging each other, saying, 'Who Dat, we dat, and all dat.' You understand?"[28]

Ordinary fans talked about sports having the power to unite people across racial and other social barriers. They believed in the concept and believed it was important for their city. People responded to open-ended questions by saying that the Saints were a rallying point to bring the city together regardless of race.[29]

Observing Saints fans provided evidence that different races of people do gather together to engage in Saints game watching. The snapshot of fans in section 630 of the Superdome revealed a mix of demographics. The crowd of people in the streets for the Buddy D dress run contained a mix of people representing various ages, races, and genders all mingling for the purpose of celebrating the Saints. The skinny man in the bar with a Mohawk haircut and numerous piercings wore the same Saints T-shirt as the polished young woman who looked like a Tulane student—yet it would be difficult to imagine that any other items in their wardrobes would be anything alike. These stories and observations provided clues for how people were interacting and how people of diverse backgrounds used Saints football as a catalyst for intermingling.

In contrast to Saints football, other signature social events in the city, most notably Mardi Gras, still display segregated characteristics. Historically, residential development in New Orleans resembled a checkerboard pattern where slave and servant quarters rested very close to the homes of the city elite. Whites and blacks lived very close to each other. The absence of a physical separation by race or class inspired New Orleans' elite to carve out a realm of privilege that was defined through membership in Carnival organizations. In 1857 the Mystick Krewe of Comus staged the first organized parade, where membership in Comus was only for wealthy white men. Segregation based on race, class and gender characterized krewes that followed.

In 1991 the New Orleans City Council proposed banning racial segregation as it pertained to membership in krewes. Despite this attempt, race and gender segregation in Mardi Gras krewes persists. For example, membership in the krewe of Rex is mostly reserved for wealthy white New Orleanians. Leaders in the African American community march in the Zulu parade. Muses, established in 2000, is one of the only all-female krewes. Saints football provided a brief, yet powerful challenge to these old-line separations. Floats from various Mardi Gras parade krewes appeared in the Super Saints Parade that took place when the Saints won the Super Bowl. This was the first and so far the only time that such a mixture of floats appeared in one parade. A Zulu parade float rolled in the same line as a Rex parade float and a Muses parade float. This was a profound commingling of local tradition in the sense that membership in Mardi Gras krewes remains deeply segregated by race, class, and gender based on historical segregation patterns in New Orleans. Therefore, seeing these traditionally segregated signature floats together in a singular parade provided a visual indication that Saints fandom allowed the city to break through traditional race, class, and gender barriers.

Despite these successes, contradictions exist within the narrative of sports as a racial unifier. Saints fans were quick to point out that they believed in sports to unite people across differences, particularly race, but there remained some question about whether or not something as seemingly frivolous as sports can make a real difference in something as complex as racism. The consequences of segregated social patterning became vivid in the images of the predominantly black population trapped inside the Superdome during Katrina. When the racial narrative surrounding Saints football reemerged in 2010 during the Saints' winning season, a *Times-Picayune* article quoted social scientists who cautioned that the significance of the Saints success as a racial unifier should not be overstated. Lance Hill, executive director of the Southern Institute of Education, a program focused on race relations,

Masked Saints fan and Kevin Kolb watch the NFC Championship game in the Superdome. Fans placed importance on the social relationships they built through their Saints fan experiences (photograph courtesy Kevin Kolb).

said, "I'd like to think anything that makes people trust each other and have more confidence in their ability to succeed as a city is a good thing, but we shouldn't fool ourselves into thinking that winning football games solves fundamental structural problems, or that a racial group will relinquish long-held grievances because of it."[30] Tulane University geographer Richard Campanella agreed and said, "Is it an illusion? Of course it is; it's a sporting event. But if this sense of optimism and unity is this universally shared, it's a powerful illusion and maybe it's not entirely illusionary."[31] The camaraderie associated with Saints football can be both illusory and not, reinforcing the complexity of negotiating meaning through sport spaces and highlighting the contradictions within the narrative of sports as a racial unifier.

One resident quoted in the article, a black Vietnam veteran living in the Gentilly neighborhood, said, "I have never seen black and white people talk like this. I saw Bourbon Street after the game and it was like seeing salt and pepper put together. It's not the end-all-be-all, but it's a good start."[32] This man's comment offered a poignant summary of the extent to which the collective identity of the Who Dat Nation can influence city race relations. He recognized that the Saints' success and shared sense of euphoria sparked positive social interactions between different races and that this was a good start towards envisioning a more collective commitment to bridge gaps between deeply divided sectors of society.

New Orleans Saints fans marked Saints football as a realm that allowed them to interact with other New Orleanians regardless of race and indicated that this opportunity for community cohesion through racial unity was a valuable part of having sports in New Orleans. Sporting moments that achieve widespread attention, as did the case with the Saints, could offer opportunities for social scientists, activists and citizens to raise more substantial questions regarding disparate racial outcomes based on structural social inequalities. Sport spaces offer a place to challenge and renegotiate bigger questions of social justice. The contradictions, questions about whether sport unites or divides, do not undermine the power of narratives about race and community cohesion or the opportunity to negotiate popular opinion about social issues through sport spaces in a way that can begin to promote social justice. The popular and powerful narrative showed that people believed community cohesion was possible where diverse urban residents could unite under the collective identity of the Who Dat Nation.

In addition to the idea of the Who Dat Nation, Saints fandom also offered places to experience face-to-face interactions among diverse people. Places where Saints fans gathered were examples of "cosmopolitan canopies." In the words of ethnographer Elijah Anderson, cosmopolitan canopies "provide an opportunity for diverse strangers to become better acquainted with people they otherwise seldom observe up close. The existence of the canopy allows such people, whose stronger reference point often remains their own social class or ethnic group, a chance to encounter others and so work toward a more cosmopolitan appreciation of difference."[33] When talking about how he thinks the Saints contribute to improving city race relations, one Saints fan offered his thoughts in a way that shows how contradictions coexisted:

> How the Saints are connected to stuff and people get into it ... it's good. It really
> is a good way to calm people down. Calm them down. Make them stop hating
> each other. It's a good way. It's not very substantive at the end of the day but it's
> still good for the soul. That's because we're all feeling the same way at the exact
> same time and it's being caused by something that's not a conflict. It was some-
> thing positive and it helped that black people could go to the stadium and buy a
> ticket wherever they wanted to from the beginning.[34]

When this man mentioned black people being able to buy a ticket since
the beginning, he was referencing the first exhibition game that New
Orleans staged in 1963 to lure the NFL. Tickets to that game were sold
on a first come, first served basis regardless of race. He discussed how
the Saints were able to integrate people where other institutions failed.
He pointed to the current school system as an institution that was supposed to be integrated but in many ways was still segregated. He said,
"It's like the other institutions that you could integrate here, didn't, but
with football, many people have to be together." This man recognized
the contradictions but still saw how narratives and interactions within
the realm of sport could be helpful. He saw Saints football as the institution where people of different races could interact.

The civility experienced during Saints games and Saints fan experiences creates expectations of continued civil engagement. It is possible that repeated positive interactions can have a lasting influence
on city social patterns. People saw community cohesion when they
saw the Who Dat Nation, and they wanted to use that cohesion to transcend the Who Dat Nation and affect other dimensions of urban life.
Using the cohesion to create a narrative of renewal for the city served
as an extremely powerful example of how a collective identity could
serve a greater purpose. The moment in 2006 when the Saints returned
to the Superdome after Katrina solidified the symbolism surrounding
the Saints and showed they could help New Orleans people feel
connected to the city of New Orleans. The Who Dat Nation emerged
as a citywide phenomenon in 2009 to connect New Orleans people
to each other. The Super Bowl celebrations brought this idea to the
forefront as people had ample opportunities to interact with others in
a positive way. Beyond the extraordinary Super Bowl–winning season,
New Orleans residents continued to interact with each other in subsequent years, using Saints football as a medium for generating sociability.

Within discourses of collective identity, people latch onto the elimination of racial tensions through sport spaces as a positive narrative connected with reproducing collective identities. People tend to seek out instances of unity and cohesion among different races within the sports crowd. To a certain extent, Saints fans embraced this message. As Saints fans gathered in public spaces during football games they created pockets of sociability throughout urban public spaces where people interacted in a positive way despite their social differences. Fan practices created a "cosmopolitan canopy" to which everyone had access through fandom. The cosmopolitan canopy was a diverse, civil space that could be inclusive. A deeper sense of collective identity emerged grounded in knowledge of the other based on face-to-face interaction. The idea of the cosmopolitan canopy is deeper than game day civility and can leave lasting impressions beyond fleeting interactions. Members of the Who Dat Nation both wanted to see a sense of racial cohesion and recognized that they experienced interactions with strangers who were different in positive ways. It is possible that this could have a lasting effect where the symbolism and interactions present in sport fan spaces can create a pattern of repetitive civil interactions.

However, the contradiction remains that viewing the collective of Saints fans as a homogenous group despite racial differences ignores structural racial outcomes. A true commitment to address structural inequality based on race and class that Hurricane Katrina exposed faded too quickly. The rebuilding of New Orleans was marked with more incidents of racial disparity than equality. Although sport fan spaces allowed people a space to envision greater community cohesion and the ability to transcend what appeared to be deep racial divides in the city they live in, this did not necessarily lead to different racial outcomes. When the narratives of race and community cohesion emerge in sport spaces, the question remains unanswered about the extent these spaces can really do to facilitate changes in city race relations. Sport spaces continue to offer a platform, both symbolic and in practice, to further negotiate and challenge ideas about social differences. The connections between fans, their city, and their home team offer an intersection for continuing discussions about the extent to which a sense of community identity can foster repetitive civil interactions.

This provokes discussion on the extent to which sport fan activities influence changes in social interaction across racial differences.

The proliferation of Saints messages in New Orleans threw a blanket over the city that seemed to wrap up New Orleanians in a unified Who Dat package, especially during the Super Bowl–winning season. But underneath the covers lies a multiplicity of voices that experience the city in different ways. People have multiple, often contradictory alliances, networks and identities that are not erased through affiliation with the Who Dat Nation. A look at how city residents created their own fan environments throughout urban public spaces leads to a better understanding of the social patterning that exists within the larger realm of Saints fandom.

5

Female Fans of Saints Football

Women of the Storm formed in 2006 as a nonpolitical alliance of Louisiana women whose families, businesses and lives were affected by Hurricane Katrina. Initially, this collective of women sought to convince each member of Congress to personally visit New Orleans after Katrina based on the premise that you could not understand the condition of the city without seeing it for yourself. Their efforts were successful; a large congressional delegation came to New Orleans, and, upon seeing the magnitude of the damage, approved federal funding for New Orleans' restoration. Women of the Storm eventually adopted a broader agenda and continued to draw attention to the needs of New Orleans, south Louisiana and the entire Gulf Coast, particularly in the area of coastal protection and restoration. On the eve of the Saints' appearance in Super Bowl XLIV, each member of Congress received by hand delivery a small, colorful football with a tag urging, "Be a Saint! Save Our Coast! Invest in America's Future!"[1]

Women of the Storm received attention for their political successes following Katrina. Women, however, are often overlooked in disaster discourses despite a growing body of research that shows women suffer disproportionately in comparison to most men when disaster strikes.[2] The scenes in the Superdome after Katrina prompted national debate on poverty and race, but omitted gender as an inequality worthy of discussion. Disasters reveal existing unequal power relations and serve as extreme versions of daily struggles. Just as women are overlooked in disaster discourses, women are often rendered invisible within descriptions of sport spaces and football fandom.

Women play a prominent role in every dimension of life in New

Orleans, including the Who Dat Nation of Saints fans that built meaningful post-disaster narratives of recovery after Katrina. While a racial narrative clearly surrounded the story of Saints football in New Orleans, defining a socially just, gendered narrative around football fandom has been more elusive. The prominent placement of women within the ranks of Saints fan activities offers an opportunity to gain a more equitable understanding of women's roles in building sports fandom.

The Who Dat Nation represents a multiplicity of voices. While many different marginalized groups deserve more attention regarding the ways in which they contribute to sports fandom, the following analysis of the Who Dat Nation focuses on female fans of Saints football. This approach targets gendered fan practices as a way to bring forward the discussion of the extent to which spaces of sport fandom can be used to negotiate meaningful collective identities through social interactions and lived experiences. Despite the way in which Saints football created a collective place-based identity and provided a means for civil human interaction, the public spaces within which fan activities occurred were not free from social structuring. The analysis leads to a more robust understanding of gender and fandom, as well as spaces of fandom that help us illuminate the gendered nature of sport fan activities and the ways in which sport fan identities are more deeply embedded within city spaces.

Women of the Who Dat Nation

While watching a Saints game at Finn McCool's Irish pub, one woman with puffy, afro-like hair talked to me about how she is the biggest Saints fan. Her enthusiasm for football was obvious when she jumped up on her barstool in cheerful jubilation at the end of the game when the Saints won on a field goal in the last seconds of play. She wore an oversized white Saints jersey, which looked tentlike on her round frame and draped past her shorts. She showed me pictures of when she went to look at the Lombardi trophy and got a personal glimpse at the Saints Super Bowl ring. After the Saints won the Super Bowl, they took the Lombardi trophy and a Super Bowl ring on tour to different locations throughout the greater New Orleans area so that fans could see these artifacts up close for themselves. This woman described her excitement as she waited in line for her personal moments with the ring and the trophy. She asked me if I knew that the Saints had a high number of female fans, saying she had heard some report that 50 percent of Saints fans were women. "That's crazy," she remarked, either in pride or in disbelief that football had so many other fans like her. She was only one of several people who quoted that ambiguous statistic to me throughout the Saints football season. According to the NFL, some 375,000 women go to NFL games weekly and 45 million tune in to televised games, accounting for almost 50 percent of the NFL audience.[3]

Despite the proliferation of women within the ranks of NFL fans, assumptions about gender norms challenge fan identity. One of the citywide celebrations surrounding the Saints Super Bowl win, the Buddy D Dress Run, showed the complexity of negotiating gender identities in sport fan spaces. During the Buddy D Dress Run, men flipped gender norms on their head while sporting dresses—an act that seemed as absurd as the Saints going to the Super Bowl. During the parade, I saw one woman dressed in black pants with a black jacket and tie. She painted a mustache across her lip in opposing satire to the men in dresses surrounding her. I told a friend the next day about the Buddy D Dress Run. She asked me why I walked in the parade. I said because it was for Saints fans. She corrected me, saying that it was supposed to be only for men. I was confused, faced with the idea that something for Saints fans, something to celebrate the Saints, was not meant for all fans. In practice, the Buddy D Dress Run was a celebration with diverse participants, including women. But the perceptions remained, as evidenced by my friend's comments, that this sport celebration was something for men where women played the role of intruders. Saints games offered a particular time and space to transcend differences in gender, race, class and sexuality. Despite this, there were still incidents of gender marginalization within Saints fandom. Many scholars argue that women experience feelings of marginalization and denigration in their consumption of organized sport.[4]

Even though examples of gender marginalization within fan practices showed how men and women diverge in their fan activities, mingling with Saints fans revealed more ways in which men and women demonstrated similarities in their perceptions of fandom. Saints fans created shared local narratives where people pointed to ways in which the powerful meanings associated with sports transcend the game itself. The narrative of post–Katrina renewal, the idea of community cohesion, the importance of interacting and building relationships are all important aspects of Saints football fandom regardless of gender. These narratives offer an inclusive vision of Saints fandom that is shared by both men and women.

Using the case of the Saints in New Orleans, a men's professional football team seemed an unlikely place to agree that all fans "Who Dat" the same regardless of gender differences. However, fan spaces in the Who Dat Nation incorporated all the actions of fan activity, and men and women appeared to engage in fan activity and speak of their attachment to the Saints similarly and in equal numbers. In addition, women carved out numerous spaces for enjoying Saints games. A closer look at the experiences of women in the Superdome and in neighborhood bars provides lessons for reconceptualizing fandom through a more socially just gendered lens.

Saints Day in the Superdome

On Saints game day, the Superdome became like a city within the city of New Orleans. With over 70,000 people inside, its population outranked all but five Louisiana cities. This domed city is highly secured, meticulously organized and spatially segregated. Tens of thousands of fans, 185 Superdome staff members and 2,500 part-time Saints game day workers who entered the building found there were spaces they were and were not allowed to occupy. Superdome entrances, concourses, elevators and seating sections, as well as locker rooms, press boxes, luxury suites and the playing field were all areas that physically designated who belonged in each space. As in any city, income disparities prevailed as the dome housed multimillionaire athletes alongside low-wage janitorial workers. Work uniforms designated respective job functions for football players, security personnel, janitorial staff, food servers and vendors, ushers and ticket takers. Other workers included Saints front office staff, and members of the media, including TV crews and videographers for the NFL. Each working person wore a credential designating which zones within the Superdome they were allowed to access.

The most exclusive areas of the sports stadium were those reserved for the football players and coaching staff. Women were seldom present on team buses, in private stadium entrances and hallways, the team locker room, and on the green turf of the playing field. In the realm of men's professional sports, women were shut out from these most sacred spaces reserved for male athletes, male coaches and male referees. Women were less likely than men to gain access to the press area or areas occupied by Saints front office staff and NFL personnel, as the National Football League receives poor ratings in hiring women for key management positions.[5] For decades, women journalists were not allowed in the press box and were banned from postgame interviews that traditionally took place in the teams' locker rooms. Women have made some progress into entering sports media career fields, but the sportscaster landscape remained male dominated.

In the early morning hours on game day, only employees with a job function were allowed to enter the dome. The stadium gates did not open to ticket-holding spectators until two hours before kick-off. Saints fans milled around the stadium exterior at tailgate parties waiting for their moment to enter the dome. Within the tailgate crowds, groups of women gathered together, making Saints game day their version of a ladies' night out. Women posed together to snap pictures in their black-and-gold game day attire. Fans jammed together as they approached the stadium entrances.

Beginning with the 2013 season, the NFL implemented a new policy that restricts the size and type of bags that spectators are allowed to bring into NFL games. Any bags brought into stadiums on game day have to adhere to small size restrictions or be completely transparent. These restrictions were supposed to increase safety and expedite security searches for fans entering the stadium gates. The new bag policy immediately struck a negative chord with female fans of the NFL who felt the rule unfairly targeted the female fan experience. Culturally in America, most women carry purses while men usually stuff items such as wallets and cell phones into pants pockets. Despite league efforts to publicize this new rule, several women were stopped at the stadium gates because their purses were not in compliance. Women were asked to throw their purses away at the entrances or return them to cars, hotel rooms, or other originating places. I watched a family unload diapers, bottles and other contents from a diaper bag and carry these baby essentials through the gates piled up in their arms because the bag was not allowed inside and they had been unaware of the rule. Other fans responded creatively to the bag policy, such as fastening straps around clear zip-lock bags to serve as a shoulder bag.

New Orleans entrepreneurs created solutions to the bag policy by offering stylish clear purse designs in their boutique shops or advertising a variety of clutches that were small enough to pass NFL security inspection. One die-hard Saints fan invented the Flak-it, a convertible garment that transforms from a purse into a vest. She did not want other women to become discouraged by the NFL bag restrictions and crafted a solution that worked with her sense of style before offering the Flak-it for sale to other women. These creative responses to restrictions placed on fans demonstrated that women adapt to make fandom fit their personal style, rather than fully capitulating to homogenizing standards. Despite these adaptations, many women remain bitter towards the NFL and are reminded of gendered restrictions every time they approach the stadium gates.

As I stood just outside the entrance gate to the Superdome, I reached into my clear purse, pulled out my two season tickets and handed one to my husband. He does not know where I keep them in the house and I only hand him a game ticket right before we go into the dome. We split up despite the enormous crowd because all people with tickets were temporarily separated by gender as they approached the Superdome gates. The entrances to get into the Superdome on game day were segregated into separate lines for men and women, so that same-gendered security personnel could perform the mandated pat-down that inspects each person entering the game. During preseason, the women's line stretched significantly longer than the men's line. This line length was reversed from regular season games, where the men's lines typically stretched longer than the women's. I sometimes had to skip over four men-only lines before finding one designated for women.

Once inside the dome I made my way up escalator after escalator, heading toward the highest level of the dome, the 600 level Terrace Seats. Levels segregated the dome seating sections: Luxury Suites, Club Level Seats, Plaza Level Seats, and Terrace Level Seats. Every spectator who entered the Superdome on game day had a seat ticket that regulated where they can and cannot go. Tickets could be obtained only through season ticket packages or on the secondary market from a season ticket holder. Ticket prices ranged from $25 per seat for the upper-level section to thousands of dollars for luxury suites that were leased out to businesses on multiyear contracts. With my ticket I could walk around the Plaza Level concourse to go to the Saints merchandise store or buy food from vendors, but I was not allowed access to other seating sections without the proper authorization. Ushers stationed throughout each seating section checked tickets to make sure fans did not occupy seats that did not belong to them. This is a post–Katrina phenomenon that accompanies a sold-out stadium. One woman spoke nostalgically of the days before Katrina when she could buy a cheap ticket on the day of the game and then sit almost anywhere because the Saints' perpetual losing status left plenty of vacant seats in the massive Superdome.

I continued riding the escalators and passed over the Club Level, where ropes and ushers protected the concourse entrance, only allowing in those with Club seating tickets. Club tickets provided access to better-quality food and beverages than the traditional hot dog stands lining the concourses and offered more amenities than regular stadium seating, such as cup holders for each seat and additional lounge areas. I passed over the 300 Level Suites and then the 400 Level Suites, each monitored with extensive security. One needed a suite ticket, received a hand stamp, and had a hole punched into their ticket to enter the Suite Level. Suite holders had their own separate entrance to the Superdome at Gate A on the ground level.

When I finally reached my seats in the 600 level, most of the men seated near me only talked to my husband, not to me. During one game a couple wanted to switch seats with us to be closer to their friends. They asked my husband permission and bought him a beer when we complied. Even though they were my season tickets, the neighboring seat holders made assumptions about fandom based on gender. During touchdowns, I watched the men around me high five each other. They did not offer high-fives to me or to the woman who sat in front of me. When these moments occurred, I missed the days when I could watch college football surrounded by my female roommates.

The overall experience of watching football in the Superdome was exhilarating. A mix of people, many of whom were women, poured their nuanced styles into communal actions such as dressing the part of a Saints fan, cheering for big moments in game play, chanting Who Dat and dancing to the popular music that blared through the dome. The cadence of four quarters of football kept the diverse collective in sync until the final game clock ran down.

Bar Hopping on Saints Game Day

Whether a person had access to the Superdome or not, a fan might prefer to watch games elsewhere where they could express their own identity. While the Superdome was tightly controlled and structured by NFL rules and regulations, the social structuring in neighborhood bars was influenced by those who spent time there. Rather than being ushered into a gender-specific Superdome security line or holding a ticket that delineated where they belonged, people found different levels of belonging and fan expression in bars throughout the city during Saints games.

The neighborhood bar served as a center of social public space that easily accommodated sports fans. The power of neighborhood institutions cannot be ignored in examining the culture of New Orleans. Bars have always been a primary location for information sharing and coalition forming. During games where the Saints were not playing in New Orleans, certain spaces transformed to accommodate throngs of people eager to huddle around television sets in a public setting to share the experience of watching the Saints play. This phenomenon also occurred among those who could not gain access into the Superdome during home games.

New Orleans' landscape lacked nationally popular chain restaurants and bars. Instead, mom-and-pop locales dotted every area of the city and provided a hub of sociability for every neighborhood. It was not easy to pinpoint what would be considered a "sports bar" in New

Clorinda Johnson holds her breath in anticipation while watching the Saints play in Super Bowl XLIV.

Orleans. Despite this, any number of locations hosted groups of people gathering together to watch games when the Saints played. In each bar or sports locale I entered, female fans of Saints football were present. People gathered to watch Saints games in places that meshed with their urban routines and lifestyles.

Bar Stop Number 1:
A "Community Center" for Socializing

Finn McCool's Irish pub, located in New Orleans' Mid-City neighborhood, became a space for entertaining and socializing. This establishment completely rearranged its indoor bar area to better serve Saints game watchers. Rather than a comfortable scattering of pub tables, extra banquet-style tables ate up every available foot of space. Dozens of folding chairs all pointed towards a large, temporary movie screen. Right before kickoff, bartenders positioned additional folding chairs in front of the large white screens. Patrons overflowed the dark, smoky bar and found additional areas to watch the game on the sidewalk outside, where another temporary movie screen broadcasted the game. Some people brought their own collapsible chairs from home and found a patch of sidewalk near the action, balancing baskets of fries and burgers on their knees while chatting with friends and watching the Saints play. When all the seats filled, people found spots to stand or lean.

Beyond the cigarette machine in a dark corner of the bar stood banquet tables. Trays of food lined these tables, given catchy names that poked fun at the Saints' opponents. The food was provided by Finn's regulars who offered it up as a complimentary buffet to anyone watching the game. About halfway through the game, the bar owner strolled the room, asking each person to choose a favorite dish among the evening's offerings. The person whose contribution got the most votes won a $20 bar tab.

Although the groups of people wearing black and gold were drawn to Finn McCool's at that particular time to watch the Saints game, more than just a football game added to the festive atmosphere in the bar that night. Two pretty young women wearing tight T-shirts emblazoned with the words "Miller Light" mingled with the people standing in line to grab a plate piled high with food. The "Miller Light girls" worked the crowd, offering free beer samples. A group called Dear New Orleans arranged a photo shoot in what was normally a darts area. Instead of dodging a gauntlet of dart throwers to gain access to the women's restrooms in the back corner, bar patrons were greeted with photo flash bulbs, a donation bucket and black markers. After making a $5 donation, fans used the black markers to write messages on hands, arms, bellies or any number of body parts that would then be photographed and posted to the Dear New Orleans website. The photos and messages served as a sort of love letter to the city of New Orleans. Almost everyone in the bar took a few minutes away from game watching to participate and decorate themselves with some sort of Saints-themed message. People chose whatever messages they wanted to convey, although almost all of them were Saints-related, such as Who Dat, Two Dat, or Saints Go All the Way.

The Saints game drew people to Finn McCool's bar on a Monday night. Mostly, the evening provided a time and location to socialize. Almost every person in the bar that night wore black-and-gold Saints gear. Only one woman wore a red San Francisco shirt in support of the opposing team. At one point the bar owner spanked her with a wooden spoon in mocking punishment for supporting the wrong team. The crowd looked like a gathering of predetermined friend groups—an off-duty bartender and her boyfriend, members of a co-ed kickball league, participants in the all-female local dance troupe called the Pussyfooters, and women athletes from the Big Easy roller derby league. Still, intermingling among the various groups was commonplace, as many people seemed comfortable in this Mid-City neighborhood bar. People roamed the area instead of staying in one spot with their eyes glued to the televisions. Patrons abandoned their seats, moved around the barroom, ventured outside to chat, and then meandered back inside. One fan described Finn McCool's as more of a community center that happened to serve drinks. The Saints game created an excuse to socialize in Finn's that night.

Bar Stop Number 2:
An Extension of the Living Room

Entering a bar called Bayou Beer Garden, I felt like I had walked off the street and into someone's living room. The bar was housed in a converted shotgun double—an architectural style of home passed on to New Orleans from Africa and Haiti, in which rooms are arranged in a row, one leading to another in such a way that a shotgun blast could go in the front door and straight out the back door. With an expansive outdoor patio, the bar offered a reprieve from the loud, dark, smoky interior characteristic of so many sports bars. On this sunny afternoon, people flocked to the outdoor patio and gathered around tables with sun-blocking umbrellas sprouting from their centers. People huddled around TVs under awnings. Dogs lounged near their owners' feet. One young woman sat at a table with her dad, while their dog lay under the table. People smuggled in po-boy sandwiches, dripping with fried shrimp.

A large group of women congregated around an outdoor TV. One woman invited me to sit with them and offered an empty chair. The woman who sat next to me wore a Touchdown Jesus necklace and a Holy Grail fleur-de-lis charm around her neck. I had chuckled at the Touchdown Jesus charm when I saw it at a festival art booth the day before. The art vendor had different necklaces portraying patron saints of almost anything from touchdowns to pets. After the Saints won their game that day against the Tampa Bay Buccaneers, this woman vowed to wear those same charms at every Saints game. She told me that when she is not in the dome, she usually watches games surrounded by female friends. All the women at the table wore Krewe Du Drew shirts except for one wearing a classy black dress adorned with white and gold fleurs-de-lis. They chatted about how much they loved that their places of employment had implemented black-and-gold Fridays, allowing them to wear Saints-themed clothes instead of their normal work attire.

The relaxed atmosphere at Bayou Beer Garden felt different from the highly regulated spaces in the Superdome on game day. People eating sandwiches and sitting with friends looked as comfortable and laid back as if they were watching the game in their own living rooms. Even

Holly Mahony enjoys a game in the Superdome. Women were fully integrated into the Who Dat Nation, populated fan spaces in numerous ways and challenged traditional conceptions of football fandom.

Jeanne Vidrine snaps a self-portrait during a Saints game. She often watches football surrounded by her female friends (photograph courtesy Jeanne Vidrine).

the dogs hovering around their owners' feet created more of a "family room" feeling, though we occupied a public space. People were able to take what made them feel comfortable and expressed their personal habits and rituals while still sharing in a public atmosphere and being around other people. The groups of women and co-ed groups of people gathered in the outdoor bar space still focused on the communal experience of watching Saints football.

Bar Stop Number 3:
The Neighborhood Man Cave

Located in the Bywater neighborhood, Markey's bar felt like a social lodge for nearby residents. I heard cheers coming from inside the little building in response to a great play, as the football game had already started. It was such a beautiful, cool, sunny day that stepping into the darkness of Markey's was a shock. A stifling blanket of smoke filled the interior. All the blinds remained tightly closed so the darkness could allow people to see the televisions better. Many patrons sat along the bar in the long narrow room, smoking cigarette after cigarette.

The bartenders, who were both women, each had their hair fashioned into curly pigtails. I watched one of them make an elaborate Bloody Mary with Worcestershire sauce, spicy green beans, and something from a spice jar. At least five people around me ordered that drink, which seemed appropriate for an early Sunday game in New Orleans. Throughout much of the game, these bartenders were the only women present in this game-watching space. Four televisions were mounted behind the bar, each tuned to a different NFL game, not just Saints football. Three larger screens at either end of the bar and one in a larger adjacent room featured Saints football.

The men sat on their barstools, ordered drinks, binge-smoked cigarettes and focused their eyes on the Saints game. There was not much movement around the bar areas; rather, most patrons remained stationary and seemed to watch in resolute isolation. As the game clock ticked on I realized the men in the bar all seemed to know each other, as though they were regulars and it just happened to be Saints Sunday. A guy walked in, shook hands with a man sitting against the wall, and then shook hands with a man sitting at the bar before going to sit on a stool in the back room. Another man with a long silver ponytail poking out from underneath his hat came in and worked his way through the bar saying hello to people he knew, shaking hands, never sitting to watch the game. It made the bar feel like an extension of the Bywater neighborhood surrounding it. Markey's was a place that existed to serve the neighborhood, rather than one that attracted people from all over the city.

Some people wore Saints jerseys and T-shirts, but there were many people wearing everyday, grungy-looking clothes. A couple of people wore "Defend New Orleans" shirts, a popular local design. One person wore a Bywater neighborhood shirt. Two men wore sunglasses the entire time, which seemed out of place in the dark room. Some people wore sports apparel for teams other than the Saints, among them a Yankees jacket and a Giants shirt. The man whose pub table I shared sipped slowly on a constant stream of Miller High Life, a popular beer choice for New Orleans drinkers, presumably for its low price. He and my husband talked a little about college sports.

People straggled into Markey's. At any given time, there were never more than ten women in the bar and all of them were accompanied by a man. The lone exception was a pair of women who came in during the second quarter to sit at the edge of the bar near the front door. Their position in the room made it look like they were poised to escape at any moment. The absence of groups of women at Markey's bar was a notable difference from other Saints spaces around the city. Markey's bar was more subdued than other game day spaces. It was easy to imagine that Markey's would not be too much different on a day without Saints football. The communal spirit of the Who Dat Nation emerged as everyone in the bar clapped for good Saints plays and touchdowns, as was characteristic of Saints watching groups regardless of venue.

A Problematic Definition of Sports Fandom

Throughout the history of Western civilization, sport has been understood as an almost exclusively male domain. A textbook published in the 1970s about the sociology of sport pointed out that "sport is perhaps the most sexually segregated of America's civilian social institutions."[6] The extent to which this has changed since that sentence was written is subject to debate. Sport served as a sign of masculinity, and arena spaces were a major site for the cultural reproduction of masculinity. Consumption of sport had to do with defining what is masculine and therefore what is not feminine. Sport as a cultural institution served as a training ground where boys learned what it means to be men, where masculinity was something that had to be taught. Boys learned at an early age that participating in athletics was an important part of developing a masculine identity. The insult "You throw like a girl" demonstrated the way in which femininity was seen as degrading and incompatible with sports participation and masculine ideals.

Fandom literature often perpetuated assumptions about masculinity and femininity that correlate with assumptions about the authenticity of fan loyalty and devotion. Fandom studies tend to reinforce an assumption where men have more knowledge of the sport itself and that is valued as the most authentic indicator of fan identity. On the other hand, women are assumed to be more interested in "inconsequential" aspects of sports such as sociability. The social aspects of game watching that are correlated with women's fan experiences are valued lower than the men's fan experiences that focus on reinforcing knowledge of the game.

A concern with violence in world football (soccer) culture sparked ethnographic studies on the male subculture of football hooliganism that formed a foundation for sports fandom studies.[7] The construction of "traditional" and "authentic" forms of fandom were built upon the idea of masculine culture as a core definition. Much fandom literature continued to define "traditional" fandom through masculinity, where stadiums are perceived as masculine spaces and fan activities function to reinforce male culture.[8]

Urban theorists examined the relationship between space and gender to characterize spaces within the built environment as adopting a gender identity.[9] Places are characterized as being masculine spaces or feminine spaces dependent upon dominating power relations. While activities within the home and family life are presented as feminine spaces, the activities of work and public life are often described as the male domain. Sports stadiums and bars are taken for granted as being masculine spaces. Urban studies texts use bars and sports stadiums as "excellent examples" to illustrate masculine spaces.[10] This demonstrates the extent to which ideas of masculinity are intertwined spatially with sports.

Early approaches to sport sociology presented theses that sport served as a masculine realm and a site for the production and reproduction of gendered power relations. This perspective continued to influence conceptual approaches to analyzing gender in sport. Feminist approaches to sport analysis explored female athletes to show ways in which women were marginalized and excluded in sport participation.[11] Most analysis of women in sport centered around the female athlete; research focused on the underrepresentation of women in sport or the uneven availability of resources for women to participate in sports. Women's sports performances were often marginalized and trivialized as inferior versions of "the real thing." Common arguments involved framing sports and the sports stadium as a domain for expressing masculinity while demonizing women, all while reinforcing hegemonic gender norms.[12]

Since most research focused on the female athlete, even less was understood about women in terms of sports fandom. Mainstream stereotypes assumed and academic fandom studies reported that sports fans were disproportionately likely to be male.[13] Traditional constructions of fandom included male culture as a core definition. The white working-class male was seen as the default fan, and therefore his behaviors were still regarded as the most authentic fan practices.[14] Although there existed more ambiguity in studying fans than in studying athletes, the practice of trivializing women seeped into the realm of sports fandom as well, where women were portrayed as inferior versions of the real fans. Because sport was defined by men and masculinity, women in sports became trespassers on male territory.[15]

This trespasser construct was difficult to avoid with the case of women as fans of NFL football. Cities spent millions of dollars to attract men's and not women's sports teams. American football was held up as the epitome of a masculine realm into which women cannot cross. Many men seem to need to establish the "fact" that no matter what gains women make in sports, they can never play football.[16] Despite the approach taken to better understand women fans of sports, theoretical conceptions of fandom did not address female sports fans in a way that seeks to appreciate difference and assess the extent to which women can influence sport fan spaces to construct and maintain alternatives to the dominant perspective of sports as a masculine realm.

What Can We Learn from the Who Dat Nation?

How can sports be a reflection of male culture when so many of the fan activities and opinions of the Who Dat Nation were created by women? When I looked at spaces across the city, they were populated with both men and women. Rigid divisions between masculinity and femininity were not always apparent when looking at the practices of Saints fans. Both genders appeared to engage in fan activities and talked of their attachment to the team similarly and in equal numbers. Women fully participated in creating fan spaces and meaningful experiences around football. Given the proliferation of women engaging in fan activ-

126

ities throughout the Who Dat Nation, fandom can no longer be taken for granted as a masculine space. Contradictions existed between what I saw in different city spaces and defining fandom through masculinity.

Both inclusionary and exclusionary practices existed among Saints fans in response to gender identifiers. These gendered practices can be seen within the social constraints that characterize places where Saints fans choose to watch games. Women fully participated in Saints events and Saints fan activities, but assumptions remained about the gendered nature of sports fandom. Throughout my participant observation at Saints games, moments occurred where I was reminded that, as a woman, people make assumptions about me as a fan. Despite the growing confidence in being able to assert that sports can make a difference in uniting across social barriers, gender conspicuously sticks out as a social divide where exclusionary rather than inclusionary practices plague women participating in sport.

Gender remains as a less visible and often misunderstood social divide within sport spaces, particularly when questioning the role of sport in constructing masculine and feminine social spaces. The stadium stands as a space that reminds us sport spaces are gendered, for example, through regulations such as gender-specific security lines. Expanding spaces of fandom to include places such as neighborhood bars or an intimate tailgate party begins to reveal different kinds of team attachment and an understanding of diverse fan behaviors that may or may not reinforce assumptions about gendered sport spaces. In the Superdome, it may be easier to see how incidents of gender marginalization, such as men failing to high-five the women seated around them, contributed to the social construction of sport stadiums as masculine spaces. Looking at places where Saints fandom manifested outside the stadium, such as neighborhood bars or city streets, begins to give voice to those who are not part of the "traditional" group of male working-class fans upon which fandom literature was built.

Looking at fan practices that took place throughout New Orleans city spaces led to a broader conceptualization of sport fandom where all have access to the Who Dat Nation. Anyone can experience fandom in multifaceted ways, and each way is a valid form of fandom. Sport spaces have a history of being characterized by hegemonic struggles over whose activities count more than others, situated within a wider social and historical context of structured inequality. Fandom can be multifaceted, where one version does not have to be a lesser version than another based on traditional measures of fan authenticity.

The women in this study see themselves as fans, not an inauthentic or lesser version of a fan. While traditional fandom studies continue to marginalize women and conclude that their fandom is a lesser version of fandom, the descriptions of the Who Dat Nation showed how sport fan spaces can be sites to renegotiate and challenge discourses of power. While the stadium is framed as a site that reproduces gendered power relations, looking beyond the stadium allows us to see nuanced fan practices that can empower and give voice to those marginalized in traditional definitions of sport fandom.

The practices and discourses of Saints fans offer a way to begin peeling back the stereotype that seeks to reinforce uneven gendered power relations. Rather than relying on the assumption that sports reproduce "natural" differences between what is masculine and what is feminine, the spaces of sports fandom offer a platform for challenging these ideas. Given the proliferation of women in the Who Dat Nation, the spaces of sports fandom can no longer be taken for granted as masculine spaces. The crowds of people gathered to watch Saints games did not comprise a sprinkling of women among a sea of men. Women fully participated in creating public social spaces and meaningful experiences around football. Accepting masculinity or conforming to masculine ideals was not a prerequisite for entering the Who Dat Nation.

With the case of Saints fans, women did not talk about a need to overcome being a woman in order to be a Saints fan. Female Saints fans did not perceive themselves as counterparts to a male fan standard. Women are fans. Women are the Who Dat Nation. The ways that they engaged with sports exemplified fandom, not an inferior version of fandom. Within the collective identity of the Who Dat Nation, having a female gender identity was not incompatible with being a sports fan.

New Conceptions of Fandom

Fandom literature did not offer a convincing framework for conceptualizing the Who Dat Nation. Studies that give voice to women fans are extremely limited and have done little to challenge the masculine foundation upon which fandom literature was constructed.[17] Shifting the discussion of fandom from team attachment to fan practices helps resolve this contradiction by allowing us to gain a deeper understanding of how diverse people create meaningful attachments to professional sports throughout city spaces.

Telling team history in terms of great catches, big wins, and coaching changes gives fans a chain of events upon which to build a common story about football and fandom. However, the drama that takes place throughout city spaces in connection with football builds fandom in a different way. Fan practices extend throughout city spaces where fandom becomes the compilation of diverse activities that reflect attachment to the team and attachment to other people through social interactions and the shared experience of rooting for the home team. Fandom is not limited to those cheering in the stadium or limited to knowledge of the game, such as quoting game statistics or player achievements. All activities that people engage in that make them feel connected to the team or connected to other people in a communal spirit of rooting for the home team count as fan activities.

Looking at the ways in which women created their own fan environments throughout urban public spaces showed nuances in how people experience fandom because they have different social identifiers or different ways of experiencing city life. At a tailgate party, one woman may talk about the best plays in Saints history while another fan is happiest to socialize and drink beer. Whether someone talks about football, eats cheese fries in a sports bar during a game, watches the game on television, cheers loudly, or silently wears a Saints T-shirt to work, all of these practices are fan activities. These indicators of fandom can take place in diverse spaces and at any time such as on game day, during routines of daily life, at the stadium, or in a neighborhood bar.

City residents created their own fan experiences throughout neighborhood bars and in the Superdome. There were multiple ways to engage in fan practices. The social activities taking place throughout the city showed that the value of professional football to a city extended beyond the confines of the publicly funded stadium. As many studies on sports fans focus on the activities that take place in stadiums on game day, the focus on spaces outside of the stadium created a new concept of fandom that incorporated many diverse people in diverse spaces. Women interacted with football in a way that was compatible with their gender identities and daily lifestyles. Saints fans socialized in preferred neighborhood bars that complemented their everyday lived experiences. They did not conform to some ideal of 'traditional' fandom.

Rather than asking women to adjust their identity to fit into definitions of fandom, it is necessary to shift how we conceptualize fandom. We need to shift our understanding of fandom as the practices of those who experience sporting events. Looking at spaces of sport fandom throughout city public spaces shows how fans create and inhabit social worlds that fit their needs. The public spaces within which fan activities occurred allowed me to examine both restrictions and opportunities for fans to assert meaningful interactions and social experiences.

Sport spaces embody constructions of urban place, gender and identity. This provokes discussion on the extent to which sport fan activities influence changes in social interaction across gender differences. This project conceptualized spaces of sports fandom as places of empowerment, spaces to challenge, renegotiate and rethink difference. This approach challenges the reproduction of sport spaces as something homogenous that fits neatly into dominant discourses of power. The findings of this study challenge the view of sport spaces as homogenizing agents where a focus on the multiplicity of voices that comprise the collective illuminate ways to appreciate differences without erasing them. This approach fleshes out the heterogeneity that comprises a collective of sports fans and seeks to appreciate those differences rather than marginalizing and rendering invisible those who engage in sport in "nontraditional" ways.

Collective experiences involved more than simply covering everyone in the same team logo. Although the collective actions of wearing team logos and colors or simultaneously cheering for the Saints created a sense of cohesiveness across an otherwise diverse crowd, Saints fandom did not wash away other identity factors. Rather, this showed us that underrepresented groups—those other than the stereotypical male sports fanatic—created fandom in multiple ways that can all be valued expressions of fandom. I was able to look at different spaces where people created and participated in fan activities outside the confines of the publicly funded stadium and at times that were not football game day. In these spaces, we are able to rethink ideas of diversity among the football crowd that both expands our conceptualization of fandom and reinforces sport spaces as a place to renegotiate and challenge notions of diversity in sport spaces.

This approach frames fandom as a performance or the practices of those who experience professional sports. Fan practices and activities extend beyond game day, beyond sports stadiums, and beyond team attachment and knowledge of the game to one that incorporates fan practices and activities into core definitions of fandom. Observing what people did throughout public spaces to engage in sports fandom gives a more accurate picture of fan activities. Although much fandom literature defines fandom through its masculinity, when I looked at spaces of sports fandom across the city, they were populated by both men and women. Both genders talked similarly about their attachments to the team. My conceptualization of fandom allows for a look at how gendered constructions of fan behavior permeate sport spaces. Even though women populated sport fan spaces, assumptions remained about the gendered nature of sports fandom. Sport spaces have a history of being characterized by hegemonic struggles over whose leisure activities count more than others, situated within a wider social and historical context of structured inequality. This research challenges assumptions about the gendered nature of sports fandom by conceptualizing fandom as incorporating multifaceted behaviors where all fan practices can be valued. Looking at the neighborhood bar or the city streets as spaces of fandom begins to give voice to those who do not conform to the "traditional" roles of male working-class fans upon which the concept of fandom has been defined.

All have access to the Who Dat Nation and can experience it in their own ways. Each way is a valid form of Saints fandom. This perspective allows us to challenge concepts of gendered sports spaces that seek to reinforce dominant power structures. When all have access to the Who Dat Nation—people who are not really sports fans, people who are newcomers to the city, people who do not live in New Orleans, anyone who is not the stereotypical male sports fanatic—all can use expressions of fandom to feel connected to something larger than themselves. It is not difficult to gain acceptance through spaces of fandom—wearing team colors, chanting, cheering, engaging with other people through football-related activities are all easy ways to enter the Who Dat Nation. I targeted gendered fandom as a way to bring the discussion forward about the power of sport spaces to challenge dominant power structures and to challenge how we conceptualize fandom.

6

*Cultural Economics
of Saints Football*

Sports and the city are intertwined. The evolution of sport and the evolution of the American city parallel one another. The rise of commercialized, professional spectator sports marked a significant development in American athletics.[1] As early American cities evolved into industrial centers, the urban working class sought out recreational activities. Popping into the local saloon for a beer, attending cinemas, or celebrating holidays at community picnics became part of American urban culture. Athletics were a large part of the recreation and leisure culture that Americans craved. Sports exemplified an approved mode of entertainment that provided an escape from the overcrowding, pollution and other ills associated with city life. Once sport became a popular leisure activity, businessmen recognized the potential for profit by promoting sporting events to urban crowds who grew accustomed to paying for entertainment. Sports entrepreneurs and politicians worked in tandem to define sports as a profit-making spectacle through horse racing, boxing and baseball.[2]

By the time professional football organizers established the name National Football League in 1922, Americans were already fully immersed in sports as a commercial and commodified product. Commodifcation means transforming something, in this case football, into a product that can be bought and sold. In contrast, football could be described as simply a game or sporting activity that cannot be owned and that everyone has a right to. The NFL, however, exemplifies an extreme case commodified sport. The term "hypercommodification" has been used to critique the current state of professional sports, emphasizing the extent to which sports have become a valuable commodity.[3] America is a capitalist society and American culture is increasingly defined as a consumer culture. Accepting the NFL brand as a business and commercialized product, rather than simply the game of football, is concomitant with the NFL as an extension of an American culture of consumerism.

Cities moved away from their industrial and manufacturing past and stepped into a new economy. This new economy has been called the cultural economy. The term "cultural economy" involves an inter-twining of economic and symbolic processes. The cultural economy includes instruments of entertainment, communication and sociability exemplified by film, music, clothing,[4] or in this case, sports. The role of Saints football as a commodified cultural form cannot be ignored when evaluating the relationship between sports and the city. New Orleans is a city bound by the reality of its place in American capitalism where both the team and the fans are located within the larger frame-work of the city as a place of cultural consumption. Scholars highlight the growth of cultural consumption as a defining factor in understand-ing the condition of cities in a shifting economy where manufacturing and production have been replaced by the consumption of experiences and pleasure.

Throughout the twentieth century, American football spread across the globe alongside music, fast food and consumer culture. No longer the realm of amateur play, sports are increasingly global, professional, commodified and driven by consumption. As a result, scholars are still trying to make sense of the contemporary characteristics of sport.[5]

Sport events are often viewed as hallmarks of cultural globaliza-tion and a vehicle to export American values. Although NFL football exemplifies a commodified cultural spectacle, very few studies look at how people in different locales in the United States are experiencing and creating value as spectators of home football games.[6] This chapter continues to highlight the perspective of sports fans and the value they place on professional sports by looking at how Saints fans interpreted the role of Saints football as a cultural commodity that is a highly com-mercialized national brand. The ways that locals embraced NFL hype and the commodification of professional football while also engineering local cultural adaptations to the economic dimensions of sport reveals the complexity of values assigned to Saints football.

Christie Anderson twirls a parasol during a Saints tailgate party.

Saints fans engaged with the reality of consumerism and adapted to this reality in meaningful ways. Fans did not resist commercialism as an inauthentic form of culture. They showed adaptations of commercialism in order to garner benefits on a level that was meaningful to them both economically and culturally. The experiences of Saints fans in the city did not always mesh well with the profit-making operations of the national NFL brand and the intentions of civic boosters to market the NFL to tourists. Saints fans did not passively accept any prepackaged marketing product the NFL passed down. They embraced aspects of sports commercialism that meshed with their own ideas of local culture and adapted elements to suit them. They rejected those that did not seem to quite fit with local ideals. Saints fans traveled along a continuum from embracing highly commercialized forms of sport consumption, to creating more local forms of consumer culture, to outright expressing that not everything of value is for sale.

Consuming the NFL: America's Game

The NFL as a business and a brand is, in many ways, one of the strongest and most financially successful in the world of sports. The 32 NFL teams ranked among the top 50 most valuable sports teams in the world, with the average team worth $1.04 billion.[7] The value of NFL teams increases every year. In order for the league to achieve and maintain a high level of financial success, the number of franchises needed to be limited and controlled, rather than operating on a free competition system. In order to get television viewers to faithfully tune their sets to professional football, people would have to be fans of the league, rather than a singular city team.[8] This understanding sparked the NFL to fiercely promote the league brand. The Super Bowl was created, not just as a season-culminating event, but also to further market the entire league as opposed to individual teams. Infusing the brand with elements of patriotism became the driving force behind marketing the national product.

Pete Rozelle intended the Super Bowl to be an advertisement for NFL football, investing the game with "traditional American values" and called it "a conscious effort on our part to bring the element of patriotism into the Super Bowl."[9] NFL commissioner Paul Tagliabue shared this view of the Super Bowl and called it "the winter version of the Fourth of July celebration."[10] The American flag stretches across the field from sideline to sideline during the pregame programming at most NFL games. The national anthem is always performed prior to kickoff by musicians with mass popular appeal. All who are in the stadium rise, men remove their caps, and a moment of silence breaks through the otherwise continuous soundscape of the football crowd. Sometimes pyrotechnics accompany the song and are meant to symbolize the "rockets' red glare" of the anthem.

The red, white and blue shield that comprises the NFL logo was first used in the 1960s.[11] The famous shield has only undergone slight modifications, most recently in 2008 to reduce the number of stars within the shield to represent the 8 conference divisions, darken the colors and revamp the look of the football that rests within the shield. The patriotic-looking NFL shield adorns every official NFL product from player uniforms to TV broadcast to cell phone background images.

Images of patriotism, fueled by infusing elements of the American flag, help brand the league as America's game. American exceptionalism defines the NFL, where the sport that is called football in the United States is specified as American football in other countries. The sport that the rest of the world calls football, the United States calls soccer. This difference underscores the idea that the game of professional football in America has rules, styles and identity that are unique to America. Even though baseball is known as America's pastime, several indicators prompt writers to assert that football is the new American pastime, surpassing baseball, basketball and hockey in the hierarchy of the "Big Four" North American sports.

The real cultural power of the NFL circulates around the ability to use football to tell compelling stories. The storylines crafted through football are classic American folktales and versions of the most-repeated narratives in the Western world. The players become unintentional actors in dramas about overcoming obstacles, bitter rivalries, rags-to-riches stories, emerging heroes, rooting for the underdog or essentially promoting traditional American values. The outcome of each game is not scripted like an American sitcom, making football unique as a form of popular entertainment. Football is exciting to watch because the drama unfolds in real time, as mediated messages intentionally insert narratives around the game. This generates some of the most powerful fantasies in our culture. "Any football fan could name several [storylines] off the top of his or her head—the traditional-rivals story, the bitter-enemies story, the wounded-hero story, the Cinderella or Ugly Duckling story, the son-challenging-the-father story, and so on."[12] NFL Films, the television and production studio owned by the NFL, emphasized this type of storytelling. NFL Films was created to document and archive football games, but in fact it is masterful at crafting folk dramas by editing montages for distinct purposes.

Despite the success of scripted, shared league narratives that reflect patriotism, each of the 32 teams in the NFL is stamped with individual characteristics. Each is located within a city that has its own unique culture, history, and fan base. As is evidenced by the Saints football team, locating football in New Orleans involved locating the Saints within the social and cultural context that is New Orleans. Instead of an archetypal fairy tale told through the lens of national football, the storyline of the Saints in New Orleans reflected real people and events, where the cultural power of the Saints lies in the ability to reflect the broader social conditions in which they were situated. Fans do not passively watch football and the drama built around it, but rather engage with it as active consumers of football.

The growth of the NFL as a business changed the ways that fans interact with football. The increased commodification of sport transformed fans into active consumers rather than passive spectators of their favorite team.[13] American sports and particularly the NFL are highly commercialized institutions. Engaging in professional sports as a fan or a spectator is often framed as a consumer activity. A person's consumption of professional sports teams involves buying tickets to watch the live games, buying and wearing team logo apparel, or purchasing food, beverage, or other consumer goods in connection with the game watching experience. Even though not all fan activities directly involve consumption, fans are primarily consumers, particularly within the confines of the larger American culture of consumerism and capitalism.[14]

Americans spend billions of dollars every year on sporting events, sports merchandise and other sports related activities. In most cities, it is not cheap to attend an NFL game. An average ticket price to attend one NFL game during the 2014 season was around $85. The average cost to take a family of four to see an NFL game is close to $500.[15]

Shirts, hats, key chains, or collars for your pet are only a few examples of the many products for sale that bear sports team logos. Nearly $8 billion every year goes towards the purchase of sports logo apparel. The NFL sells between $2.5 and $3.5 billion annually in team products.[16] Merchandising is a highly visible sign of the extent to which sports entities have been commodified. One of the most obvious expressions of fandom involves dressing up in team colors and team apparel to mark affiliation and show loyalty to the home team.

In the early days of the NFL, the term "team apparel" applied only to players' uniforms. Team apparel evolved and fans flocked in person and online to find and buy jerseys as an official symbol of team affiliation. The team jerseys that mimic what the players wear on the field rest on the upper tier of the team merchandise hierarchy. The NFL tightened control over its brand and licensing agreements to solidify NFL merchandise as a specialty item. After a ten-year deal with Reebok expired, Nike emerged as the official uniform provider of the NFL starting in 2012. Nike reportedly paid $1.1 billion to lock in a five-year contract as the NFL's exclusive provider of on-field apparel. Nike will pay $220 million per year to the NFL for those sponsorship rights, which is considerably more than the $25 million per year Reebok paid.[17] The NFL was able to extract this fee from Nike, which anticipated reaping vast profits from fans eager to buy the same apparel that their favorite football players wear. Fans happily paid the retail price in order to have a new style and the shiny, silver sticker that marks their coveted item as an officially licensed product of the NFL.

The extent to which culture becomes transformed into something that is commodified and consumed raises questions about whether authentic local culture can survive amongst such developments. The NFL is first and foremost a national product. Even though each team retains a local city identity, they are all united under the NFL banner and logo, a singular national television contract, and the rules and regulations of one governing body. Football fan culture continues to adapt in response to the commodification of sport. We can learn lessons from the Who Dat Nation that show how NFL fans react to the highly commercialized nature of the most popular professional sports league in America.

Selling the Black-and-Gold City

Across the city of New Orleans, black and gold Saints team colors abound. The New Orleans Saints sold the most licensed products of any NFL team on NFLshop.com in 2010, the year the Saints won the Super Bowl.[18] Despite the popularity of officially licensed gear, people wearing some sort of black-and gold-costume, rather than a traditional Saints jersey was a common sight for Saints games. Two fans gladly posed for a picture as I snapped a shot of their floor-length nun costumes displaying the names Sister Mary Who and Sister Mary Dat. At one Saints game, a woman had her silver hair tucked under a hat that boasted Saints logos on one side and Cleveland Brown logos on the other side. Her pink football jersey had also been refashioned with one half Saints jersey sewn together with one half Cleveland Browns jersey. Her team loyalties were divided that day as her favorite football stars competed with each other on the field.

During another game, two young women in black-and-gold tutus occupied the seats next to me. Women wearing black-and-gold tutus were a common sight in the Superdome on game day. One lady wearing a black-and-gold tutu was toting her baby in an infant carrier. The baby also wore a black-and-gold tutu. Together they looked like a big cloud of festive tulle. Creative costuming was an expression of fandom that defied commercialism as fans found ways to express their fandom without the use of corporately controlled logos.

One factor steering Saints fans towards locally produced products or choosing handmade Saints themed costumes was price. Branded as a specialty item, officially licensed NFL gear is expensive. In 2010 an "authentic Reebok New Orleans Saints team jersey" retailed for $239. One could pick up a "replica New Orleans Saints team jersey" for $109. When Nike took over the apparel contract, different styles of Saints jerseys ranged in price from $299 to $99. In contrast to these high-priced items, small New Orleans shops offered Saints-themed T-shirts that are not officially licensed NFL products for around $25. Or, one can rummage through items in one's closet and pull together black and gold pieces to show Who Dat pride on game day. As an extension of New Orleans celebratory culture, many adults tuck boxes of costumes into their closets. These costumes are at the ready for a variety of local events that encourage creative costuming. For example, dressing in costume on Fat Tuesday (Mardi Gras) is a tradition. Costuming in black and gold is a Saints game day tradition. These rituals are not reserved for children but rather serve as a normal playscape for New Orleans adults.

One woman who described her Saints game day outfits said, "Sunday mornings I tend to get up particularly excited and figure out which Saints outfit I'm going to put together. I decide if I'm going to wear a jersey or if I'm going to do some festive black-and-gold party clothes with a little sparkle and a little fringe and that sort of thing. There's always an element of fancifulness to it. It's not just jeans and a black shirt." The commercialized brand did not control fan identity. Fans wanted something compatible with their personal identity as well as their fan identity. I saw women wearing Saints outfits that included corsets, tutus, go-go boots, gold lamé tights, and black-and-gold fleur-de-lis hair clips. These types of costuming represented personal forms of public self-expression.

In addition to fans wanting to wear team apparel that was compatible with their identity, Saints fans also wanted something that was an expression of New Orleans culture. Buying Saints-themed products at a local art market or from a small T-shirt shop was an expression of fandom that supported local New Orleans artists and small businesses. This was something that the official NFL brand could not provide. For example, parasols are a part of New Orleans culture. Flashily decorated umbrellas are fundamental in second-line celebrations. Hoisting a black-and-gold parasol in the air or dancing around after Saints touchdowns was what Saints fans did because it was part of local ritual. In the late 1980s Saints team owner Tom Benson influenced fans with his "Benson Boogie," a celebratory shuffle performed while twirling a black-and-gold parasol in the air. Twirling parasols in the air was a part of New Orleans culture that had also become enmeshed within Saints fan culture. Street vendors sell handcrafted parasols near the Superdome on game day, representing an extension of this local cultural form of commercialism.

Fans Interpret Economic Impact

New Orleanians found several ways to capitalize on the widespread demand for all types of Saints-themed goods. On game day, the city sidewalks leading up to the Superdome were scattered with street vendors. Crafters offered bracelets, beads, buttons, top hats, and elaborate parasols—all decorated in Saints black and gold. During the Saints–Atlanta Falcons game, several of the parasols for sale were decked out in red and black feathers and sparkles to entice buyers supporting the opposing team. One group sold decorated paper grocery bags for fans to wear over their heads. Instead of the brown paper bags that hid Saints fans in shame in the 1980s, these bags were yellow, had a cutout to show the wearer's face, and boasted the words We Dat.

Creeping closer to the Superdome, many people positioned coolers on the sidewalks to sell beer and water. One guy sold beers out of his cooler, two for $5. Two blocks closer to the dome, a woman sold beers for $4 each, although I heard one man talk her price down to a $3 beer. I asked if she was always on this corner selling beers for Saints games. She said yes and explained that she had to get a $1,500 annual permit from the city. Before she was able to get this permit, she had to establish herself as a company with a liquor license. The process she explained sounded so formal for what, on the surface, looked like a very informal way for a resident to make a few extra dollars.

A handful of other groups trying to make a few dollars greeted Saints fans on the sidewalks leading up to the Superdome. I stopped and donated $1 to one of these groups, a boys' sports team raising money for uniforms. Face painters roamed the areas where tailgaters mingled, offering an artistic design in exchange for tips. Two women wove in and out of the parties of tailgating fans, carrying a wicker basket full of praline candy, selling them for $2 each. In Finn McCool's bar during a Saints game, a woman walked around to the bar patrons selling hand decorated black-and-gold pillar candles for $15 each. The man who I saw hoisting a "touchdown baby" doll into the air at the Rendezvous bar transformed this quirky ritual into a way to make money. A year later, I ran into him at a local art market. He sold tiny gold, brass, silver and pewter "touchdown baby" jewelry for $40 to more than $150. He said his "touchdown baby" business was doing really well.

At art markets throughout the city, several different vendors offered the Who Dat version of their regular art products. One of the jewelry vendors had a Saints-themed line of jewelry she created, including a replica Lombardi trophy. Another vendor sold "scrappy dolls," a hand-sewn rectangular cloth doll with dangling scraps of fabric for the doll's arms and legs. I inquired about the dolls and she explained that her mother had made scrappy dolls for her nine children. Now one of those children made her own scrappy dolls for sale at craft markets. She pointed out that she made black-and-gold scrappy dolls with fleurs-de-lis for eyes, instead of button eyes. She retold stories of how some people held their scrappy dolls in their laps throughout entire Saints games for good luck. In these instances the commodification of a cultural form, turning the Saints into product and profit, was still an expression of Saints fandom that reflected local cultural particularities.

The ways in which Saints fans talked about economics revealed that they thought economic impacts were present and important. But they were present and important on a scale much smaller than the way academic scholars talk about citywide economic impact. Multiple people offered their "expertise" on how a Saints win or loss affects the local economy. If the Saints won, then the French Quarter bartender could expect to take home more tips. If the Saints lost, that same bartender would make less money because Saints fans would not feel as elated and ready to continue the celebration. Whether or not this informal

Symbols of American patriotism infiltrate most NFL game presentations as the league strives to cultivate fans of the national brand. Photograph taken at the NFC Championship game on January 24, 2010.

win-loss economic theory is true, several different fans repeated it. This further reinforced that New Orleans residents believed there was some connection between the Saints and city economics. This example also showed that a unit of economic measurement as small as one bartender's evening tips is the level of pecuniary measurement that matters to urban residents. The ways in which local people bought and sold Saints products illustrated different ways that New Orleanians adapted to the commodification of sport and found economic value on a smaller scale.

People living in New Orleans believed that fans from visiting teams made a positive contribution to the local economy. As fans of the opposing team trudged down the steps of the Superdome seating section past rows and rows of Saints fans, it was common to hear some light heckling that frequently included statements like "Go spend money," encouraging the out-of-town guests to go to the French Quarter and pump more of their tourist dollars into local attractions.

After the Saints lost to the Atlanta Falcons in 2010, a large group of Atlanta fans congregated in one parking lot on Poydras Street near the Superdome. They posted a banner designating their claimed parking lot spaces as a Falcons party, making it clear they weren't finished celebrating even though the game had ended. On this game day Atlanta fans happily spread themselves throughout the French Quarter, excited their team had won the game. As I walked to the spot where I could catch a bus home, several Atlanta fans cat-called "Who dat?" and "We Dat!" in my direction, mocking my position as a losing Saints fan. I was an easy target as one of only a few people wearing a Saints jersey on Canal Boulevard, a busy street for tourists in the French Quarter. When I reached the bus stop on the corner of Canal and Tchoupitoulas, one woman yelled back to the people wearing Atlanta Falcons jerseys, saying, "Thank you! Go spend money!," indicating a local appreciation for any tourist dollars that come into the city. There was a certain irony involved in that exchange, if your point of view was that even though Atlanta won the game that day, ultimately New Orleans won in terms of economic benefit.

One reason why Saints fans did not entirely oppose the heightened commercialism was because they believed in the role of the NFL to market messages necessary to stimulate New Orleans tourism industry and believed that it held some value. For example, one Saints fan said, "It brings legitimacy to the city. Without a team, New Orleans is more of a small market. There is a quality-of-life issue regarding professional sports teams. Some businesses factor that into the decision to relocate to the area. I also think it aids in tourism, the most dominant industry in the city right now."

NFL games are national events staged for TV audiences, local residents, and visiting fans. The NFL kickoff weekend held in New Orleans in 2010 demonstrated how this commercialized product was perceived and experienced by local fans.

NFL Kickoff Game 2010

The NFL has a history of featuring the previous year's championship team in an opening game to mark the beginning of a new season. The kickoff game ritual as it is carried out today started in 2002 as a signature event to feature football, concerts and other ceremonies. As the Saints were the previous season's Super Bowl winners, the NFL selected New Orleans as the site for the opening kickoff game for the 2010 NFL season. The first game of each new season grew into a spectacle unlike other games that occur throughout the year. Driven by national network television broadcasts and celebratory events staged throughout downtown New Orleans, the NFL was eager to create hype for a new football season while Saints fans were eager to celebrate their championship team. As the NFL infused New Orleans with its version of a celebration, city residents found their commercialized version lacking in flavor and ignoring what New Orleanians value.

The day before the 2010 NFL kickoff game, I went to the NFL Fan Fest held in the Jackson Brewery parking lot in the French Quarter. New Orleans stages festivals throughout the year to celebrate all manner of things. Some festivals, like Jazz Fest, are mainstream, celebrating the cultural heritage of music in New Orleans. Others celebrate more obscure things, like wrinkly green vegetables at the annual mirliton festival. The NFL Fan Fest staged in the French Quarter did not resemble other festivals that I have attended in this same French Quarter location in the sense that this fest was littered with national sponsors.

Every booth or attraction was sponsored, and existed for the sole purpose of advertising a product such as Pepsi, General Motors, Verizon, or Febreze. This contrasted sharply with local names that decorated regular New Orleans festivals, such as Ochsner (health system), Rouses (supermarkets), and Entergy (utilities).

While walking past the booths someone handed me a free Pepsi. I was invited to step into the Coors beer tent and throw a football to win a prize. Insulated drink holders and Coors logo temporary tattoos were really advertising rather than prizes. At another booth I spun a prize wheel, only to win a coupon for fifty cents off of a Febreze product. The only element that felt local at all in the Fan Fest was radio personality Bobby Hebert broadcasting a live show from a tent on the small festival site. Bobby Hebert, nicknamed the Cajun Cannon, is a retired Saints quarterback and fan favorite sportscaster. His explosion of joy in the stadium press box during the Saints game against the Jets in 2010 further endeared him to Saints fans. The NFL press box has a strict rule that members of the media cannot cheer for either team while performing their duties in the press box on game day. Much to the delight of football fans, the Cajun Cannon has been ejected from the LSU press box for failing to contain his passion for the home team. Bobby Hebert's tent was the only element at Fan Fest attracting any crowd of people.

A few blocks down from this Fan Fest, crews were busy setting up stages and barricades for the concert to take place the next day in Jackson Square. Decatur Street, a main thoroughfare through the French Quarter, was blocked off, even to pedestrian traffic. To call this blockage highly inconvenient to local traffic movement in the busy French Quarter would be an understatement. Jackson Square, which would normally be crowded with wandering tourists and local vendors selling original artwork, palm readings or buggy ride tours of the Quarter, was closed—barricaded by fancy banners and security guards. Saint Louis Cathedral, whose doors would normally be open for anyone to take a peek or offer a prayer, was closed. Paper signs taped to posts on the corners of Jackson Square read in plain black and white ST. ANN BUSINESSES OPEN. Store owners on St. Ann Street posted these signs fearing that the barricades would deter people from coming into the stores so close to Jackson Square. It is ironic that small local businesses were threatened by this large-scale sporting event, since a positive economic impact for the host city is supposed to be one of the main benefits of staging this type of celebration.

French Quarter businesses, artists and street vendors were upset about the NFL taking over their space without any communication or even a courtesy notice. One manager of a shop along Jackson Square said, "We're all about this city and supporting the success of the Saints, but when we are neglected and cast aside, it's demoralizing. Nobody came to us with any information whatsoever. We weren't consulted in any way. Basically, the NFL was given free rein and had no restrictions whatsoever. This is disconcerting for the business owners and residents."[19] Observing the scene at Jackson Square that day, I understood their complaints as the normal tourist heart of the French Quarter had been shut down and barricaded to prepare for the NFL spectacle.

Some business owners lost customers while others struggled to manage parking problems and crowds. The main complaint was that they were not notified of what would be taking place and therefore could not properly plan to manage the event in a way that did not adversely affect their normal daily operations. A local gallery owner who commented on the event said, "I'm all in favor of promoting the city, but when you come into our front yard, we want you to invite us to the party."[20] Jackson Square is a public space where local culture clashes with tourism on a daily basis. Although the NFL activities were not the only incident of contested space in Jackson Square, the *Times-Picayune* reported that "complaints reached a fever pitch after the NFL threw their kickoff concert without serving notice to the neighborhood."[21] After the concert in Jackson Square, local business owners organized a task force to draft recommendations on how to best maintain Jackson Square and inform local residents and businesses about events taking place there. One task force organizer said, "We are trying to make sure the city's most iconic site is protected and respected for the future."[22]

The NFL barricade around Jackson Square was erected in preparation for events that would take place throughout the day prior to the Saints facing the Minnesota Vikings in the Superdome on Thursday, September 9, 2010. The NFL teamed up with local Mardi Gras float creator Kern Studios to produce a Mardi Gras–style parade to roll

Saints fans display creativity in costuming on game day. Many expressions of Saints fandom seek to reinforce New Orleans' celebration-oriented culture and do not rely on officially licensed NFL products. Photograph taken in the French Quarter prior to the NFL kickoff game on September 9, 2010.

through the French Quarter two and a half hours before kickoff. Activity organizers reported that "given New Orleans' tradition of parades and music and food and football, we decided to combine all those things into a single celebration."[23] However, this production of a celebration lacked some local nuances that characterize true local celebrations. For example, New Orleanians objected to the lack of local musical talent scheduled for the game night concerts, since NBC chose to schedule artists that had a broad appeal nationally. New Orleans is home to some of the greatest musicians in the world. An event that was supposed to celebrate and showcase New Orleans cast aside local musical talent as ill suited for the national production. One editorial writer compared the musical lineup to "bland alphabet soup" rather than a "flavorful gumbo."[24]

Despite the highly commercialized, NFL-directed production of events, the celebrations offered several different opportunities for Saints fans to express themselves and engage with Saints football. The newspaper warned there was no way that ticket holders to the Superdome could watch the parade, see the concert, and get to the dome in time to see the banner-drop honoring the Saints' Super Bowl win. I woke up feeling anxious and stressed, trying to decide where to be and what to do to observe as much as I could about how Saints fans were experiencing this out-of-the ordinary day.

At 11 a.m., I went to the NFL Shop for Women on Magazine Street. This was a temporary boutique, the first of its kind, erected as an experiment by the NFL. Two rocking chairs adorned the porch leading to the front door of the tiny store, carved out of a shotgun house in one of New Orleans' more posh shopping districts along Magazine Street.[25] The small boutique was full of shoppers. I asked the store clerk if it was busy for game day. She replied, "It's busy every day." She said that every morning when she came to open the shop, there were already people waiting at the door. All the store workers wore Saints shirts. Shoppers were calm—a mix of black and white women—all already wearing some sort of Saints or black-and-gold attire. The only two men in the store followed their women around and seemed out of place in the small, crowded boutique. One could buy all sorts of items emblazoned with the official NFL Saints logo—shirts, cocktail dresses, a bikini, nail polish, necklaces, shorts, jeans, or sunglasses. The merchandise offerings were adequate, but not as enticing as the offerings at local shops that feature Saints shirts with more New Orleans flair. I spent $20 for the least expensive item—a black T-shirt with the word SAINTS scrawled across the front—and went home to paint my toenails black and gold before heading out for the festivities.

On my way home I drove through downtown, past the Superdome.

Hordes of people on the downtown streets wore black and gold. If not as blatant as a jersey, less subtle outfits paid tribute to the Saints—a businessman wearing a black suit with a gold tie or a yellow shirt with a black belt. Tailgate parties, tents, and even a black-and-gold party bus occupied the parking lots surrounding the Superdome. The football game would not start for at least seven more hours.

I caught the 4 p.m. bus from my house to the French Quarter. Most other people on the bus were not wearing Saints gear or black-and-gold clothes. It was a reminder that despite the hoopla, some city residents were simply performing their daily routines, going to and from work, not possessed by the Saints mania that the local news made ubiquitous. The number 55 bus stopped several blocks shy of its normal route down Elysian Fields, as those streets were blocked by the staged parade and by the temporary concert stage on Decatur Street.

Although the parade was not yet in motion, I walked past all the stationary parade floats. Former Saints stars Michael Lewis and Deuce McAllister posed for pictures with the few fans lucky enough to be walking by as the players were mounting their parade floats. The local paper later reported, "The sponsor-branded pre-game floats no doubt caused locals to moan."[26] A float emblazoned with the Snickers candy bar logo did not arouse as much interest as a typical Mardi Gras float throwing satirical punches at New Orleans elected officials. I walked down the sidewalk, taking a slow two-hour stroll through the French Quarter to the Superdome to see all the people and the spectacle. Spectators lined up along the street, waiting for the parade to roll. The sidewalk contained several kids with their families eager to see the Saints parade. Black and gold, fleurs-de-lis, Saints gear and costumes decorated members of the crowd.

People spilled out of French Quarter bars, gathering together to celebrate Saints football. Bars and restaurants erased the daily specials from their sidewalk chalkboards and instead scribbled the words REPEAT DAT—an informal slogan used during the season following the Saints' Super Bowl win, willing the team to try and win the Super Bowl again.

After the pregame parade and concerts were over, people arranged themselves into their more normal Saints game-watching routines. They met friends at bars, squeezed into Superdome seats, or returned home to watch the game in the family living room. The New Orleans Saints hosted the Minnesota Vikings in a type of rematch of the preceding NFC Championship game. The Saints won that night 14 to 9. Throughout the rest of the season, the Saints won 11 games and lost 5. They entered the playoffs as a wild-card team but were knocked out in the first round by the Seattle Seahawks. Speculation that the Saints could "Repeat dat" and win back-to-back Super Bowls ended with the 2010 NFL season.

I Own Who Dat

As Saints fans settled into normal routines of game watching during the post–Super Bowl winning season, the NFL made a move that stunned the Who Dat Nation. The NFL claimed they owned rights to the popular local phrase. This assertion kicked off a conflict over ownership of "Who Dat" that stretched into a lengthy legal battle.

With the success of the Saints' 2009 season leading up to the team's first Super Bowl win in 2010, the phrase "Who Dat" journeyed out of the living rooms of hardcore Saints fans, spread across New Orleans and Louisiana, and found its way to a national audience of people watching the television broadcasts of NFL games. Saints fans craved anything that said Who Dat—from the words simply printed on a T-shirt, to a clever shirt design saying *Horton Hears a Who Dat* that paid homage to the Saints and writer Dr. Seuss, author of the children's book *Horton Hears a Who!* The words "Who Dat" blanketed the city of New Orleans, appearing on bus stop benches, artwork, daiquiri shop signs, necklaces, posters, and T-shirts.

Consumption of Who Dat products was not only a reflection of a winning season but also symptomatic of the voracity with which residents bought symbols of New Orleans post–Katrina. The fleur-de-lis and other symbols of Saints football easily combined to show loyalty to the team and, ultimately, a commitment to the city. One store that demonstrated this affinity for New Orleans, called Fleurty Girl, had only been open for two months when the owner received notice from the NFL that she was to stop printing "Who Dat" shirts and to destroy all the inventory she already had. Another New Orleans store called

Storyville received the same letter. The local media quickly began reporting a David and Goliath narrative that pitted tiny local businesses against the giant NFL. Operating Fleurty Girl was a second job for a young New Orleans mother who was commuting from Baton Rouge when news cameras set up outside her small shop on Oak Street to cover the growing discontent over the intellectual property questions surfacing over "Who Dat."

The NFL issued cease-and-desist letters to small New Orleans businesses that sold these consumer goods, claiming that Who Dat was an NFL-owned trademark and ordering them to stop selling unlicensed Saints merchandise. The NFL cited a 1988 trademark the Saints organization had filed with the state of Louisiana and said they had exclusive rights to the phrase. According to an article in the *Times-Picayune*, the letter said that "any combination of design elements (even if not the subject of a federal or state trademark registration), such as team colors, roman numerals, or other references to the Saints are also trademark violations."[27] Without a licensing agreement, the official marks and logos of the New Orleans Saints are off limits. The NFL assserted that the privilege of using Saints marks and logos in product or advertising campaigns is reserved for companies that enter into sponsorship agreements with the Saints and pay the price for this right.

The use and protection of intellectual property is an important issue to the sports industry. Patents, copyrights and trademark laws are all designed to protect intellectual property. The purpose of copyright is to protect those who have put time and energy into some creative project and to ensure those creators receive the financial benefits of their work. It is an economically motivated law. Trademark law protects the owner of a team name, emblem and logo and prohibits other businesses from palming off ersatz goods as products of the original source. By legal definition, a trademark is "any word, name, symbol or device or any combination thereof adopted and used by a manufacturer or merchant to identify and distinguish goods ... from those manufactured or sold by others."[28] Trademarks are supposed to serve a variety of purposes, such as designating the source of a product, signaling a certain standard or quality, or protecting the public from confusion or deception so that consumers are able to purchase the products and services they want.

It was a common practice for NFL teams to legally protect their trademarked and copyrighted marks and logos. The Saints organization regularly sent cease-and-desist letters to companies that were using the Saints name and logos in their advertising or merchandising plans without first obtaining permission to do so through paying hefty licensing or sponsorship fees. According to an NFL spokesman, "Any unauthorized use of the Saints colors and other marks designed to create the illusion of an affiliation with the Saints is equally a violation of the Saints trademark rights because it allows a third party to 'free ride' by profiting from confusion of the team's fans, who want to show support for the Saints."[29] Saints fans were not confused, as the league spokesperson suggests, by the market being flooded with Who Dat merchandise. Fans as consumers were keenly aware of the difference between officially licensed NFL merchandise and something black-and-gold with a fleur-de-lis on it.

Although the NFL protecting its marks and logos was common practice, attempting to claim the rights over the phrase "Who Dat" shocked and offended New Orleanians. They believed Who Dat lived within the public domain where no one should have exclusive trademark rights to it. The people of New Orleans, the members of the Who Dat Nation, viewed the actions of the NFL as an attack. They viewed it as an attempt to steal something that belonged to them. The NFL sent cease-and-desist letters to only two New Orleans T-shirt stores, Fleurty Girl and Storyville. They may have been narrowly targeted letters challenging only a few pieces of merchandise, but to Saints fans it felt like an assault on their culture. Saints fans displayed their backlash in a multitude of ways.

The words DEFEND WHO DAT quickly appeared on sidewalk chalkboards posted outside local businesses. At an annual neighborhood festival, a craft vendor sold hand towels stitched with the words I OWN WHO DAT. Saints fans balked at the NFL's perceived arrogance and bristled at an entity with superior legal and monetary resources. They sardonically questioned whether they should be asked to stop using the fleur-de-lis symbol or the colors black and gold altogether in order to point out the absurdity of being asked not to use a symbol that was so ubiquitous and laced with intangible meaning. The general feeling among New Orleanians was that no one should own Who Dat because it was something that belonged to the people of New Orleans. According to a man quoted in the local media, "In my opinion, I don't see how you can take something that is New Orleans, that has been around as long as I can remember and call it your own. They don't own dat phrase, or dat language, or dat nation. It's not a phrase. It's a people. It's a community. It's the way we talk."[30]

Even members of the Louisiana congressional delegation got involved in demanding that the NFL leave Who Dat alone. The most vocal of these opinions came from Louisiana Senator David Vitter, who penned a letter to NFL commissioner Roger Goodell demanding the NFL drop threats of legal action against local mom-and-pop merchants selling Who Dat T-shirts.[31] Vitter asserted he would print T-shirts that read "WHO DAT say we can't print Who Dat!" and challenged the NFL to come and get him. Although this may sound humorous, he acted as a spokesperson on behalf of the Who Dat Nation, who felt that trying to claim trademark ownership over Who Dat was absurd. Vitter's voice gained the most traction in the local media, although politicians across party lines agreed with his sentiments. The Who Dat controversy may be one of the only issues that Louisiana Democrats and Republicans wholeheartedly agreed upon. They rushed in to defend the Who Dat Nation. Senator Mary Landrieu asked the NFL to stop exploiting a phrase that had been part of Louisiana's culture for more than a century.[32]

Determining the exact legal boundaries of Who Dat remained elusive. A trademark is generally assigned to the first person who showed that he or she used it in commerce and registered the mark. However, pinpointing the origins and ownership of Who Dat was not clear. A rough timeline illustrates how Saints fans tried to make sense of the origins of Who Dat. Some sources claim the roots of Who Dat reach far back into black cultural history, including minstrel shows from the 1800s, jazz chant lyrics, and stage entertainment. In the 1970s black schools used the Who Dat chant. It has been traced back to a few New Orleans high schools, but mostly to chants heard at St. Augustine High School football games. The St. Augustine band, "The Marching 100," is often referred to as the best and most popular marching band in New Orleans. The cultural power of that respected institution is very strong throughout New Orleans. In 1983 a TV news feature on the St.

154

Augustine Purple Knights featured the football players chanting, "Who dat, who dat, who dat talkin' about beatin' St. Aug?! Who dat?! Who dat?!" In 1980 a similar chant surfaced among the Cincinnati Bengals that went, "Who dey? Who dey? Who dey think they gonna beat dem Bengals?" Culturally, the phrase had overlapping points of origination.

Most of the formal action regarding Who Dat as intellectual property took place in the 1980s. In 1983 brothers Steve and Sal Monistere registered a business called Who Dat Inc. with the Louisiana Secretary of State, intending to use the phrase on records, tapes, T-shirts, and bumper stickers. In that same year, Steve and Sal Monistere produced and copyrighted a recording of the popular song "When the Saints Go Marching In" that incorporated the Who Dat chant. The recording featured celebrated New Orleans musician Aaron Neville and a group of Saints players known as the "Singing Saints." Also in 1983, Who Dat Inc. sued Tees Unlimited for copyright infringement over Who

Barricades emblazoned with NFL sponsor logos block access to Jackson Square in preparation for NFL kickoff activities in 2010. This area surrounding Jackson Square in the French Quarter would normally be vibrant with tourists, artists, palm readers, brass bands and pedestrian traffic.

Owners whose storefronts abut Jackson Square posted signs when the NFL disrupted daily activities throughout the French Quarter in preparation for the 2010 NFL kickoff game. They feared the barricades blocking access to Jackson Square would deter people from coming into their stores.

Dat T-shirts. A judge ruled that neither side had exclusive rights to the phrase and both were allowed to sell the shirts. In 1988 the New Orleans Saints registered a Who Dat mark with the Louisiana Secretary of State for advertising and business purposes. The Saints routinely sent cease-and-desist letters to businesses using the Saints name or fleur-de-lis logos without permission, but no one gave much thought to Who Dat until the Saints were on their way to the Super Bowl.

In 2010, the day after the Saints won the NFC Championship game, the NFL filed to use Who Dat with the Florida Secretary of State. The Super Bowl would be played in Miami and the NFL was preparing to capitalize on the excitement of the Who Dat Nation. Local news media started delving into the controversy, polling lawyers and law professors for speculation on how this controversy would end and digging up history on the phrase. None of the information brought to public attention about registering Who Dat marks in the 1980s dissuaded fans from the insistence that the phrase was invented by the fans for the fans. Store owners, like the rest of the Who Dat Nation, really thought it was a phrase that belonged to the people, not the NFL or any other single business entity.

In January 2010 the NFL issued the now infamous cease-and-desist letters. Within days, the league attempted to clarify its position on intellectual property and explain that its intention was to protect the phrase when used in conjunction with league or team marks, logos or for advertising purposes. Several months after sending the initial cease-and-desist letters, the NFL backed off of its legal claim over the phrase. Saints fans celebrated this as a victory for New Orleans.

Sorting out all the legal details of ownership may not be entirely complete since protecting intellectual property is an active and ongoing issue. Who Dat Inc. and the NFL entered into a settlement where both entities were granted legal rights and protections to sell Who Dat merchandise. Even though the NFL eased up on its attempts to seize exclusive rights to the Who Dat phrase, Who Dat Inc. issued more than 300 cease-and-desist letters claiming copyright infringement to a variety of businesses. Several small businesses were involved in lawsuits surrounding usage of Who Dat. The reality was that sales of the contested items generated far less revenue for the small businesses than legal fees and everyone settled their own disputes. Using trademarks is not always contested business. Who Dat Inc. logged roughly forty partners who pay them royalties. These are business agreements between companies that are accustomed to paying royalties to various trademark owners. Some sought the licensing agreement before ever using the phrase for commercial gain. These individual disputes over Who Dat generally play out in court.

Fans of the New Orleans Saints continue to insist that Who Dat belongs in the public domain where any one entity cannot own it. New Orleanians feel that they won the Who Dat ownership battle with the NFL. There was no sweeping court decision declaring Who Dat part of the public domain, but Who Dat is still ubiquitous in New Orleans.

From the perspective of Saints fans, control and complete commodification of Who Dat would not be possible for two main reasons. First, the phrase started with the fans. A corporation manufacturing a new marketing slogan to sell merchandise did not create it. Second, Saints fans have demonstrated extreme creativity in displaying Who

Dat messages throughout New Orleans. Crafting outfits to wear to Saints games, offering original Who Dat creations at local art markets, and even spray-painted murals gracing the sides of otherwise uninviting urban structures all showcased the phrase Who Dat. The phrase was laced with the cultural power to symbolize New Orleans people. As one Saints fan said, "It's not a phrase. It's a people. It's a community." His thoughts reflected the belief that the NFL could not possibly take something or claim to own something that New Orleanians felt belonged to them. The Who Dat Nation and being a Who Dat was more of a feeling for New Orleanians than a commodity. Chanting the phrase and wearing Who Dat T-shirts was something that New Orleanians did to create a sense of collective belonging with fellow residents. Following this line of thought, it appeared impossible for an outside entity to try to assert ownership over something that was so freely used and emotionally interpreted.

Turning Who Dat into a commodity was not the issue for Saints fans. Saints fans and New Orleanians have carved out numerous ways of turning Who Dat into a commodity. For example, vendors at local art markets started slapping the phrase Who Dat onto any number of creative items for sale from paintings to light switch covers to jewelry. Saints fans craved these items. Purchasing an item from an art market or local boutique represented another extension of New Orleans culture. Buying and wearing a Who Dat themed T-shirt from Fleurty Girl, Dirty Coast, or Storyville—local shops whose T-shirt phrases play on local customs—represented embracing something that was New Orleans. In contrast, NFL ownership over Who Dat undermined what Saints fans considered not only a New Orleans cultural expression but also a New Orleans right.

Another reaction to the Who Dat controversy involved perceiving the NFL actions as a large national corporation trying to assert dominance over small local businesses. Fans criticized the NFL for waiting until they saw an opportunity to profit from Who Dat before trying to assert ownership. The phrase had been part of the local lexicon for decades or longer, yet the struggles over who had the right to profit from the phrase did not emerge until the Saints found unprecedented success on the field followed by record-breaking merchandise sales.

The NFL's action represented a fundamental conflict between a national entity's branding and profit-seeking strategies and the traits, characteristics and nuances of a local market. The NFL underestimated the myriad ways in which Who Dat had permeated the city landscape and captured the hearts of local residents as a true identifier of place. Although the Saints organization was an NFL team and NFL product, the NFL was oblivious to the ways in which local Saints fans engaged with their home team. This disconnect between the national organization and the local environment provided evidence that sports fans had agency in creating local cultural practices around a national product in a way that creates value. The Who Dat controversy showed that the corporate drive for commodification was not all consuming and that there existed the possibility for local resistance and meaningful, grassroots expressions of fandom.

7

Rebuilding the Broken City

In the days after Hurricane Katrina, a makeshift grave appeared on the corner of Magazine and Jackson streets in Uptown New Orleans. Beneath a modest wooden cross, outlined with stacks of bricks and covered with a white sheet, the black spray painted words *Here Lies Vera* and *God Help Us* rested as a heart-wrenching reality of Hurricane Katrina. Vera Smith was killed by a hit-and-run driver on a Tuesday night after Katrina made landfall. Her body lay in the street for four days, the city authorities too overwhelmed by Katrina's destruction to provide help. Neighbors decided to bury her themselves, covering her with a sheet and crafting a makeshift grave out of bricks. The temporary gravesite went on to become a spontaneous memorial bearing a large metal cross, small offerings from neighbors, and a sign bearing Vera's name along with the date August 29, 2005. It stood as a remembrance of tragic events during Hurricane Katrina.

After the Saints won the Super Bowl, Vera's memorial was joined by a new memorial structure that paid tribute to the victory. A year later, a third structure was added to mark the Deepwater Horizon oil spill, an event that had devastating effects on the New Orleans region. The disaster occurred in April 2010 when a rig explosion caused oil to flow into the Gulf of Mexico for three months. The explosion killed eleven people and sent an estimated 4.9 billion barrels of crude oil into the gulf. The gushing oil and dispersants used to contain it caused extensive damage to marine habitats and the gulf's fishing and tourism industries. Occurring two months after the Saints' Super Bowl win, the oil spill disaster sobered the mood of New Orleanians and threatened to erase the feelings of progress that had been made since Katrina. Including an altar for Saints football in this triad of informal monuments served as powerful evidence of the level of importance at which New Orleanians placed Saints football within contexts of disaster, survival and remembrance.

That corner on Jackson and Magazine streets has been redeveloped and no longer holds the monuments. A modern brick building that houses a restaurant called Charcoal's Gourmet Burger Bar is now situated at the corner. Like many areas of the city, that corner looks very different than it did before Katrina.

Rebuilding New Orleans Through Tourism

Nearly all aspects of New Orleans' built environment have undergone transformation in some form. From large-scale infrastructure redevelopment projects to rehabilitated corner stores, New Orleans was put back together piece by piece. Many New Orleanians took their gumption and insurance money (if they had any) and started rebuilding their homes without a guiding plan from a charismatic and decisive mayor. Urban planners cringed when homeowners rebuilt right on top of an empty slab, while neighbors raised their houses several feet off the ground. Residents who wanted to come home just could not wait while civic leaders and planning experts fumbled through several different iterations of blueprints for rebuilding New Orleans. Residents grew incensed when an initial plan for rebuilding called the BNOB, or Bring New Orleans Back plan, plotted green dots over their neighborhoods to designate that the place where their house once stood would be better served as a park space. To make matters worse, many of those green dots lay on top of low-income and African American neighborhoods. The anger over this injustice galvanized neighborhood groups and led to a degree of civic engagement not seen in many other cities. New Orleans did not have a history of predictable land use plans, which are critical for informing and guiding the influx of public and private investments that flow into cities after disasters.[1] Without a solid land use plan, mapping the future of New Orleans would be like trying to put together a jigsaw puzzle with no picture to follow. Leaders faced the challenge of identifying the projects that would be most critical to New Orleans' recovery in order to channel limited resources.

Organized redevelopment in New Orleans immediately after Katrina focused on large projects, like the Superdome, at the expense of smaller, more widespread aspects of recovery that shape daily life such as grocery stores, schools, playgrounds, local businesses, and other neighborhood-level institutions. Not every project could be funded. The decision to steer resources towards the Superdome and sports-related development was not surprising, even though it may sound questionable when compared to funding for resources such as schools or hospitals.

Outside of the disaster context, sports have assumed a key place in wider urban development strategies and urban tourism promotion. Cities responded to an economic shift away from industrial capitalism and turned their attention towards postindustrial forms of consumption. As the U.S. manufacturing industry dwindled and shipped jobs overseas, so grew the tourism industry. In response, some cities sought to become entertainment destinations. Politicians worked with businesses and entrepreneurs to produce the kind of city that would attract residents, companies and visitors.

In many cities, tourism became a main strategy of urban revitalization as local governments tried to sell the city to potential consumers.[2] Rather than relying on the consumption of goods, cities emphasized the consumption of experiences and pleasure.[3] As a result, urban redevelopment efforts focused on the intersection of culture and economics. Art galleries, convention centers, and sports stadiums are examples of cultural infrastructure built as part of urban revitalization strategies that emphasize entertainment and commodified cultural forms. Many cities turned to the development of cultural commodities in order to stimulate a tourist economy, revitalize an urban area, and create an enhanced city image.

Between 1980 and 2004, 34 cities in North America invested in new sports facilities in downtown or areas near downtown to drive development and redevelopment of urban districts.[4] The economic development rationale behind investing large amounts of public subsidies into sports facilities relies on the idea that the stadium will spark redevelopment in the area in which it is located. Strong emphasis is placed on city image as an important factor in urban development as cities compete with each other to attract businesses, visitors and residents.

This message scribbled outside a bar in the French Quarter is an example of the many ways in which "Who Dat" became part of the local lexicon. The informal usage of the phrase was so ingrained within New Orleans' daily culture that Saints fans felt outraged when the NFL tried to claim ownership claim over the saying.

New Orleans' renewal after Katrina relied on remaking New Orleans as a city worthy of visitors in order to revitalize a tourism-based economy. City officials emphasized rebuilding tourist spaces and promoting New Orleans as a renewed place to visit, work, play and live. In addition to promoting a positive city image to lure visitors and new residents to the city, many believed it was important to keep New Orleans on the national agenda in order to lobby federal support. "Katrina fatigue" signaled that the willingness of outsiders to help in New Orleans recovery subsided quickly after news cameras turned their lenses towards other events. Even several years after Katrina hit, New Orleans still needed help from the federal government, national nonprofit organizations, and the state of Louisiana to continue the long recovery process. No city has the capacity to recover from a disaster of this magnitude on its own.

The national appeal of NFL football provided a platform for bringing New Orleans and Katrina back into the nation's consciousness. The literature of sport and urban development often emphasizes the power of sports to promote an enhanced city image to national audiences. Even when impact reports show that the benefits of investing in sports do not produce anticipated economic benefits through job creation or spillover effects, the value of publicity lingers as a marker of success. The promotional power of sports and the ability of large-scale sporting events to promote an enhanced city image are often touted as an extremely valuable benefits that are worth even more than the multimillion-dollar economic impacts projected onto these events.

Public investments in sports teams and facilities are symptomatic of postindustrial cities looking to gain a competitive edge in a changing world economy. Sports teams are viewed as commodities that are supposed to stimulate tourist-oriented development and growth, revitalize downtown areas, promote enhanced city images, and create urban spectacles or a celebratory atmosphere. The case of the Saints in New Orleans displayed all of these characteristics of sport as a cultural commodity. New Orleans civic leaders felt investing in the Saints would be worth the price paid.

The Price of Renewing the Sports Landscape

Eleven days after Hurricane Katrina made landfall, I sat in the Bank of America Stadium in Charlotte, cheering the Saints as they played an emotional game against the Carolina Panthers. Over 700 miles away from where the Saints were playing, New Orleans officials donned hazmat suits and entered the Superdome. It had been left in shambles from storm damage and from being used as an ill-prepared shelter for thousands of city residents. Mere days after the last of the stranded people had been evacuated from the place, these officials speculated the Saints may have played their last game in the Superdome.

Despite the dire outlook in the first few weeks after the storm, a commitment to rebuild the Superdome, invest in sports development, and secure the Saints' position in New Orleans was made quickly. As a result of this intentional investment, New Orleans' position as a prominent sports landscape is more powerful now, more than ten years after Katrina, than it has ever been.

In the months before Katrina hit New Orleans, Saints owner Tom

Benson and the state of Louisiana were haggling over a new lease agreement as Governor Kathleen Blanco sought to restructure a deal that was becoming more of a burden to fund with public money. In 2001 Benson inked a contract with Louisiana's then-governor Mike Foster in which the state committed $187 million over a 10-year period to keep the Saints in New Orleans. This guaranteed the Saints a direct annual subsidy payment that started at $12.5 million and escalated to $23.5 million in the final years of the deal. Although this payment structure was generous in comparison to other agreements between NFL teams and their host cities, it was not uncommon.

Throughout the 1990s, U.S. cities entered into a stadium construction boom. Some $18 billion went into constructing big-league sports facilities, with over half of this money coming from public funds. Cities are faced with the choice of either subsidizing the team or losing the team to another city. This threat of team relocation exists under normal circumstances and is not unique to New Orleans post-disaster context. New Orleans and Louisiana had been forced to keep up with the rising growth of the NFL. Governor Kathleen Blanco had been outspoken against the public subsidy deal that her predecessor constructed with the Saints prior to Katrina. However, very soon after Katrina she issued an executive order to fast-track funding so the Superdome could reach renovation goals in time for the 2006 NFL season. The post–Katrina renovations to the Superdome were also largely funded by FEMA, the Federal Emergency Management Agency.

There are a lot of resources that come into a community after disaster. Attention is paid to community, volunteer labor, community mobilization and federal and state funding. All of the monetary investments are often accompanied by the rhetoric of coming back better and stronger. It is difficult to answer with any accuracy exactly where all federal relief money went after Katrina. After Katrina, the federal government spent $120.5 billion on the gulf area, including the Louisiana, Alabama and Mississippi Gulf Coast regions. The majority of that money, $75 billion, went to emergency relief operations rather than rebuilding. Other areas that received FEMA funding include environmental historic preservation, hazard mitigation, and housing assistance. In Louisiana, $11.9 billion in FEMA public assistance funds helped rebuild public infrastructure damaged by hurricanes Katrina and Rita.[5] To break down that approximate $11.9 billion further: $3.88 billion for education and learning facilities, $1.04 billion for public safety facilities, $5.87 billion for general infrastructure such as roads, parks, and sewer and water facilities, $1.16 billion for health care facilities.

Steering money towards sports-related developments was only a piece of a larger revitalization puzzle. Even though the Saints are the main tenant of the Superdome and it exists primarily to support Saints football and generate private wealth for Tom Benson, the Superdome is a state-owned facility. Less than two months after Katrina hit, Governor Blanco asked federal officials to pay for $2.3 billion to repair damage to state facilities such as universities, courthouses and other state buildings. The Superdome was included on that list of state facilities with early estimates speculating $125 million to $200 million would be needed to restore the iconic facility. Historically, FEMA reimburses state and local governments for their losses and emergency costs. FEMA is required to pay 75 percent reimbursement for costs not covered by insurance; however, that amount is negotiable, as shown by the federal government's covering 100 percent of New York's costs after the September 11 terrorist attacks.[6] FEMA has paid for sports stadium repairs after disaster in other cities. For example, after the 1994 earthquake in Los Angeles, FEMA paid $100 million to repair the Los Angeles Memorial Coliseum and $6 million to replace the scoreboard at Anaheim Stadium.

Federal relief funding for Superdome repairs was a catalyst for the Saints to leverage additional state funding for initial Superdome repairs after Katrina and initiate additional upgrades to the facility. Some $336 million worth of renovation is the often-quoted number associated with all the Superdome renovations and upgrades that have occurred since Katrina. Of that $336 million, $156 million came from FEMA and $121 million came from the state.[7] Because of the funding that came into Louisiana after Katrina, local leaders had different pools of money to play with in order to support sports developments. Beyond the immediate commitments to restore the Superdome after Katrina, the financial relationship between the Saints organization and the state of Louisiana continued to operate in a way that used public funds to greatly benefit the private accumulation of wealth for Benson, while simultaneously growing New Orleans' entertainment landscape.

Growth of a Sports Empire

Four years after Katrina, the Saints' lease agreement with the state of Louisiana was once again due for renewal and renegotiation. Post-Katrina investments had been made to renovate the Superdome and lure the Saints back to the city. Louisiana was in a position where it had little bargaining power for the task of securing the Saints' future in New Orleans. After a year of negotiations, the Saints announced in April 2009 that they had reached a new deal with the state. The 15-year lease agreement would keep the Saints in New Orleans through 2025. The agreement was complex and involved a mix of public and private interests that would not only keep the Saints in New Orleans but also included more renovations to the Superdome and a real estate trans-action concerning property adjacent to the Superdome. Even though the new agreement relied less on direct payments to the Saints from the state than the previous deal, the state will funnel roughly $392 mil-lion to Benson over the length of the agreement.[8] The entire transaction between the state and Tom Benson was one of the largest downtown real estate transactions since Katrina. The deal was lucrative for Benson and helped make him one of the wealthiest men in Louisiana.

One component of the deal involved state approval of $85 million in funding for upgrades to the Superdome. These upgrades included expanding the concourse and concession areas, adding two ground level bunker clubs, installing new electrical video and audio systems, widening the exterior ramps, expanding the team retail store, relocating the press box to make way for 16 additional suites and 3,100 stadium seats, and constructing a permanent staircase at Champions Square.[9] The staircase at Champions Square serves as a grand entrance into the stadium. The renovations were intended to generate additional revenue for the team by creating more seats and suites to sell as well as better facilities for making money on concessions and merchandise. The Saints anticipated making $12 million in additional revenue attributable to stadium renovations over the course of the year. If the team falls short of that mark, the state will make up the difference with a maxi-mum payment of $6 million.[10]

A cornerstone of the deal involved a real estate transaction wherein the Benson family purchased property adjacent to the Superdome and further subleased the property back to the government. At a price tag of $42.1 million, they purchased the 26-floor Dominion Tower building, a 2,000-space parking garage and the 400,000-square-foot New Orleans Centre Mall. These buildings rested on land adjacent to the Superdome and stood empty and shuttered for five years following Katrina. The area around the Superdome had once been described as a bustling hub of business and commerce for the city. The long-term vision in redeveloping this space was to create a destination retail, restaurant and entertainment district.

Dominion Tower was renamed Benson Tower and the New Orleans Centre Mall property was converted into Champions Square. Champions Square was the centerpiece in a plan between the Saints and the Louisiana Stadium and Exposition District (LSED) to build a sports and entertainment zone around the Superdome in order to breathe life

A makeshift memorial on the corner of Magazine Street and Jackson Street in New Orleans paid tribute to three monumental events in New Orleans history: the Saints' first Super Bowl win (left), Hurricane Katrina (center), and the Deepwater Horizon oil spill (right). This illustrates the extent to which Saints football lies at the heart of disaster and recovery narratives.

into the upper Poydras corridor of downtown New Orleans. Champions Square sits on 60,000 square feet of land adjacent to the Superdome. The state appropriated $10.5 million to demolish most of the mall and renovate the plaza and invested over $12.5 million to create Champions Square. The state subtracted the expense of this renovation from the Saints' remaining subsidy payment that was owed to the team under the old contract. However, the Superdome Commission agreed to pay a $2.3 million annual lease to promote and manage the plaza, garage and remaining mall structures.[11] The $13.5 million construction project began in January 2010 with the demolition of a patch of the dormant New Orleans Centre mall, which had been closed since Hurricane Katrina. Officials supporting the project hoped this space would become a year-round entertainment district. The Superdome Commission chairman, Ron Forman, said, "Our hopes and dreams are that this [opening for the 2010 season] is just the first phase. But as we lead up to the 2013 Super Bowl, we'll have a major sports district that will be open 365 days a year, 24 hours a day that will be another major attraction for economic development."[12] The construction project was financed by $10.5 million in inducement payments the Saints were scheduled to receive under their lease agreement with the state. LSED was responsible for paying the balance, which was expected to be recovered through revenue generated by the square.

Champions Square is a 121,000-square-foot festival plaza that includes a 2,100-space parking garage, a large concert stage and LED video screen, food and beverage tents and two VIP lounges. As with many urban development plans, the vision for this sports district project was to inspire future investment in downtown. Champion Square serves as an outdoor party venue throughout the year for various events in addition to Saints games. The creation of Champion Square transformed a Katrina-derelict space into a space for sports entertainment.

Another part of the real estate deal guaranteed Benson that as many as 50 state agencies would relocate and rent office space in the new Benson Tower at an agreed-upon rate that was higher than market value rent for comparable office space downtown. State agencies that occupy this building include departments such as Public Safety, Children and Family Services, Civil Service and Revenue, and the Louisiana Workforce Commission. The state agencies are paying for 15-year leases that started at a rental rate of $24 per square foot and account for about $7.7 million in payments to Benson each year. Before this relocation, the state paid roughly $4.6 million in office lease costs.[13]

In 2014 the *Times-Picayune* generated some criticism about the portion of the lease agreement that required state agencies to occupy Benson Tower. According to the Louisiana Legislative Auditor's Office, the state pays $8.1 million every year to lease 17 floors of the building. Some of this space, as much as 25,000 square feet, or $625,000 in annual payments, are being made on unused office space. More than ten years after Katrina, government agencies that lease office space in Benson Tower are paying higher-than-average rent for the space. This includes paying for some offices that sit vacant. Benson assumed little risk in this real estate deal as the government committed to lease the office space in Benson Tower.

In addition to the government funding, private investments also contributed to the Saints' financial success. In October 2011 the Saints announced that they had sold the naming rights for the Superdome to the Mercedes-Benz company. The 10-year naming rights agreement carried a $60 million price tag. Tom Benson has been a longtime dealer of Mercedes-Benz cars and owns dealerships throughout the greater New Orleans region as well as in San Antonio, Texas.

A newly installed LED light system around the exterior of the dome projected the Mercedes-Benz logo large enough to see from blocks away, with the interstate traffic receiving a particularly good view. Enormous lighted Mercedes-Benz signs rested atop the giant scoreboards on each end of the Saints' playing field. Interior walls of the Superdome that were previously blank displayed floor-to-ceiling ads for various Mercedes-Benz vehicles. Throughout professional sports in general, corporate logos of all types splashed across sports fields and stadium infrastructure as teams activated sponsorship agreements. The timing of an NFL game is strung together by a series of advertising promotions as much as it progresses through a series of first downs in each quarter of play. The National Football League's revenue-sharing business model assures that a portion of tickets sold for Saints games enters a revenue stream that is shared with the league. Revenue from the sale of sponsorships and luxury suites, however, remains with each individual team.

Even before Mercedes-Benz emerged as a financial partner for the Saints, naming rights were addressed in the Saints contract with the state. Under the contract, if the Saints sold a naming rights deal for the Louisiana Superdome, proceeds from that sale would go towards offsetting some of the public subsidy payments that the state owed to the Saints. At the time this deal was struck, the Saints had never in their history been able to attract any corporate entities that were interested in a stadium naming rights sponsorship. Prior to Katrina and the Saints' Super Bowl win in 2010, any sponsorship deals with the Saints were tough sells. The team relied on piecing together smaller sponsorship contracts than those enjoyed by teams in other NFL cities. According to the lease agreement, the Saints would get the first $1 million of net revenue from the naming rights deal, with a 50–50 split of the remaining revenue between the team and the state, although the state's share would come in credits to offset the subsidy payments owed to the team, rather than cash.[14] The entire deal between the Saints and the state of Louisiana that leverages public money to support New Orleans professional sports was creative and lucrative for Benson.

This naming rights deal prompted corporate executives and the Louisiana governor to restate the narrative of renewal surrounding this football venue. Louisiana Governor Bobby Jindal continued to promote this narrative as he provided the following statement to the local news media covering the announcement of the Superdome naming rights deal: "This sends a great signal about the continued comeback of the city of New Orleans and the state of Louisiana. It speaks to a commitment to rebuild better and stronger after the storm. Everybody across the country remembers the iconic images of the Superdome after Katrina. This is just one more national or even international sign that we are coming back."[15]

Tom Benson's sports empire grew even more in 2012 when he purchased the city's National Basketball Association (NBA) team, the Hornets. Two years earlier, former NBA owner George Shinn looked to sell the franchise to an out-of-town investor that may have been looking to move the team to San Jose, California. Benson's purchasing the Hornets secured local ownership for the NBA team but also gave Benson even more negotiating power over the state as the owner of both professional sports franchises in New Orleans. In 2013 Benson rebranded the NBA team from the Hornets to the New Orleans Pelicans. A new name, new logo and colors accompanied a $54 million renovation to the New Orleans Arena.[16] In 2014 Smoothie King signed a 10-year, $40 million deal to obtain naming rights to the arena. Since Katrina, Benson has solidified his personal wealth and position as a powerful business-man by leveraging both professional sports franchises to obtain lease agreements with the state and rehabilitate the downtown area sur-rounding the Superdome and New Orleans Arena.

Ten years after Katrina, an image of the Superdome at night, bask-ing in glowing LED lights, transmitting the Mercedes-Benz logo across its vast domed roof, showcases just how far this iconic building has come since its days as the "shelter of last resort." The Superdome is now one of the most modern stadiums in the country. The narrative of renewal surrounding this building continues to resurface as Katrina recedes farther into the past with every year. Professional sports in New Orleans continue to offer a platform to promote New Orleans as a big-league city. Sporting events hosted in the Superdome since Kat-rina include 2008 and 2014 NBA All-Star Games, 2012 NCAA Men's Final Four, 2013 NCAA Women's Final Four, the 2013 NFL Super Bowl, and the annual Bayou Classic. In addition, the Sugar Bowl continues to bring big games to the city annually, including the upcoming 2018, 2021 and 2024 college football playoffs scheduled to be held there. The Sugar Bowl is one of six bowls in the college football playoff semifinal rotation. The Sugar Bowl has also secured a prime television spot each year for the next decade. Images of a vibrant and renewed New Orleans are cast into the national spotlight as thousands of media outlets turn their cameras towards these events. Each time the media shines its light onto sports in New Orleans, civic and business leaders restate the narrative of renewal and use the success of the sporting landscape as a barometer to show progress since Katrina.

Hosting Super Bowl 2013

New Orleans hosted the Super Bowl in February 2013, providing another platform for fueling the narrative about New Orleans' cultural and economic renewal. This time, however, the Saints were not competing. Narratives of renewal surrounding the city of New Orleans continued in a different way. Rather than local media capturing the emotions of city residents and reflecting on their experiences, as was the case in 2006 when the Saints returned from Katrina and 2009 when the Saints went on to win the Super Bowl, the focus turned towards national media coverage and promoting a positive image of the city. This image was not concerned with the experiences of residents or realities of life in New Orleans.

Media narratives surrounding the New Orleans–hosted Super Bowl served as a vehicle to promote the messages of civic boosters. PR from the mayor, the Super Bowl Host Committee, and the Tourism and Marketing Board served to promote a pristine city image that lacked regard for diversity of cultural expression and everyday lived experiences. These stakeholders fully admitted their intentions to use the Super Bowl as a performance space to craft a message that New Orleans is an excellent place for visitors. Quotes in the paper that exemplify this intention include "Boosters for New Orleans will circulate at the event, pressing a theme with visiting journalists that the city is a great place to live, work, visit and host more Super Bowls."[17] Public relations professionals were recruited to serve as volunteers promoting the city. Numerous news headlines and articles about Super Bowl XLVII quoted Mayor Mitch Landrieu as a civic leader promoting a positive city image.[18] Mayors are often the most vocal proponents of sports-related urban development efforts.[19]

More than 5,000 credentialed media members descended upon the Super Bowl host city. The week leading up to the game was a time when national media cameras pointed to festivities surrounding the event, such as parties and themed entertainment areas like Super Bowl Boulevard and the NFL Experience. These are interactive football-themed experiences are open to members of the public in the weeks leading up to the Super Bowl. New Orleans was the backdrop for news coverage of these events.

Several different television segments paid tribute to New Orleans as the host city. Television personality and former chef Anthony Bourdain devoted an episode of his Travel Channel show to New Orleans, providing a tour of New Orleans food options from fine dining to "dives." TV shows broadcasting from New Orleans incorporated local

New Orleans figures and football personalities into their programming. A local TV anchor for WWL-TV, Angela Hill, appeared on a CBS show called *The Talk*. She showcased gifts that highlight New Orleans Mardi Gras parade culture. These gifts included signature parade throws from two popular parading krewes: a glittery shoe from the Krewe of Muses and a decorated coconut from the Zulu Social Aid and Pleasure Club.

On Super Bowl Sunday, CBS aired a show that included a story about the popular New Orleans dish called gumbo, and enlisted the help of Wynton Marsalis, a local musician with national appeal. CBS reported an audience of 4 million for a late-morning show called *New Orleans: Let the Good Times Roll*.[20] The local press evaluated the show as "a thoughtful, tuneful tele-tour of our streets, kitchens, clubs and history that should stream on a loop on every website that comes up when you Google 'New Orleans,' 'music,' 'food' or 'fun.'"[21] Music, food and fun were the aspects of New Orleans cultural economy that the media projected to an outside audience.

Stories focused on the fanfare and party aspects of New Orleans' image. Some talked about fans flocking to the French Quarter bars and restaurants after the game.[22] New Orleans' festive image was solidified with a commentary dedicated to "the city that always had more fun per square inch than any place I know."[23] These types of messages sought to promote a positive image of the city, but did not offer much of substance.

Underneath this image of New Orleans as a place of good times and revelry lurked the realities of life in New Orleans. As the NFL infused New Orleans with its version of a celebration, city residents found the NFL's commercialized version lacking in substance and ignoring what New Orleanians value. Three points of evidence reflected this conflict. First, the narrative of post–Katrina renewal mentioned in Super Bowl–related media did not reflect local residents' recovery experiences. Secondly, the use of city space for Super Bowl–related events interrupted the everyday experiences of some city residents rather than reflecting what it is like to be a New Orleanian. Lastly, local discourse surrounding these events developed into an "us versus them" story, with local residents expressing the opinion that their needs were made secondary to those of tourists or outsiders.

Super Bowl 2013: Local Perceptions

Media outlets reporting from New Orleans during the week leading up to the Super Bowl referenced Katrina several times. For example, Mayor Mitch Landrieu was quoted as saying, "It will be a great opportunity for us to show what the city of New Orleans looks like after Katrina."[24] Another example: "The city wanted to do this up right to say thanks to the rest of America (including, yes, the NFL), for all the post–Katrina recovery cash and volunteer sweat that came this way and will have to keep coming if the generation-long task is to be completed. The rest of America (including, yes, the NFL through its media partners) wanted to say thanks to New Orleans for pulling through and remaining."[25] Another reporter said, "People ask me who I'm cheering for today, and my answer is the people of New Orleans for the job they've done bringing this city back." He continued, "Only those who were here in the days after Katrina can understand what they've accomplished."[26]

Juxtaposing images of the Katrina disaster with images of sports victories had become common practice at high-profile events in the years following the storm. However, the Katrina-related messages associated with the 2013 Super Bowl did not resonate with local residents. The commentary between one New Orleans sportswriter and his readers exemplified a disconnect between Super Bowl-related Katrina recovery messages and New Orleanians' experiences. This article carried forward the narrative of renewal that grew from the Saints' return to New Orleans post–Katrina through their 2009 Super Bowl–winning season. Jeff Duncan wrote, "We can show the world how far we've come after Hurricane Katrina, that we truly are a city of progress and enlightenment. Or we can revert to the cloistered close-mindedness that often characterized us pre–Katrina." "This week is about something much bigger than the Saints or Bountygate or season ticket prices. It's about New Orleans. The NFL awarded its marquee event to New Orleans largely as a reward for our inspiring post–Katrina recovery."[27]

Within the first twelve hours of this article posting online, readers published 172 comments. More than 250 comments remained on the news archive several weeks after publication, many criticizing the author's usage of Katrina recovery in connection with the 2013 Super

Bowl. One fan post that exemplified these thoughts read, "Your suggestions are not for those of us who survived intact. Those of us who remember the storm. Those of us who remained or returned. Those of us who lost. You have forgotten, Mr. Duncan, that it is we, the Saints fans, that are the heroes—the very citizens you are childishly chiding. We rebuilt this city. We paid for the team. Of course we did, we are the fans."

References to "Bountygate" and NFL commissioner Goodell were a topic that received considerable media attention during the 2013 Super Bowl. The NFL had been conducting investigations into the New Orleans Saints organization since 2010 to determine if they had been engaged in a "pay for performance" system wherein players were encouraged to injure specific opponents. If successful, the Saints players would be compensated. The bounty scandal became known as

Champions Square hosts Saints fans prior to a game. The state of Louisiana and the Saints partnered to build a sports and entertainment district adjacent to the Superdome in order to breathe life into the upper Poydras corridor of downtown New Orleans.

Bountygate. The Saints were slammed with penalties for operating a bounty program that ran from 2009 through 2011 that paid bonuses to players for hits that knocked their opponents out of the game. The punishments passed to the team included suspending Saints head coach Sean Payton for one year, General Manager Mickey Loomis for eight games, Coach Vitt for six games, and former coach Greg William

Dominion Tower, adjacent to the Superdome, was purchased by Saints owner Tom Benson in 2009 and renamed Benson Tower. Prior to the redevelopment of Benson Tower, the building had stood empty and derelict following Katrina.

indefinitely. The Saints also lost second-round draft picks for 2012–2013 and were fined $500,000.[28] Sanctions had also been delivered against Saints players. However, backed with the power and support of the NFL players' union, the league eventually cancelled the penalties incurred by players allegedly involved in Bountygate.

Goodell's tenure as NFL commissioner ushered in a focus on player safety, pushing for rule changes to protect players on the field and levy heavier fines against players for hits ruled too savage for the game. As a result, several former and current NFL players have filed lawsuits against the NFL and various equipment makers, alleging the parties were insufficiently diligent in making player safety a priority. Saints fans were disappointed in members of their beloved team.[29] This was a scandal that threatened to diminish the strength of the Who Dat Nation.

Many Saints fans turned their anger towards the league, targeting commissioner Goodell as the source of their disappointment. Saints fans wanted to show the nation that New Orleanians could battle through adversity. Posters that read FREE SEAN PAYTON popped up in local apparel stores such as Dirty Coast. The NFL commissioner has a considerable amount of power in determining rules violations and punishments for NFL member conduct. He is also the figurehead for the entire league.

Many Saints fans and media narratives paint the penalties handed to the Saints as a message the commissioner was looking to send, using New Orleans as an example of what would happen should football players and personnel fail to adhere to league rules. New Orleanians cast Roger Goodell as the villain in a constructed narrative that pitted the league against the city. Who Dats still hold his predecessor Paul Tagliabue up on a pedestal, as the commissioner who insisted the Saints return to New Orleans after Katrina. Even though Tom Benson had been cast as the enemy of the Who Dat Nation in the days after Katrina, Benson had long since redeemed himself in the eyes of Who Dats as the owner who brought them Drew Brees, Sean Payton and the Saints' first Super Bowl win. Saints fans needed a new face to blame for circumstances in which the realities of being a member of the NFL conflicted with what Saints fans value. Goodell became a symbol of aspects of the national product that Saints fans did not particularly care for. Blaming Goodell gave a name and face to the frustrations of the Who Dats.

Goodell's poor reputation among Saints fans spilled over into narratives about the city hosting the commissioner of the NFL as a guest. A headline read, "Will New Orleans Welcome Roger Goodell for Super Bowl 2013?"[30] Prior to the Super Bowl, the NFL announced that head coach Sean Payton would be reinstated a little early from his season-long suspension that was handed down as punishment for Bountygate. This early release was not enough to appease Saints fans. One news article quoted a Saints fan as explaining, "My first thought was 'I think Roger Goodell is just doing it before the Super Bowl to make the fans happy because he doesn't want to come here. He's afraid.'"[31] Another article explained, "Fans of the hometown Saints have been—and in many cases, continue to be—livid at Goodell for the discipline he imposed on the team this season for the so-called bounty scandal."[32] "Musician Kermit Ruffins told the *Times-Picayune*, "There's a lot of angry cats down here, and I'm thinking most folks don't have a problem letting someone know how they feel."[33]

Mercedes-Benz bought the naming rights to the Superdome in 2011. The 10-year naming rights agreement came with a $60 million price tag and contributed to the Saints' financial success in post–Katrina New Orleans.

On the streets, fan disapproval for the NFL commissioner was apparent in anti–Goodell T-shirts for sale in French Quarter and other local shops. Signs hanging in restaurant windows bore a picture of the commissioner and words that said "Do not serve this man." These signs were comical but also served as an outlet for Saints fans to express their feelings of protectiveness over their team and their home city.

The 2013 Super Bowl coincided with the 2013 Mardi Gras season. In New Orleans, Mardi Gras is not one day but rather weeks of parades and revelry enjoyed by locals. Many parades poke fun at current events or carry satirical themes, and some floats display politically charged messages. One particularly irreverent krewe, the Krewe du Vieux, touts political, satirical and sexually themed floats. In light of the Super Bowl being in town, Krewe du Vieux featured a float depicting Roger Goodell being eaten by a giant vagina. The media coverage of the Super Bowl framed these sentiments as a public relations problem. Commentator Jeff Duncan wrote, "The last thing we need is an ugly incident to mar the festivities. That'd be a major setback to our burgeoning positive image."[34] Saints fans, however, were proud of their comical backlash against the NFL.

Super Bowl 2013: Temporary Urban Renewal?

The Super Bowl is no longer just a championship football game. The Super Bowl includes multiple events, entertainment, and sponsorship elements that take over city streets for more than a week leading up to the game. Looking at how Super Bowl 2013 used urban spaces in the weeks leading up to and during the event reveals more information about the vibrant cultural attachments communicated through sports events in New Orleans. The Super Bowl changes the urban landscape for the duration of the NFL stay in the host city. The Super Bowl has grown to an entertainment event of massive scale that disrupts daily city life. This disruption is not always welcome.

The NFL created additional entertainment spaces in the French Quarter and Central Business District spanning from the Superdome to the Mississippi River. One example of an NFL created entertainment space was Super Bowl Boulevard. Super Bowl Boulevard is an entertainment space constructed in downtown areas of Super Bowl host cities. The area is open to the public and features interactive football-themed activities and sponsorship elements. Super Bowl Boulevard took over Woldenburg Park along the Mississippi River in the French Quarter. It drew an estimated 150,000 people.[35] The construction of additional entertainment spaces in the French Quarter is somewhat ironic, as New Orleans' French Quarter is one of the most celebrated tourist entertainment spaces in the world. When the city of Jacksonville, Florida, hosted the Super Bowl in 2005, a "restaurant row" had to be created in the industrial downtown area because there were not adequate amenities near the stadium to accommodate the normal Super Bowl crowd. In a city like New Orleans that already comes equipped with numerous amenities that appeal to large tourist crowds, the necessity of additional themed entertainment landscapes is questionable. This is particularly questionable when considering the costs incurred in hosting the Super Bowl. New Orleans had to do more than just open the doors to the city. The Super Bowl host committee was on the hook for fundraising approximately $13.5 million to invest in the games. This is a much smaller budget than most cities invest in producing the Super Bowl.[36]

Much like the events of NFL Kickoff Weekend in 2010, Jackson Square in the French Quarter transformed into a space for spectacle. CBS set up its broadcast studios in Jackson Square for the week in order to run live shows. Much to the chagrin of locals, CBS plastered the base of Andrew Jackson's statue with logo signage. CBS used the staging area to hype various new sports ventures, including at least 50 hours of shows on its revamped CBS Sports Network cable channel.[37] The takeover of space for national broadcasting was not about promoting New Orleans but rather about promoting the CBS sports network. The network transformed the space for its own gain, with little regard for how that space is actually used and interpreted by locals.

News stories only hinted at local conflicts pertaining to the Super Bowl events by commenting on traffic delays, noting the Saints' fans dislike of the NFL commissioner, and allotting two sentences of information about homeless people being displaced to accommodate the event. Large sections of Poydras Street and Canal Boulevard, main thoroughfares through downtown New Orleans, were blocked off and closed entirely as the Superdome boundaries were extended into the streets to accommodate game day security lines. The road blockages are not just for game day, but rather begin weeks in advance of the game. Commuters to downtown ended up stuck in lengthy traffic delays as they attempted to get to work every morning.

In addition to street blockages imposed by the NFL footprint, the city of New Orleans saw a construction boom immediately preceding the event as several hotels and other service-oriented businesses underwent renovations to prepare for the influx of upscale clientele that follows Super Bowls. Mayor Mitch Landrieu insisted that several infrastructure development projects be finished before Super Bowl day. The hundreds of millions of dollars in infrastructure investments occurring at this time included a $305 million upgrade to Louis Armstrong International Airport, $52 million renovation at the Ernest N. Morial Convention Center, $45 million expansion of the Loyola Avenue streetcar line, $13.2 million improvements on state roads, and $11.3 million in French Quarter street repairs.[38] These city improvements would have taken place even if New Orleans hadn't hosted the Super Bowl, but their deadlines were moved up so the projects would be ready in time for the event. The eyesores and inconvenience that come with city construction zones were a burden to local residents and looked bad for visitors.

Attempts to clean up the tourist areas of the city prior to the Super Bowl were numerous. The city planned to put fences up to prevent people from living on the streets before and during the Super Bowl.[39] Homeless citizens were cleared out of their normal resting places underneath the interstate near the Superdome. Though it is difficult to find concrete information on the scope of homeless removal associated with hosting Super Bowls, displacement is a common problem connected with sporting mega-events. Homelessness is a larger city problem that does not come and go with Super Bowls. The media attention bestowed upon mega-events offers opportunity to highlight a myriad of conditions already present within the urban fabric.

In addition to refashioning city streets to better suit the event, it seemed the NFL looked to refashion the demeanor of New Orleans service workers. As part of the NFL Fans First initiative, the league hosted free classes aimed at preparing service industry workers to be better hosts for Super Bowl visitors. In partnership with the Disney Institute and the New Orleans Convention and Visitors Bureau, free training sessions were offered at the Ernest N. Morial Convention Center in order to encourage service industry managers and workers to polish their presentations for Super Bowl 2013 visitors. Although the NFL presumably meant well, it is difficult to ignore the underlying message: that New Orleans service workers could use some polishing in order to properly serve under the NFL brand. New Orleans residents felt that those in charge seemed to care more about tourists and Super Bowl guests than citizens.

Ironically, the convention center was the site of so much post–Katrina misery and injustice. In February 2013, however, it became a site for teaching New Orleans service workers how to put their best foot forward for tourists. It also transformed into the NFL Experience. The NFL Experience took over the Ernest N. Morial Convention Center from January 30 through February 3, covering more than 850,000 square feet of space.[40] Although the Convention Center was not as important as the Superdome as a site of post–Katrina renewal, the transformation of this space marked a significant step towards tourism revival.

New Orleanians were continuously asked to make changes in order to stage a successful Super Bowl. Mardi Gras parade schedules were rearranged to make way for Super Bowl Sunday. Rearranging parade schedules served to reinforce a divide between what locals usually do and what the Super Bowl coming to town wants them to change.

The amount of media outlets converging upon New Orleans to cover the Super Bowl events changed the use of urban spaces for a temporary period of time. This did not happen completely harmoniously, but rather produced contested spaces. This negotiation over physical city space contributed to the formation of the "us versus them" dichotomy. Locals felt their needs were secondary to impressing tourists. This dichotomy hints at a subtle collective citizen identity forming around sports-related narratives, but does not share the intensity of a collective identity formed around Saints football. The extent to which local residents feel burdens associated with hosting mega-events is difficult to pinpoint.

All local residents are not affected equally by the Super Bowl. The takeover of downtown spaces for Super Bowl events disrupted what was already there at varying costs to different local citizens. The Greater New Orleans Sports Foundation and the Super Bowl host committee members are all New Orleans citizens doing what they think is good for their city by promoting a positive image through national media. The homeless man displaced to clear the way for Super Bowl traffic is also a New Orleans citizen. The frustrated downtown worker who was delayed in traffic for one hour because of road blockages erected for the Super Bowl is also a New Orleans citizen. The local bank vice presidents buying up Super Bowl tickets to give to their clients are also New Orleans citizens. The families who went to the convention center to enjoy the NFL Experience are New Orleans citizens. All have different interpretations of the how the Super Bowl hosted in New Orleans made an impact.

Despite this diversity of experiences, the Super Bowl is still touted in the media by civic boosters as being good for New Orleans as a whole because it brings economic benefit. The New Orleans Super Bowl reportedly resulted in a $420 million economic impact.[41] However, the economic impact touted by the media and civic boosters has been refuted as exaggerated by different economic impact evaluations conducted in other football cities. Often, the economic impact does not live up to the hype. Therefore, fleshing out how local residents interpret benefits received from hosting mega-events would be the more appropriate question to explore. In some instances, the smaller economic exchanges that are important to local residents are usurped for the economic or promotional gain of the NFL or nonlocal vendors.

The economic benefits to local small business owners may fall short of expectations. In the same day that the newspaper reported a $420 million economic impact from hosting the Super Bowl, a local shop owner told me that the shops in the French Quarter, including his, were not making the kind of sales he expected. It was not just a gut feeling that business was slow. He spit out hard dollar figures comparing the cost of inventory he ordered to cover expected sales and the deviation from actual sales. His shop is located along busy Decatur Street in the French Quarter, the tourist hub of New Orleans and the epicenter of Super Bowl events. While we were standing outside his shop, I overheard the adjacent business owner complaining about the lack of business rolling into her shop.

Sports media surrounding Super Bowl 2013 was used to promote the idea of economic gains associated with this mega-event, especially when aligned with Mardi Gras festivities. This emphasis on economic gains aligned with Mardi Gras is ironic considering that one of the few academic sources[42] that shows Super Bowls can have a positive economic benefit explains that the benefit occurs because the game happens during an otherwise slow tourist time in a city.

Super Bowl 2013: The Blackout Bowl

The positive hype perpetuated by the media took an abrupt change during the Super Bowl game when a power outage in the Superdome shut off half the stadium's interior lights. The Superdome sat dimly lit while the football game was delayed for 34 minutes. Despite this unusual situation, members of the crowd remained calm. Media coverage of the game generally settles down after the half-time show, and several reporters had already vacated their posts inside the Superdome. When the blackout occurred, they rushed back through the secure perimeter, as now there was a new story to cover. Unfortunately, the Blackout Bowl, as some media outlets dubbed the incident, gave the national media an excuse to turn against New Orleans and criticize the city for allowing a failure to happen during an otherwise perfect event. Perhaps New Orleans had not come so far since Katrina after all? The Superdome had once again been cast into darkness. Some questioned whether New Orleans should be allowed to host a Super Bowl again. Like the event itself, the negative publicity was only temporary. The lights came back on. The teams finished the game. The NFL packed up and left town. New Orleans is still one of the best places in the United States at entertaining tourists and hosting mega-events. The city made a bid to host the 2018 Super Bowl, a game that would have coincided with New Orleans' tricentennial celebration. However, the league awarded the 2018 game to Minneapolis.

The immeasurable value of worldwide publicity is consistent with literature on sports mega-events and the city. But what is the value of promoting a message with little regard to how well that message reflects local culture and diversity within local culture? The narrative of cultural and economic renewal continued as the city of New Orleans hosted the 2013 Super Bowl. However, the 2013 Super Bowl was not a focal point of collective urban identity for New Orleans residents in the same way as football events featuring the Saints. While sports narratives reflected through the Saints served as a vehicle for telling a story about New Orleans culture, the 2013 Super Bowl media discourse perpetuated a narrative of renewal that was devoid of local cultural richness. The 2013 Super Bowl served as a vehicle for delivering polished messages of a positive city image. Rather than reflecting the experiences of New Orleanians, the discourse surrounding the 2013 Super Bowl hosted in New Orleans perpetuated an "us versus them" narrative that pitted local residents against visitors, outsiders and tourists. Through football spaces, New Orleans could not shed its historical image as a place that is somehow different from the rest of the country.

Revisiting the Narrative of Renewal

Both the marketed city images and the messages that New Orleanians fostered amongst themselves contributed to creating the narrative of renewal. Good or bad, sport spaces had the ability to reflect what was happening in the city in a particular moment. The messages delivered through the Superdome demonstrated this complexity as the dome delivered a negative image of the city in the days during Katrina and a positive image of the city as the Saints returned to play football. Sport spaces will not automatically deliver an "enhanced city image" but rather continue to be a space that reflects situational relevance. In addition, there are contradictions in using Saints football to deliver messages about city recovery. Even though city rebuilding after disaster thrives on the power of architecture and celebratory festivals to symbolize recovery, "the downside of such an emphasis is that dominant symbols can be allowed to mask the less visible parts of the city, especially as marketed to outsiders."[43]

The Superdome experienced rebuilding and recovery at a rapid pace, which was in direct contrast to the neighborhoods surrounding it and the citizens struggling to rebuild their lives years after the storm made landfall. This reality does not undermine the fact that the narrative of renewal was powerful and real in helping New Orleanians feel recovered but rather underscores the complexity of how issues of social justice can be negotiated through sport spaces. The Superdome was an important symbolic space for transforming negative images into positive ones. The symbolism of a refurbished Superdome and the success of the Saints football team perpetuated through dominant media narratives was reflective of local residents need for a symbol to rally around in support of the city of New Orleans.

The experience in New Orleans shows that "promoting an enhanced city image" is too simplistic to explain the complexities of how different outlets produced and delivered contradictory messages about New Orleans' recovery. On one hand, city images were marketed messages delivered to a national audience in order to promote the idea that New Orleans was recovered enough to be a vibrant place for tourists. The value in this type of message had economic implications, as the Saints are part of the tourism-based economy on which the city relies. On the other hand, there were messages created by and for New Orleanians about the city's recovery. These fostered a narrative of renewal rooted in real emotions and experiences where the Saints were a symbol of hope that helped with the psychological and emotional aspect of city rebuilding. Regaining the tradition of Saints football was something that helped New Orleanians feel reconnected to their home or feel like they were getting back to their old selves. City residents were not always concerned with projecting these messages of recovery to an outside audience but rather with fostering a message among themselves that said, "We can recover" and "We are a city people that has the perseverance to do so."

Through the "home team," sports become rooted in place and offer a platform for unveiling narratives about city image and urban life. As evidenced by the story of the Saints in New Orleans, powerful local narratives emerge that are complex, multifaceted and offer insight into collective urban identities. Sports may seem like an unlikely place to talk seriously of city recovery. However, using professional football to craft stories that are absorbed as part of popular culture can be a very powerful medium. The political and economic importance placed on reviving the New Orleans tourism industry within the post–Katrina recovery context cannot be ignored. Fueled by the national marketing power of the NFL, the Saints football team lies at the epicenter of New Orleans' tourism-marketing landscape. In many ways, New Orleans pursued its revitalization through redefining and promoting its tourist image.

Dominant narratives surrounding Saints football described the presence of professional football in New Orleans as a beacon of hope for cultural and economic revival. The decision to invest in retaining Saints football in New Orleans, renovate and upgrade the Superdome and redevelop adjacent Benson-owned properties were all done to secure the future of New Orleans image as a big-league city. Serving as host city for the Super Bowl marks the pinnacle of big-league status in America. For New Orleans, hosting the 2013 Super Bowl served as a barometer to measure redevelopment and communicate messages about city recovery.

The presence of the Saints in New Orleans will continue to be paradoxical. The narrative of renewal will offer hope even as it obscures the reality of hard times faced in the rebuilding process. It will showcase the multimillion-dollar football player salaries and wealth of the team owner while many New Orleanians live in poverty. The Superdome, mega-events like the Super Bowl, and the money and glamour associated with the NFL will paint a picture of New Orleans as a city that is vibrant, even as the money and vibrancy is unevenly dispersed. In the decade since Katrina, New Orleans rebuilt the Superdome and surrounding area, hosted a Super Bowl, and continues to craft a strong community culture around Saints fandom. The challenges of a sluggish and ongoing recovery were worse than the storm itself. In contrast, the return of professional sports and the rebuilding of the Superdome stood as a positive recovery story and vehicle to deliver messages about New Orleans' cultural and economic viability.

If we look only at the superficial story of football in New Orleans, we will see a city that rose out of flood and devastation to rebuild a winning team and big-league status. We will see a city that can rise to the challenges of adversity and host some of the greatest sporting events the world has to offer. If we peel back the layers of this rags-to-riches narrative, we can uncover an even more compelling story of

188

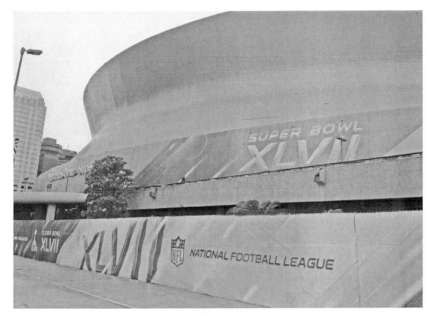

Temporary signage marks the Superdome as the site of Super Bowl XLVII. The national appeal of NFL football provided a platform for bringing New Orleans and Katrina back into the nation's consciousness.

lived experiences for the people of New Orleans who endured prolonged disaster. The story of Saints football in New Orleans is not the classic Cinderella story, but rather a series of contradictions that when confronted show the potential of sport to highlight pre-existing problems. Our challenge moving forward is to embrace the contradictions, confront the problems facilitated through sport spaces and commit to emphasizing the unique position of sports to influence positive changes in the urban landscape. As I penned the final edits for this book, New Orleans was in the midst of the ten-year anniversary of Hurricane Katrina. A barrage of remembrance and events commemorating what happened here accompanied myriad analysis of how far the city has come and comments about the outlook for New Orleans' future. The assessments are a mix of elements of city life that have improved and those that have not. The Saints football team played a role in the construction and representation of collective identity through a narrative of renewal in New Orleans after Katrina. The story of football became a study of urban culture in which integrative discourses construct a collective urban identity through sport.

The history of the Saints organization in New Orleans introduces how the Saints fit into the larger urban framework of life in New Orleans. While most sports team histories focus on coaching tenures, star players, and great defeats and triumphs on the playing field, this case presents the history of the Saints as a factor in the political, economic, and social events taking place in the city and larger society around them. The history of the team coincides with the history of the city in which it lives. The year 2005 marked a new chapter in the story of the Saints wherein Hurricane Katrina sparked a narrative arc that extended throughout the Saints' relationship with New Orleans. Before, the Saints story was one of the growing business of professional sports, focused on cultivating fans and situated within a historical context of city race relations. For the Saints and for New Orleans, Hurricane Katrina in 2005 and the handful of tumultuous years that immediately followed began to consume their story. People in New Orleans talk about events in their lives as happening either pre–Katrina or post–Katrina.

The Superdome after a $1.6 million LED light system was installed in October 2011. The Superdome has undergone more than $336 million in repairs since Katrina and served as a cornerstone for building a narrative of renewal around Saints football.

Like all of New Orleans, the history of the Saints has been split into a pre– and post–Katrina dichotomy.

Since those horrible days in 2005, the Superdome has been refurbished and transformed from a symbol of despair into a symbol of hope. Once an emblem of all that went wrong, the Superdome has since been used as a symbol of success in recovery. Contradictions remain in using Saints football to craft and deliver messages about city recovery. Those who were in the Superdome during Katrina continued to live with the trauma they experienced. Years later, many were traumatized anew when they could not come back to New Orleans or returned to find their neighborhoods irreparably changed. The Superdome remains as a powerful icon of the New Orleans landscape that can remind us of both the injustices made visible by Katrina and victories won for city recovery.

The city continues to recover at an unequal pace. In the aftermath of Hurricane Katrina, tension blanketed the city and New Orleanians were dispirited as they realized how hard it was going to be to overcome a myriad of obstacles in lengthy rebuilding processes. Using Saints football as a space to negotiate racial narratives and speak about relevant concerns continued in the time frame surrounding Hurricane Katrina, the recovery of New Orleans, and the Saints' first Super Bowl win. People used the Saints' successes and a shared sense of euphoria to tell stories about greater community cohesion and the ability of New Orleanians to transcend what appeared to be deep racial divides. At the same time, contradictions existed between these narratives and structural class and racial outcomes that led to an uneven post–Katrina recovery process. Within this extreme case, sport spaces become a platform to discuss the extent to which a collective urban identity and shared positive experiences can heal a community.

Chapter Notes

Chapter 1

1. National Football League, "History," www.nfl.com/history/chronology/1869-1910.

2. Most information on league history was taken from the chronological history on the official NFL website, www.NFL.com. See also Michael Oriard, *Brand NFL: Making and Selling America's Favorite Sport* (Chapel Hill: University of North Carolina Press, 2007).

3. National Football League, "History," www.nfl.com/history/chronology/1931-1940.

4. National Football League, "History," www.nfl.com/history/chronology/1951-1960.

5. Michael Oriard, *Brand NFL: Making and Selling America's Favorite Sport* (Chapel Hill: University of North Carolina Press, 2007).

6. Oriard, *Brand NFL*, 12.

7. National Football League, "History," www.nfl.com/history/chronology/1961-1970.

8. *Ibid.*

9. *Ibid.*

10. Oriard, *Brand NFL*.

11. *Ibid.*

12. For descriptions of the political and cultural connections of early sports in New Orleans, see Dale Somers, *Rise of Sports in New Orleans, 1850–1900* (Baton Rouge: Louisiana State University Press, 1972).

13. Mark J. Souther, "Into the Big League: Conventions, Football and the Color Line in New Orleans," *Journal of Urban History* 29, no. 6 (September 2003).

14. Michael S. Martin, "New Orleans Becomes a Big League City: The NFL-AFL Merger and the Creation of the New Or-

leans Saints," in *Horsehide, Pigskin, Oval Tracks and Apple Pie: Essays on Sport and American Culture*, ed. James A. Vlasich (Jefferson, NC: McFarland, 2006), 119–131.

15. Dave Dixon's autobiography includes extensive firsthand accounts of bringing the Saints to New Orleans and building the Superdome; see Dave Dixon, *The Saints, the Superdome and the Scandal.* (Gretna, LA: Pelican, 2008).

16. Charles Kenyatta Ross, *Outside the Lines: African Americans and the Integration of the National Football League* (New York: New York University Press, 2000).

17. Richard Lapchick, *100 Pioneers: African-Americans Who Broke Color Barriers in Sport* (Morgantown, WV: Fitness Information Technology, 2008).

18. Ross, *Outside the Lines.*

19. Alan Levy, *Tackling Jim Crow: Racial Segregation in Professional Football* (Jefferson, NC: McFarland, 2003).

20. Souther, "Into the Big League," 711.

21. Levy, *Tackling Jim Crow.*

22. Souther, "Into the Big League."

23. Dixon, *The Saints, the Superdome and the Scandal.*

24. *Ibid.*, 48.

25. *Ibid.*

26. *Ibid.*

27. Souther, "Into the Big League."

28. Dixon, *The Saints, the Superdome and the Scandal.*

29. *Ibid.*

30. Martin, "New Orleans Becomes a Big League City," 119–131.

31. *Ibid.*, 69–70

32. *Ibid.*

33. Copy of the prayer obtained from wwltv.com, http://www.wwltv.com/story/news/local/2014/08/25/14288486/, October 29, 2013.

34. Peirce Lewis, *New Orleans: The Making of an Urban Landscape* (Charlottesville: University of Virginia Press, 2003). See also Andrew Chafin, "Louisiana Superdome: Newest Wonder of the World," Louisiana Superdome Commission, 1975.

35. Karen Kingsley, "New Orleans Architecture: Building Renewal," *The Journal of American History* (December 2007), 716–725.

36. Lewis, *The Making of an Urban Landscape*, 93.

37. Martin, "New Orleans Becomes a Big League City," 128.

38. Chafin, "Louisiana Superdome."

39. See, for example, Lewis, *The Making of an Urban Landscape.*

40. *Times-Picayune,* January 23, 2010.

41. "Saints to Play Four Games in Baton Rouge, Three in San Antonio," *Times-Picayune,* September 12, 2005.

42. Many professional sports teams do not open their books even when they are funded with public money. *Forbes* is the only consistent source available to the public that publishes NFL team values every year. See *Forbes,* "The Business of Football," www.forbes.com/nfl-valuations (accessed 2016).

43. Ed Anderson, "Landrieu Has Doubts About Sports Bonds," *Times-Picayune,* January 28, 1994.

44. Jeffrey Meitrodt, "Saints Dome Deal Called Fair, About Average for NFL, Football Experts Claim," *Times-Picayune,* October 6, 1994.

45. For an analysis of the political economy surrounding the willingness of governments to subsidize professional sports, see Charles Euchner, *Playing the Field: Why Sports Teams Move and Cities Fight to Keep Them* (Baltimore: Johns Hopkins University Press, 1993). See also Michael Danielson, *Home Team: Professional Sports and the American Metropolis* (Princeton, NJ: Princeton University Press, 1997) for a description of how city residents place symbolic values on their home teams.

46. Roger Noll and Andrew Zimbalist, eds. *Sports, Jobs and Taxes* (Washington DC: The Brookings Institute, 1997).

47. Much academic literature that examines the relationship between sports and the city focuses on the public subsidies paid to retain professional sports teams. For examples see Austrian and Rosentraub, "Cities, Sports and Economic Change," *Journal of Urban Affairs* 24, no. 5 (December 2002): 549–563; Robert Baade, "Professional Sports as Catalysts for Metropolitan Economic Development," *Journal of Urban Affairs* 18, no. 1 (1996): 1–17; John Crompton, "Public Subsidies to Professional Team Sports Facilities," in *Sport and the City,* ed. Gratton and Henry (New York: Routledge, 2001): 15–34; Delaney and Eckstein, *Public Dollars, Private Stadiums* (New Brunswick, NJ: Rutgers University Press, 2003); Mark Rosentraub, *Major League Losers* (New York: Basic Books 1999); Noll and Zimbalist, *Sports, Jobs and Taxes.*

48. Jeffrey Metroidt, "Spending Cuts into Saints Profits," *Times-Picayune,* October 3, 1999.

49. "Saints, Spurs Center of Threats," *Times-Picayune,* October 29, 1999.

50. Aaron Kuriloff, "The Dome at 25," *Times-Picayune,* July 30, 2000.

51. Jeff Duncan, *From Bags to Riches: How the New Orleans Saints and the People of Their Hometown Rose from the Depths Together* (Lafayette, LA: Acadiana House, 2010).

52. Greg Thomas, "Saints Want to Raze Iberville Development, but Morial Says Favored Stadium Site Is Off-Limits," *Times-Picayune,* June 28, 2001.

53. Oriard, *Brand NFL.*

54. Baade, "Professional Sports as Catalysts for Metropolitan Economic Development"; Crompton, "Public Subsidies to Professional Team Sport Facilities in the USA"; Delaney and Eckstein, *Public Dollars, Private Stadiums*; Arthur Johnson and Allen Sack, "Assessing the Value of Sports Facilities," *Economic Development Quarterly* 10, no. 4 (November 1996): 369–381; Rosentraub, *Major League Losers.*

55. For an excellent and thorough assessment of the relationship between professional sports and the political, economic and social forces in American cities, see Danielson, *Home Team*; also see Euchner, *Playing the Field.*

56. *Times-Picayune,* January 25, 2010.

Chapter 2

1. Southern District Institute Transportation Engineers (SDITE), "Overview of the Louisiana Contraflow Plan," http://sdite.org/presentations2006/2A-Wols

hon—Louisiana-Contraflow-Plan.pdf (accessed May 2015).

2. Russell, *Times-Picayune*, August 28, 2005.

3. SDITE, "Louisiana Contraflow Plan," sdite.org.

4. Jeff Duncan, "Refuge of Last Resort," *Times-Picayune*, August 27, 2006.

5. James Varney, *Times-Picayune*, September 27, 1998.

6. For some firsthand accounts of being in the dome during Katrina, see Paul Harris, *Diaries from the Dome* (New York: Vantage Press, 2008); D'Ann Penner and Keith C. Ferdinand, eds. *Overcoming Katrina: African American Voices from the Crescent City and Beyond* (Basingstoke: Palgrave Macmillan, 2009).

7. New Orleans Sewer and Water Board, "Drainage System Facts," www.sbno.org/history_drainage_facts.asp (accessed June 2015).

8. John Barry, *Rising Tide: The Great Mississippi Flood of 1927 and How It Changed America* (New York: Simon & Schuster, 1998).

9. *Times-Picayune*, August 29, 2005.

10. Numerous articles, *Times Picayune*, August 29, 2005.

11. *Times-Picayune*, August 30, 2005.

12. *Ibid.*

13. *Times-Picayune*, September 1, 2005. Vivid descriptions can also be found in Michael Eric Dyson, *Come Hell or High Water: Hurricane Katrina and the Color of Disaster* (New York: Basic Civitas, 2006).

14. Penner and Ferdinand, *Overcoming Katrina*, 144.

15. Richard Lapchick, "Sport as a Bridge across the Racial Divide," 10th Annual National Conference: Different Perspectives on Majority Rules, 2005.

16. Penner and Ferdinand, *Overcoming Katrina*, 144.

17. Harris, *Diaries from the Dome*, 31.

18. *Ibid.*, 17

19. For one man's story that reveals the swift and unjust incarceration efforts that took place in response to Katrina, see Dave Eggers, *Zeitoun* (San Francisco: McSweeney's Books, 2009).

20. Penner and Ferdinand, *Overcoming Katrina*, 145.

21. Lola Vollen and Chris Ying, eds. *Voices from the Storm: The People of New Orleans on Hurricane Katrina and Its Af-*termath (San Francisco: McSweeney's Books, 2008), 245.

22. Penner and Ferdinand, *Overcoming Katrina*, 145.

23. Larry Bradshaw and Lorrie Beth Slonsky, "Trapped in New Orleans by the Flood—and Martial Law," *The Socialist Worker*, 2005.

24. "Guard Halts Superdome Evacuations," *Times-Picayune*, September 3, 2005.

25. Richard Lapchick, "Hurricane Katrina and a Saintly Rescue," in *Learning Culture through Sport: Perspectives on Society and Organized Sport*, Sandra Spickard Prettyman and Brian Lampman, eds. (Lanham, MD: Rowman and Littlefield, 2010).

26. *Ibid.*

27. Allison Plyer, "Facts for Features: Katrina Impact," The Data Center, last modified Aug 28, 2014, www.datacenterresearch.org.

28. I have been involved in almost every trip that Hope for Stanley has made to New Orleans. For more information see www.hopeforstanley.org.

29. *Ibid.*

30. *Ibid.*

31. *Ibid.*

32. "City Park History," New Orleans City Park, www.neworleanscitypark.com/new-orleans-city-park-history (accessed May 2015).

33. "Katrina Hits Louisiana Schools Hard," *CNN*, September 10, 2005.

34. Robert Bullard and Beverly Wright, eds. *Race, Place and Environmental Justice after Katrina.* (Boulder, CO: Westview Press, 2009).

35. Allison Plyer, "Facts for Features," www.datacenterresearch.org (accessed May 2015).

36. Kingsley, "New Orleans Architecture," 721.

37. *Ibid.*, 724.

38. Alan Donnes. *Patron Saints: How the Saints Gave New Orleans a Reason to Believe* (New York: Center Street, 2007), 46–47.

39. *Times-Picayune*, September 25, 2006.

40. Jeanne Vidrine, interview by author, New Orleans, February 20, 2011; see also *Times-Picayune*, April 4, 2010; *Times-Picayune*, September 10, 2010.

41. *Times-Picayune*, September 25, 2006.

42. Interview with a Saints fan, January

17, 2010. Name of interviewee withheld by mutual agreement.

43. Kevin Kolb, interview by author, New Orleans, January 28, 2011.

44. *Times-Picayune,* November 11, 2009.

45. Kolb, interview; Casey Knoettgen, "We Are the Who Dat Nation: football Fandom, City Identity, and Urban Renewal in New Orleans' Public Realm" (Ph.D. diss., University of New Orleans, 2010).

46. Holly Mahony, interview by author, New Orleans, June 15, 2011.

47. Kolb, interview.

48. *Times-Picayune,* April 3, 2010.

49. Dixon, *The Saints, the Superdome and the Scandal,* 7.

50. *Sporting News,* September 29, 2006.

51. Internet questionnaire response from a Saints fan, January 21, 2011. Internet questionnaire participants' identities were withheld by mutual agreement.

52. *Ibid.*

53. Interview with a Saints fan, February 1, 2011. Name of interviewee withheld by mutual agreement.

Chapter 3

1. Colley Charpentier, "Saints Fans Recall Surly Treatment at Soldier Field," *Times-Picayune,* December 28, 2007.

2. For a good example of a scholarly measurement of Katrina's impact, see John Logan, "The Impact of Katrina: Race and Class in Storm-damaged Neighborhoods," Brown University's American Communities Project, www.s4.brown.edu/Katrina/report.pdf (accessed May 2015).

3. *Washington Post,* September 10, 2005.

4. *Times-Picayune,* February 5, 2010.

5. *Times-Picayune,* September 16, 2010.

6. Interview with a Saints fan, September 8, 2011. Name of interviewee withheld by mutual agreement.

7. *Times-Picayune,* January 24, 2010.

8. *Times-Picayune,* 2009.

9. *Times-Picayune,* January 27, 2010.

10. *Times-Picayune,* February 2, 2010.

11. *Times-Picayune,* February 7, 2010.

12. *Times-Picayune,* February 1, 2010.

13. Kolb, interview.

14. *Times-Picayune,* February 4, 2011.

15. Jeralyn Wheeler, interview by author, New Orleans, January 29, 2011.

16. Vidrine, interview.

17. Interview with a Saints fan, Febru-

ary 1, 2011. Name of interviewee withheld by mutual agreement.

18. Wheeler, interview.

19. *Ibid.*

20. *Times-Picayune,* February 10, 2010.

21. *Times-Picayune,* August 10, 2010.

22. "In New Orleans, Saints Fans Stage Funeral for the Aints," *Houma Today,* February 22, 2011, www.houmatoday.com (accessed February 2011).

23. Spike Lee, *If God Is Willing and da Creek Don't Rise,* DVD, HBO Documentary Films, 2010.

24. *Ibid.*

25. Questionnaire response from a Saints fan, January 21, 2011. Internet questionnaire participants' identities were withheld by mutual agreement. Knoettgen, "We Are the Who Dat Nation."

26. *Times-Picayune,* January 26, 2010.

27. *Times-Picayune,* November 30, 2009.

28. *Times-Picayune,* January 25, 2010.

29. *Times-Picayune,* August 10, 2010.

30. National Football League, Super Bowl XLIV press conference transcripts, Miami, Florida, February 3, 2010. I obtained credentialed access to the NFL media center during several Super Bowls and was able to obtain all printed transcripts provided to members of the media from the NFL to use in their various news reporting outlets.

31. *Ibid.*

32. *Ibid.,* February 4, 2010.

33. *Ibid.,* February 1, 2010.

34. A case study of Pittsburgh Steelers fans living in Fort Worth, Texas, found that "one of the most organized attempts for sports fans to reconnect with home occurs in American football bars," Jon Kraszewski, "Pittsburgh in Fort Worth: Football Bars, Sports Television, Sports Fandom and the Management of Home," *Journal of Sport and Social Issues* 32, no. 2 (2008), 139–157.

35. National Football League, Super Bowl XLIV press conference transcripts, February 1, 2010.

36. *Times-Picayune,* February 9, 2010.

37. Donnes, *Patron Saints,* 101.

38. Super Bowl XLIV press conference transcripts, February 1, 2010.

39. Vidrine, interview; Knoettgen, "We Are the Who Dat Nation."

40. Super Bowl XLIV press conference transcripts, February 5, 2010.

41. *Times-Picayune*, January 25, 2010.
42. Wheeler, interview; Knoettgen, "We Are the Who Dat Nation."
43. Questionnaire response from a Saints fan, January 21, 2011. Internet questionnaire participants' identities were withheld by mutual agreement. Knoettgen, "We are the Who Dat Nation."
44. *Times-Picayune*, September 16, 2010.

Chapter 4

1. Lyn Lofland. *The Public Realm* (New Brunswick, NJ: Transaction, 1998), 65.
2. Elijah Anderson. *The Cosmopolitan Canopy* (New York: W.W. Norton & Company, 2011).
3. See the ethnographic study of Scunthorpe United football (soccer) matches, Tom Clark, "'I'm Scunthorpe 'Til I Die': Constructing and (Re)negotiating Identity through the Terrace Chant," *Soccer and Society* 7, no. 4 (2006): 494–507.
4. *Ibid.*; see also Jon Kraszewski, "Pittsburgh in Fort Worth"; Benjamin Rader, "The Quest for Subcommunities and the Rise of American Sport," *American Quarterly* 29, no. 4 (autumn 1977): 355–369; Gordon Waitt, "The Olympic Spirit and Civic Boosterism: The 2000 Sydney Olympics," *Tourism Geographies* 3, no. 3 (2001): 249–278.
5. Anderson conceptualized nations as imagined communities: "It is imagined because the members of even the smallest nation will never know most of their fellow members, meet them, or even hear of them, yet in the minds of each lives the image of their communion," Benedict Anderson, *Imagined Communities* (New York: Verso, 1983): 6.
6. *Times-Picayune*, February 2, 2010.
7. *Times-Picayune*, November 21 2010.
8. *Times-Picayune*, November 12, 2010.
9. *Times-Picayune*, November 21, 2010.
10. Questionnaire response from a Saints fan, January 21, 2011. Internet questionnaire participants' identities were withheld by mutual agreement.
11. Vidrine, interview.
12. *Times-Picayune*, January 8, 2011.
13. Vidrine, interview.
14. Three scholars whose work influenced my understanding of the subject include Elijah Anderson, *Cosmopolitan Canopies*; Lyn Lofland, *The Public Realm;* and William F. Whyte, *Street Corner Society* (University of Chicago Press, 1993).
15. Lyn Lofland researches urban public spaces and analyzes interactions among strangers.
16. Social scientist William H. Whyte used the term "triangulation"; see William H. Whyte, *The Social Life of Small Urban Spaces* (New York: Project for Public Spaces, 1980).
17. Lofland, *The Public Realm*, 8.
18. Questionnaire responses from Saints fans, January 21, 2011. Internet questionnaire participants' identities were withheld by mutual agreement; see also Knoettgen, "We Are the Who Dat Nation."
19. Kolb, interview.
20. Questionnaire responses from Saints fans, January 21, 2011. Internet questionnaire participants' identities were withheld by mutual agreement.
21. *Ibid.*
22. Interview with a Saints fan, February 1, 2011. Interview participant identity was withheld by mutual agreement.
23. *Times-Picayune*, February 2, 2010.
24. *Ibid.*
25. *Times-Picayune*, February 9, 2010.
26. See also any publications by Richard Lapchick on race and sport in society. His social justice activism using sport lies at the heart of my theoretical and practical approaches to sport in society.
27. As a graduate student in the DeVos Sport Business Management program at the University of Central Florida, I heard from several influential guest speakers in the sports industry. Bill Curry was a keynote speaker on more than one occasion.
28. "In New Orleans, Saints Fans Stage Funeral for the Aints," *Houma Today*, February 22, 2011, www.houmatoday.com.
29. I did not ask any questions about race relations or race in interviews or survey questions. Participants spoke of race and brought up the subject on their own without being prompted by research questions. Interview and survey questions were designed to ask about Saints fandom, not race. Yet participants spoke about race anyway; see Knoettgen, "We Are the Who Dat Nation."
30. *Times-Picayune*, February 2, 2010.
31. *Ibid.*
32. *Ibid.*

33. Anderson, *Cosmopolitan Canopies*, 276.

34. Interview with a Saints fan, September 8, 2011. Interview participant identity was withheld by mutual agreement.

Chapter 5

1. "Overview," Women of the Storm, www.womenofthestorm.net (accessed May 2015).

2. See Elaine Enarson's body of work on disaster through a gendered lens, such as Emmanuel David and Elaine Enarson, *The Women of Katrina* (Nashville, TN: Vanderbilt University Press, 2012). Rachel Luft has done work that looks at gender inequality and Hurricane Katrina, including teaching courses on the subject at the University of New Orleans. Institute for Women's Policy Research, "Fact Sheet: Women, Disasters and Hurricane Katrina," www.iwpr.org (accessed June 2015).

3. Mark Yost, *Tailgating, Sacks, and Salary Caps: How the NFL Became the Most Successful Sports League in History* (Chicago: Kaplan Publishing, 2006).

4. Pat Griffin, *Strong Women, Deep Closets: Lesbians and Homophobia in Sport* (Champaign, IL: Human Kinetics, 1998); Susan Birrell and Cheryl Cole, *Women, Sport, and Culture* (Champaign, IL: Human Kinetics, 1994).

5. The Institute for Diversity and Ethics in Sport publishes empirical, quantitative assessments that look at race and gender composition of leadership and management positions in sports; see Richard Lapchick, "2014 Racial and Gender Report Card: National Football League," www.tidesport.org.

6. Harry Edwards, *Sociology of Sport* (Homewood, IL: The Dorsey Press, 1973).

7. See, for example, Gary Armstrong, *Football Hooligans: Knowing the Score* (New York: Oxford International Publishers, 1998).

8. See, for example, Wann, Daniel, Merrill Melnick, Gordon Russell and Dale Pease, *Sports Fans: The Psychology and Social Impact of Spectators* (New York: Routledge, 2001).

9. For authors who confront gender in urban planning, see Dolores Hayden, *The Grand Domestic Revolution* (Cambridge, MA: MIT Press, 1981); Daphne Spain, *Gendered Spaces* (Chapel Hill: The University of North Carolina Press, 1992).

10. M. Gottdiener and Leslie Budd, *Key Concepts in Urban Studies* (Thousand Oaks, CA: Sage, 2005), 81.

11. Birrell and Cole, *Women, Sports and Culture.*

12. Griffin, *Strong Women, Deep Closets.*

13. Wann et al., *Sports Fans.*

14. Katherine Jones, "Female Fandom: Identity, Sexism, and Men's Professional Football in England," *Sociology of Sport Journal* 25 (2008), 516–537.

15. Griffin, *Strong Women, Deep Closets.*

16. Mariah Burton Nelson, *The Stronger Women Get, the More Men Love Football: Sexism and the American Culture of Sports* (New York: Avon, 1994).

17. For exceptions, see Kim Tofoletti and Peter Mewett, eds. *Sport and Its Female Fans* (New York: Routledge, 2014); see also Jones, "Female Fandom." Jones focused her research on female fans at male sporting events (soccer in England) to illustrate that women experienced a tension between fan identities and gender.

Chapter 6

1. For an excellent urban history on how commercialized sport and the American industrial city grew up together, see Steven Riess, *City Games* (Urbana: University of Illinois Press, 1998).

2. *Ibid.* Riess, *City Games,* provides historical accounts of how organized and sanctioned gambling transformed leisure activities into commercialized sports.

3. Richard Giulianotti, "Supporters, Followers, Fans, and Flaneurs: A Taxonomy of Spectator Identities in Football," *Journal of Sport and Social Issues* 26, no. 1 (2002), 25–46.

4. Gibson, Chris, and Lily Kong, "Cultural Economy: A Critical Review," *Progress in Human Geography* 29, no. 5 (October 2005), 541–561.

5. "Assessing the Trajectory and Challenges of the Sociology of Sport," *International Review for the Sociology of Sport* 50, no. 4–5 (June–August, 2015).

6. For exceptions see Kraszewski, "Pittsburgh in Fort Worth"; Knoettgen, *We Are the Who Dat Nation*; and Daniele C. Lindquist, "'Locating' the Nation: Football Game Day and American Dreams in Central Ohio,"

Journal of American Folklore 119, no. 474 (2006), 444–488. In addition, I participated in a sports panel at the 2015 Popular Culture Association conference where other scholars shared preliminary results from research into sports fandom that shows potential to view NFL fandom through new and different lenses.

7. "NFL Team Values: The Business of Football," *Forbes,* last modified September 7, 2011. www.forbes.com/lists/2011/30/nfl-valuations-11_land.html.

8. Oriard, *Brand NFL.*

9. *Ibid.,* 22.

10. *Ibid.,* 23.

11. "Uniwatch: History of League Logos," ESPN. Last modified July 23, 2014. www.espn.go.com.

12. Oriard, *Brand NFL,* 27.

13. For analysis on how sports fandom has changed as a result of the increased commodification of sport, see Richard Giulianotti, "Supporters, Followers, Fans and Flaneurs"; Francis Lee, "Spectacle and Fandom: Media Discourse in Two Soccer Events in Hong Kong," *Sociology of Sport Journal* 22 (2005), 194–213; John Horne, *Sport in Consumer Culture* (Basingstoke: Palgrave Macmillan, 2006).

14. Garry Crawford, *Consuming Sport: Fans, Sport and Culture* (London: Routledge, 2004), argues that fans are first and foremost consumers, especially if we are subscribing to the belief that consumption is of central importance to capitalist societies.

15. Team Marketing Report produces and publishes reliable information on the business of sport, including a trademarked "Fan Cost Index." The FCI for 2014 was $478.52, which is an estimated price for a family of four to attend a game. See www.teammarketing.com.

16. Numbers vary based on source of reporting and contain variations from year to year. See Yost, *Tailgating, Sacks and Salary Caps* for a more scholarly account of the business of football. *Sports Business Daily* and *Fortune* periodically report on NFL merchandising numbers.

17. Erik Siemers, "Nike's NFL Apparel Deal Valued at $1.1B," *BizJournal,* March 11, 2011. www.bizjournals.com/portland/blog/2011/03/nikes-nfl-apparel-deal-valued-at-11b.html.

18. CNBC.com, April 14, 2010.

19. *Times-Picayune,* September 5, 2010.

20. *Ibid.*

21. *Times-Picayune,* October 11, 2010.

22. *Ibid.*

23. *Times-Picayune,* August 15, 2010.

24. *Ibid.*

25. For an interesting and concise summary of shotgun houses, see Richard Campanella, "Shotgun Geography: The History behind the Famous New Orleans House," *Times-Picayune,* February 12, 2014.

26. *Times-Picayune,* September 11, 2010.

27. Jaquetta White, "NFL Says It Has Exclusive Rights to 'Who Dat,'" January 29, 2010.

28. Doyice Cotton, et al., *Law for Recreation and Sport Managers* (Dubuque, IA: Kendall/Hunt, 2001).

29. "NFL Orders Shops to Stop Selling Who Dat Gear," January 27, 2010. www.wwltv.com.

30. *Times-Picayune,* January 29, 2010.

31. "U.S. Senate Candidates Agree on Who Dat Controversy," *Times-Picayune,* January 29, 2010; and "Who Dat Nation Triumphs as NFL Drops Trademark Lawsuit," January 30, 2010.

32. Jaquetta White, "Who Dat Nation 1, NFL 0 in Merchandise Fight," *Times-Picayune,* January 31, 2010.

Chapter 7

1. Bob Collins, "No More 'Planning by Surprise': City Planning in New Orleans Ten Years after Katrina," New Orleans Index at Ten, The Data Center, last modified June 24, 2015. www.datacenterresearch.org.

2. Kevin Fox Gotham, "Marketing Mardi Gras: Commodification, Spectacle, and the Political Economy of Tourism in New Orleans," *Urban Studies* 39, no. 10 (2002), 1735–1756; Gotham examines Mardi Gras in New Orleans and uses the concepts of commodification and spectacle as a basis for understanding the rise of the tourism industry, place marketing and the transformation of cities into entertainment destinations.

3. For an authoritative urban theory on consumption and the postmodern city, see David Harvey, *The Condition of Postmodernity* (Cambridge: Blackwell, 1990).

4. Timothy Chapin, "Sports Facilities as Urban Redevelopment Catalysts," *Journal of the American Planning Association* 70, no. 2 (2004), 193–209.

5. "Louisiana Recovery," Federal Emergency Management Agency, www.fema.gov/louisiana-recovery (accessed May 2015).

6. Michael Grunwald and Dan Morgan, "La. Wants FEMA to Pay for Majority of Damage to State Property," *The Washington Post,* October 28, 2005. www.washingtonpost.com.

7. Ryan Jones, "Superdome Received Nearly $1 Million for Final Hurricane Katrina–Related Repairs," www.nola.com, June 20, 2012.

8. Dan Alexander, "Billionaire Saints Owner Tom Benson to Score $400 Million Revenue Boost from Agreement with State," *Forbes,* July 31, 2013.

9. "Analysis of Benson Tower Lease," Louisiana Legislative Auditors, September 2014. I have been into the renovated Superdome many times.

10. Alexander, "Billionaire Saints Owner."

11. *Times-Picayune,* August 12, 2010.

12. *Times-Picayune,* August 15, 2010.

13. *Times-Picayune,* September 8, 2014.

14. *Times-Picayune,* October 3, 2011.

15. *Ibid.*

16. Different news sources quote different values for the arena renovations between $31 million and $54 million.

17. Quote from Mark Romig, president of the New Orleans Tourism and Marketing Corporation and co-chair of media for the New Orleans Super Bowl Host Committee.

18. Waller, www.nola.com, December 11, 2012; Rainey, www.nola.com, October 25, 2012.

19. For analysis of the role of mayors in the politics of professional sports, see Gene Burd, "Mediated Sports, Mayors, and the Marketed Metropolis," in *Sporting Dystopias,* ed. Ralph Wilcox (Albany: State University of New York Press, 2003), 35–64.

20. www.nola.com, January 8, 2013.

21. *Ibid.*

22. Alexander-Bloch, www.nola.com, February 4, 2013.

23. www.nola.com, January 8, 2013.

24. Waller, www.nola.com, December 11, 2012.

25. www.nola.com, January 8, 2013.

26. *Ibid.*

27. Jeff Duncan, "At Super Bowl 2013, Roger Goodell Should Be Hailed As a New Orleans Hero for Helping Save a Cosmopolitan City," www.nola.com, January 22, 2013.

28. James Varney, "New Orleans Saints Severely Penalized by NFL for 'Bounty' Program," *Times-Picayune,* March 21, 2012; Katherine Terrell, "New Orleans Saints Bounty Scandal Timeline," *Times-Picayune,* December 11, 2012.

29. For more firsthand accounts and descriptions of how Bountygate worked to diminish Saintsmania, see Brandon Haynes, "A Gateway for Everyone to Believe" (Ph.D. diss., University of New Orleans, 2013).

30. *Ibid.*

31. Whittacker, www.nola.com, January 22, 2013.

32. *Ibid.*

33. *Ibid.*

34. Jeff Duncan, www.nola.com, January 22, 2013.

35. www.nola.com, February 4, 2013.

36. Adriana Lopez, "New Orleans Is Stepping Up Its Game for Super Bowl XLVII," Forbes.com, October 9, 2012.

37. www.nola.com, January 8, 2013.

38. Mark Waller, "Super Bowl 2013 Drove $480 Million in Spending in New Orleans," www.nola.com, last updated October 24, 2013.

39. www.nola.com, October 30, 2012.

40. Scott, www.nola.com, January 22, 2013.

41. Waller, www.nola.com, December 11, 2012.

42. For economic assessments of the impact of Super Bowls and other sporting events, see publications by Matheson and Baade, such as Victor Matheson and Robert Baade, "Padding Required: Assessing the Economic Impact of the Super Bowl," *European Sport Management Quarterly* 6, no. 4 (January 2007), 353–374.

43. Lawrence Vale, "Restoring Urban Vitality," in *Rebuilding Urban Places after Disaster: Lessons from Hurricane Katrina,* eds. Eugenie L. Birch and Susan M. Wachter (Philadelphia: University of Pennsylvania Press, 2006), 156.

Bibliography

Anderson, Benedict. *Imagined Communities: Reflections on the Origin and Spread of Nationalism.* New York: Verso, 1983.

Anderson, Elijah. *The Cosmopolitan Canopy: Race and Civility in Everyday Life.* New York: W.W. Norton & Company, 2011.

Armstrong, Gary. *Football Hooligans: Knowing the Score.* New York: Oxford International, 1998.

Austrian, Z., and M. Rosentraub. "Cities, Sports and Economic Change: A Retrospective Assessment," *Journal of Urban Affairs* 24, no. 5 (December 2002), 549–563.

Baade, Robert. "Professional Sports as Catalysts for Metropolitan Economic Development," *Journal of Urban Affairs* 18, no. 1 (1996), 1–17.

Barry, John. *Rising Tide: The Great Mississippi Flood of 1927 and How It Changed America.* New York: Simon & Schuster, 1998.

Birrell, Susan, and Cheryl Cole. *Women, Sport, and Culture.* Champaign, IL: Human Kinetics, 1994.

Bullard, Robert, and Beverly Wright, editors. *Race, Place and Environmental Justice after Katrina: Struggles to Reclaim, Rebuild, and Revitalize New Orleans and the Gulf Coast.* Boulder, CO: Westview Press, 2009.

Burd, Gene. "Mediated Sports, Mayors, and the Marketed Metropolis," in *Sporting Dystopias,* edited by Ralph Wilcox. Albany: State University of New York Press, 2003, 35–64.

Chafin, Andrew. "Louisiana Superdome: Newest Wonder of the World," Louisiana Superdome Commission, 1975.

Chapin, Timothy. "Sports Facilities as Urban Redevelopment Catalysts," *Journal of the American Planning Association* 70, no. 2 (2004), 193–209.

Clark, Tom. "'I'm Scunthorpe 'til I Die': Constructing and (Re)negotiating Identity through the Terrace Chant," *Soccer and Society* 7, no. 4 (2006): 494–507.

Cotton, Doyice, John Wolohan, and Jesse Wilde. *Law for Recreation and Sport Managers.* Dubuque, IA: Kendall/Hunt, 2001.

Crawford, Garry. *Consuming Sport: Fans, Sport and Culture.* London: Routledge, 2004.

Crompton, J. L. "Public Subsidies to Professional Team Sports Facilities in the U.S.A.," in *Sport in the City: The Role of Sport in Economic and Social Regeneration,* edited by Chris Gratton and Ian Henry. New York: Routledge, 2001.

Danielson, Michael N. *Home Team: Professional Sports and the American Metropolis.* Princeton, NJ: Princeton University Press, 1997.

David, Emmanuel, and Elaine Enarson. *The Women of Katrina: How Gender, Race and Class Matter in an American Disaster.* Nashville, TN: Vanderbilt University Press, 2012.

Delaney, K., and Eckstein, R. *Public*

Dollars, Private Stadiums: The Battle over Building Sports Stadiums. New Brunswick, NJ: Rutgers University Press, 2003.

Dixon, Dave. *The Saints, the Superdome and the Scandal.* Gretna, LA: Pelican, 2008.

Donnes, Alan. *Patron Saints: How the Saints Gave New Orleans a Reason to Believe.* New York: Center Street, 2007.

Duncan, Jeff. *From Bags to Riches: How the New Orleans Saints and the People of Their Hometown Rose from the Depths Together.* Lafayette, LA: Acadiana House, 2010.

Edwards, Harry. *Sociology of Sport.* Homewood, IL: The Dorsey Press, 1973.

Euchner, Charles. *Playing the Field: Why Sports Teams Move and Cities Fight to Keep Them.* Baltimore: Johns Hopkins University Press, 1993.

Forbes. "NFL Team Values: The Business of Football." Accessed 2016. www.forbes.com/lists/2011/30/nfl-valuations-11_land.html.

Gibson, Chris, and Lily Kong. "Cultural Economy: A Critical Review," *Progress in Human Geography* 29, no. 5 (October 2005), 541–561.

Giulianotti, Richard. "Supporters, Followers, Fans, and Flaneurs: A Taxonomy of Spectator Identities in Football," *Journal of Sport and Social Issues* 26, no. 1 (2002), 25–46.

Gotham, Kevin Fox. "Marketing Mardi Gras: Commodification, Spectacle, and the Political Economy of Tourism in New Orleans," *Urban Studies* 39, no. 10 (2002), 1735–1756.

Gottdiener, M., and Leslie Budd. *Key Concepts in Urban Studies.* Thousand Oaks, CA: Sage, 2005.

Griffin, Pat. *Strong Women, Deep Closets: Lesbians and Homophobia in Sport.* Champaign, IL: Human Kinetics, 1998.

Harris, Paul. *Diaries from the Dome: Reflections on Fear and Privilege during Katrina.* New York: Vantage Press, 2008.

Harvey, David. *The Condition of Postmodernity.* Cambridge: Blackwell, 1990.

Hayden, Dolores. *The Grand Domestic Revolution: A History of Feminist Designs for American Homes, Neighborhoods, and Cities.* Cambridge, MA: MIT Press. 1981.

Horne, John. *Sport in Consumer Culture.* Basingstoke: Palgrave Macmillan, 2006.

Johnson, Arthur T., and Allen Sack. "Assessing the Value of Sports Facilities: The Importance of Noneconomic Factors," *Economic Development Quarterly* 10, no. 4 (November 1996), 369–381.

Jones, Katherine. "Female Fandom: Identity, Sexism, and Men's Professional Football in England," *Sociology of Sport Journal* 25 (2008), 516–537.

Kingsley, Karen. "New Orleans Architecture: Building Renewal," *The Journal of American History* (December 2007), 716–725.

Knoettgen, Casey. "We Are the Who Dat Nation: Football Fandom, City Identity, and Urban Renewal in New Orleans' Public Realm," Ph.D. diss., University of New Orleans, 2010.

Kraszewski, Jon. "Pittsburgh in Fort Worth: Football Bars, Sports Television, Sports Fandom and the Management of Home," *Journal of Sport and Social Issues* 32, no. 2 (2008), 139–157.

Kuklick, Bruce. *To Everything a Season: Shibe Park and Urban Philadelphia 1909–1976.* Princeton, NJ: Princeton University Press. 1991.

Lapchick, Richard. "Hurricane Katrina and a Saintly Rescue," in *Learning Culture Through Sport: Perspectives on Society and Organized Sport,* edited by Sandra Spickard Prettyman and Brian Lampman. Lanham, MD: Rowman and Littlefield, 2010.

_____. *100 Pioneers: African-Americans*

Bibliography

Who Broke Color Barriers in Sport. Morgantown, WV: Fitness Information Technology, 2008.

_____. "Sport as a Bridge Across the Racial Divide." 10th Annual National Conference: Different Perspectives on Majority Rules, 2005. Accessed February 2010, http://digitalcommons.unl.edu/pocpwi10/21.

Lee, Francis. "Spectacle and Fandom: Media Discourse in Two Soccer Events in Hong Kong," *Sociology of Sport Journal* 22 (2005), 194–213.

Levy, Alan. *Tackling Jim Crow: Racial Segregation in Professional Football.* Jefferson, NC: McFarland, 2003.

Lewis, Pierce. *New Orleans: The Making of an Urban Landscape.* Charlottesville: University of Virginia Press, 2003.

Lindquist, Daniele Christensen. "'Locating' the Nation: Football Game Day and American Dreams in Central Ohio," *Journal of American Folklore* 119, no. 474 (2006), 444–488.

Lofland, Lyn. *The Public Realm: Exploring the City's Quintessential Social Territory.* New Brunswick, NJ: Transaction, 1998.

Martin, Michael S. "New Orleans Becomes a Big League City: The NFL-AFL Merger and the Creation of the New Orleans Saints," in *Horsehide, Pigskin, Oval Tracks and Apple Pie: Essays on Sport and American Culture,* edited by James A. Vlasich, 119–131. Jefferson, NC: McFarland, 2006.

Matheson, Victor, and Robert Baade. "Padding Required: Assessing the Economic Impact of the Super Bowl," *European Sport Management Quarterly* 6, no. 4 (January 2007), 353–374.

National Football League. "History." Accessed June 2015. www.nfl.com/history/chronology.

Nelson, Mariah Burton. *The Stronger Women Get, the More Men Love Football: Sexism and the American Culture of Sports.* New York: Avon Books, 1994.

Noll, Roger, and Andrew Zimbalist. "Build the Stadium—Create the Jobs," in *Sports, Jobs, and Taxes,* edited by Roger Noll and Andrew Zimbalist, 1–54. Washington, DC: The Brookings Institute, 1997.

_____, and _____. "The Economic Impact of Sports Teams and Facilities," in *Sports, Jobs, and Taxes.* 55–91. Washington, DC: The Brookings Institute, 1997.

Oriard, Michael. *Brand NFL: Making and Selling America's Favorite Sport.* Chapel Hill: University of North Carolina Press, 2007.

Penner, D'Ann, and Keith C. Ferdinand, eds. *Overcoming Katrina: African American Voices from the Crescent City and Beyond.* Basingstoke: Palgrave Macmillan, 2009.

Rader, Benjamin G. "The Quest for Subcommunities and the Rise of American Sport," *American Quarterly* 29, no. 4 (autumn 1977): 355–369.

Riess, Steven A. *City Games: The Evolution of American Urban Society and the Rise of Sports.* Urbana: University of Illinois Press, 1998.

Rosentraub, Mark. *Major League Losers: The Real Cost of Sports and Who's Paying for It.* New York: Basic Books, 1999.

_____. *Major League Winners: Using Sports and Cultural Centers as Tools for Economic Development.* New York: CRC Press, 2010.

Ross, Charles Kenyatta. *Outside the Lines: African Americans and the Integration of the National Football League.* New York: New York University Press, 2000.

Somers, Dale. *The Rise of Sports in New Orleans, 1850–1900.* Baton Rouge: Louisiana State University Press, 1972.

Souther, Mark J. "Into the Big League: Conventions, Football and the Color Line in New Orleans," *Journal of Urban History* 29, no. 6 (September 2003).

Spain, Daphne. *Gendered Spaces*. Chapel Hill: University of North Carolina Press, 1992.

Tofoletti, Kim, and Peter Mewett, eds. *Sport and Its Female Fans*. New York: Routledge, 2014.

Vale, Lawrence J. "Restoring Urban Vitality," in *Rebuilding Urban Places after Disaster: Lessons from Hurricane Katrina*, edited by Eugenie L. Birch and Susan M. Wachter. Philadelphia: University of Pennsylvania Press, 2006, 149–167.

Vollen, Lola, and Chris Ying, eds. *Voices from the Storm: The People of New Orleans on Hurricane Katrina and Its Aftermath*. San Francisco: McSweeney's Books, 2008.

Waitt, Gordon. "The Olympic Spirit and Civic Boosterism: The 2000 Sydney Olympics," *Tourism Geographies* 3, no. 3 (2001): 249–278.

Wann, Daniel, Merrill Melnick, Gordon Russell and Dale Pease. *Sports Fans: The Psychology and Social Impact of Spectators*. New York: Routledge, 2001.

Whyte, William F. *Street Corner Society: The Social Structure of an Italian Slum*. Chicago: University of Chicago Press, 1993.

Whyte, William H. *The Social Life of Small Urban Spaces*. New York: Project for Public Spaces, 1980.

Yost, Mark. *Tailgating, Sacks, and Salary Caps: How the NFL Became the Most Successful Sports League in History*. Chicago: Kaplan, 2006.

Index

Numbers in **bold italics** refer to pages with photographs.

205

Index